THE PIONEER IN THE AMERICAN NOVEL, 1900–1950

The Pioneer

in the
American Novel
1900-1950

BY NICHOLAS J. KAROLIDES

UNIVERSITY OF OKLAHOMA PRESS
NORMAN

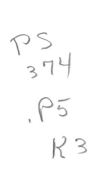

The paper on which this book is printed bears the watermark of the University of Oklahoma Press and has an effective life of at least three hundred years.

LIBRARY OF CONGRESS CATALOG CARD NUMBER: 67–15573

Copyright in microfilm 1964 by Nicholas J. Karolides, assigned to the University of Oklahoma Press, 1967. Book copyright 1967 by the University of Oklahoma Press, Publishing Division of the University. Composed and printed at Norman, Oklahoma, U.S.A., by the University of Oklahoma Press. First edition.

To Inga

.

Preface

THE American frontier is closed, the grand dream of Manifest Destiny accomplished, the violent, brilliant chapter in American history ended. The Census Bureau signaled the beginning of the end in 1890 when it declared officially that "the unsettled area had been so broken into by isolated bodies of settlement that there can hardly be said to be a frontier line." To be sure, vast reaches of territory behind the frontier line continued to draw land-hungry men and women in the succeeding decade, but the final goal was at hand.

However, the full harvest of the pioneer movement had yet to be reaped. Led by Frederick Jackson Turner, who first formulated his thesis in his famous paper of 1893, "The Significance of the Frontier in American History," historians have amassed evidence to show the effect of the frontier in shaping the culture and character of America. The influence of the frontier was judged to be widespread and many faceted, causing the transformation even of the character of the people: certain traits were strengthened and new ones formed to meet the demands of the environment. The frontier influenced the character and direction of the government, not only in its structure but also in its democratic processes. The entire flavor of American life and culture was redirected—in the breakdown of class patterns, the introduction of new mores, the distinct separation from European influences, and the broadening of the economic framework of society. In short, the effects of the frontier were seen in all areas of life.

The patterns of action and personality of our nation and people fostered by the frontier not only affected our cultural ancestors but exert at least residual cultural effect upon present-day Americans. This effect is partly due to absorption of the pioneer image through environment and educational situations which promote historical concepts, attitudes, preferred roles, acceptable behavior patterns, and patriotic ideals which stem from a frontier heritage. The effect is due also to modern communications media, which identify more explicitly the attitudes and characteristics of this earlier period as aspects of the American heritage and way of life and as foundations of present characteristics. The combined effect upon the public is unmeasurable, but the fact that Turner's thesis is being constantly disseminated is certainly significant in the inculcation of ideas and attitudes about the frontier.

The twentieth-century novel has been an important force in structuring our image of the American pioneer hero. The pioneer figures prominently in the novel; he has been a popular literary subject since James Fenimore Cooper brought him fame and popularity. Although, as will be seen, certain locales and types receive significantly greater literary attention than others, the major events and locales of our history and legend are all represented with frequency. Popularization of epic periods and figures has had both sweeping appeal and an extensive effect on the public's image of the nation's past. Authors, including some with considerable reputation and acclaim, have recreated the life of the frontier, developing understanding of the people and insight into their goals, attitudes, and reactions. Novelists have tended to focus on this particular era, and since novels are so widely read, the image of the frontier which they present has become a major source for the concept of the pioneer held by the public as a whole.

The question here is not of accuracy or authoritativeness but rather of the received impression: the image of the frontier and the pioneer as presented to the reader's mind. The public, imbued with the nature of its cultural heritage and assuming an implicit relationship of the past to the present, responds to and accepts the image presented. To the degree that there is reiteration of themes and characteristics will there be strength and solidification of impression.

How then is the frontier depicted in the twentieth-century novel? What image—or images—of the pioneer is being disseminated? What were his special traits, his values, attitudes, objectives? An analysis of the conception of the pioneer in the novel will aid in comprehending how Americans see their past and how they see themselves in relation to their heritage of a way of life and a national character.

Generally, my intellectual debts in the development of this work are many and unaccountable; they trace a personal history. I am, however, particularly indebted to Professor Louise M. Rosenblatt of New York University, whose advice and critical analysis helped to formulate the basic direction and style of the work, and Professors John C. Payne and Fred C. Blanchard (whose father was himself a pioneer) of New York University, who read and commented on the document in process. I am personally indebted for the encouragement and assistance to associates, family, and friends, especially those at Devon's Fancy, Amagansett, New York, who helpfully bore with my reading and writing for several summers. My fullest gratitude goes to Inga, who beyond wifely encouragement contributed her unerring sensitivity to language to smooth over many rough lines in the final document. To all, my boundless appreciation.

NICHOLAS J. KAROLIDES

River Falls, Wisconsin
June 10, 1966

Contents

THE PIONEER IN THE AMERICAN NOVEL, 1900–1950

1

Plots and Conflicts

From the ragged ribbon of coastal settlements, the pioneers had crossed the Appalachian chain in steady streams and had conquered the Ohio and Mississippi valleys. Later, drawn by the dual magnets of gold and land, they had suffered the arduous overland trek to California and Oregon. Then the surging tide had backed up to fill sections of the vast reaches of prairie and mountain. At last there remained only empty pockets of less desirable land to which a man could turn. The American frontier had closed.

Like a mirror facing the past, the literature of America effected a grand reopening of the frontier in the years following its official close. Since 1900, many novels have chronicled and recreated the early American drama. More and more pioneers take to the pages to scout and trail the woods, to cross the plains and mountains, to trap the seemingly ubiquitous beaver, to plow the prairie. With each succeeding decade, the number of such novels does not lessen but rather increases.

Certain areas and periods have received more literary attention than others in the novels of the frontier. The forest frontier is the most prominent locale of pioneer fiction. Almost half of the novels used in this study take place in the forest environs. Of these the area of greatest frequency is the Old Northwest Territory, followed closely by the Kentucky-Tennessee region, the dark and bloody ground. Western New York and Pennsylvania share much of what remains. The entire southern forest region,

3

encompassing all of the area between the original tidelands states and the Mississippi River, receives minimal attention as does the forest region of the Oregon Territory. Oregon, however, figures prominently as a goal in another large group of novels dealing with the overland trail theme.

The remainder of the novels is divided among several groups, the most prominent being the novels of the prairie country, those of the overland trail, and those taking place in the mountains and open ranges. These three have an approximately even distribution in the novels. The works concerned with the overland trail cover both prairie and mountain country en route to Oregon and California. The settings in the prairie novels are principally of the Midwest, though a few stray into the Southwest. The locale of the mountain group covers both the southwestern ranges and those of the northern areas, the headwater country of the Missouri and Mississippi rivers. A final, relatively smaller group is concerned with the mining areas of California.

PLOTS

Two fairly distinct plot patterns emerge in the delineation of the forest frontier, although each of these has its own variations. The first of these depicts the scout-hunter, that free agent and samaritan of the woods; the second pattern deals with the forest-leveler, the farmer. There is of course some similarity in the design of these plot patterns because of the sameness of environment and the fabric of history upon which they are both embroidered. The problems and methods of life are basically similar as are the responses to environmental pressures. There is also an overlapping area of skills, since the incipient farmer often must perform the woodsman skills that are outstanding in the scout. The chief variance derives from a basic difference in goals and values. However, in this area there is also some overlapping: the hunter, in some novels, shifts his goals, usually because of a woman's influence, to assume the status of the farmer pioneer; in other instances, the trees cast their spell over the farmer, drawing him away from the clearing.

The stories centering on the scout hero frequently have him involved in Revolutionary War and anti-Indian activities. The plot includes the elements of battles, forays and scouting trips—trailing and spying—through the woods. At times the scout becomes an appendage of a military force in some guise, either leading it or providing necessary food and information. Examples of this type of novel are M. Thompson's *Alice of Old Vincennes* and *The Forest and the Fort* by Hervey Allen.

Similarly, the pioneer may be involved in the defense of a settlement or a group of settlers. In these cases, various hardships are presented: brutal attack, scalping, privation, forced marches. Heroic and astounding feats are woven into the action as is a thread of romance. In the more contemporary novels, the romance is interlaced with sex. Examples of this type are Zane Grey's *The Last Trail* and James Boyd's *Long Hunt*. In a particular variation of this theme, the hero acts as the protector and rescuer of an individual, often his secret beloved. It is his task to rescue the fair damsel who has fallen into the hands of hostile Indians or a villainous renegade and to escort her safely through the wilderness. Typical of these is J. A. Altsheler's *The Wilderness Road* and Dale Van Every's *Bridal Journey*. These, of course, contain many of the other elements cited.

Another typical design has as its point of departure the capture by Indians of the hero and his subsequent captivity among them. This capture usually occurs when the pioneer is a child or a young adult, and the captivity serves to provide him with instruction in the ways and skills of the Indian. He becomes—for most intents and purposes—an Indian. Complications are provided, in a few novels, by his marriage to an Indian girl. Usually, however, he escapes to his true cultural heritage, as in Burton Stevenson's *The Heritage*, or to be culturally re-educated, as in *The Forest and the Fort* by Hervey Allen. With their special skills in language, woodcraft and understanding of Indian ways, these figures maintain significant roles as language interpreters or scouts for the army. Special conflicts of loyalty and choice as well as the various trials of the frontier are other aspects of the plot.

The unusual and deceptively simple plot of Walter D. Edmonds' *In the Hands of the Senecas* depicts the travail and reactions of a group of women captives. Two other novels, *Red Morning* by Ruby Frey and *Strife Before Dawn* by Mary Schumann, devote considerable space to such captivity. A basic subplot in each hinges upon the enforced marriage of the heroine to an Indian and the subsequent reaction of her white husband to this upon her release or escape.

The second basic pattern of the forest frontier novels is relatively less diversified. Basically, this chronicles the life of a family in its attempt to establish a permanent home in the wilderness. The crude island of opened space, hacked out of the close surrounding trees, is besieged and beset. The pioneer and his family face brutal work, illness, privation, isolation, and death; they are the pawns of war being buffeted by Indians with varying degrees of ferocity. In dire times they are forced to remove to forts for protection; this situation is found in such separated areas as New York, in Edmonds' *Drums Along the Mohawk*, and Oregon, in Archie Binns' *Mighty Mountain*, despite the essentially dissimilar nature of the Indians on these two frontiers. In about half of these novels the Indian problem is more muted, forming but a general background to the day-by-day struggle and adventure with primitive existence. *The Trees*, by Conrad Richter, and *Lamb in His Bosom*, by Caroline Miller, illustrate this approach.

The spotlight in these forest frontier novels is on the development of the home or early settlement, which directs the general tone of the novels. There is, however, a necessary correlation with other novels of the forest frontier due to the environment and shared events. Furthermore, the settler hero is often only one step removed from the offstage forest. The pioneers in *The Great Meadow* by Elizabeth M. Roberts and *Green Centuries* by Caroline Gordon, for example, are equally adept in trailing the woods and guiding the plow. In Helen Todd's *So Free We Seem*, the hero reverts to this wilder role, disappearing into the darkness of the forest and leaving the slight clearing to his wife and family. Louis Zara's *This Land Is Ours* depicts a pioneer who successfully fills the role of adopted Indian, knowledgeable and trusted campaign scout, hunter, and sometime husbandman.

A close relative of the hunter-scout of the forest frontier is the hero who figures prominently in the novels in which the locale is the mountain and river country of the Southwest and the Far West. This pioneer is a particular breed of hunter-scout whose special occupation is trapping. When the mountains are emphasized as the setting, the characterization is that of a mountain man, a specialized version of the trapper. Aside from a slightly exaggerated code and pattern of life, the habits of the mountain man and the trapper are similar as are the plot structures of the novels. Like the forest-runner, with whom he shares lone habits and natural instincts, the mountain man is a wanderer enjoying a free, unencumbered life. Either with some close friends or alone—as he matures he prefers fewer people—he traps and hunts, faces the elements or the Indians, and sows wild oats at the yearly roundup. Invariably he becomes a "squaw man." His stronger alienation from civilization and the greater distance separating him from it cause a deeper and lasting quality in his associations with the Indians. This is illustrated in *The Big Sky*, by A. B. Guthrie, and *The Long Rifle*, by Stewart E. White, in which the heroes elect to live with their adopted tribes.

Occasionally this character becomes involved in military matters, taking on the role of scout or hunter for an outpost, as in Richard Roberts' *The Gilded Rooster*. The mountain man also appears in other novels as a secondary figure—usually as a guide to a covered-wagon train or as an elder-statesman type; although he maintains faint vestiges of his early glamor and his stark individuality, he is but a faded tintype of the man he once was.

Some of these trappers settle down before they fade away. A

few of them develop fur trading posts after their initial experiences on the fur runs. As the country develops and the furs become less accessible, the fur post takes on some semblance of farm life as in Janet Lewis' *The Invasion* and August Derleth's *Wind Over Wisconsin*. Another group, generally ex-mountain men, go from that wild trade to a kind of ranching-homesteading. Typical are the heroes of R. Raynolds' *Brothers in the West* and Wilbur Steele's *Diamond Wedding*, in which the heroes end their solitary existence by marrying and settling down to found a homestead. They face various calamities and personal hardships involved in such moves, their adjustment to the encroachments of organized society being the greatest difficulty. A few of these heroes return to their wandering ways.

The prairie country serves as the background for another series of novels. As with those stories which catalogue the first opening of the forest frontier by the prospective agrarian, these novels primarily detail the early settlement of prairie country by the farmer. In keeping with historical accuracy, this period is considerably later; generally the time of initiation is the mid-nineteenth century. The background problems of the plot, therefore, are different. There is no Revolutionary War, with its associated fears, battles and hardships; the War Between the States and its issues lend some emotional and political color, but the war is not fought before the pioneer's doorstep. In these novels, too, the Indian makes but sporadic appearances and is rarely of the devastatingly fear-inspiring nature as on the forest frontier, though hints of fearful events do exist. The problems dealt with are those that go along with the creation of livelihood and a home out of a raw, uncompromising wilderness. Heat, drought, hunger, blizzards, locusts, loneliness: these are the trials in the building of a life on the prairie. The novels of Bess Streeter Aldrich, *A Lantern in Her Hand, Spring Came on Forever*, and *Song of Years*, typically represent the events and problems of this frontier series.

Closely related to these are a few works which focus attention upon the immigrant on the frontier, notably those of Willa Cather—*O Pioneers* and *My Antonia*—and Ole Rolvaag's *Giants in the Earth*. Although the ramifications of the plot are essentially the same, the additional element of the foreign origin of the characters lends special prominence to these novels. Emphasis on psychological and social adjustments in addition to the physical problems also creates a distinctive tone in these novels.

Somewhat specialized are the Oklahoma novels. The "boomers" forced the opening of Oklahoma in 1889 after most of the surrounding country had been settled. The pioneering period of this situation was decidedly foreshortened as a result of the rapid development of community life. The Indian situation also takes on a variant attitude: these Indians had already been pacified; their resistance was not warlike. The special problems created by this situation, in terms of this study, have little direct consequence as the number of these novels is limited. The one widely known work is Edna Ferber's *Cimarron*.

The overland trail preceded these developments. The detailing of the tedious, hazardous trip westward to Oregon, California, and Deseret makes up the bulk of these works; from Emerson Hough's *The Covered Wagon* to A. B. Guthrie's *The Way West*, the basic material is the same. The massed wagons snake westward from Missouri, edging slowly across the plains, straining over the mountains. There are problems: the fording of rivers, too little food for man and vegetation for beast, dust, weariness. Some of the wagon trains lack guides and take the wrong trail as in John Weld's *Don't You Cry for Me*. Possessions are left ruthlessly along the way; disease and death overtake the weak; Indians account for others. Free land, however, lures them onward. The sense of destiny and patriotism strengthens the purpose of the Oregon bound, gold, the California bound; the Mormons have their religious fervor and their escape from persecution. When nothing else remains, an indomitable will forces them, and they trudge on for the final miles.

There is a point of common identity in these novels and those

9

of the prairie, as well as a few of the forest-leveler. This relationship derives from the essentially farmer-type character and motivation of the majority of the overland travelers. There is little similarity of events.

A final group of novels, though comparatively few in number, sets the scene in California during the height of the gold rush. They usually describe the hero's attempt to find his fortune of gold. There are adventures: the finding of a rich lode, the bandit raids, the magical pull of the gaming tables, and the ambushes on the trail. There is usually a romantic twist, heightened in the later novels—though all of them precede the quarter-century—by the dubious reputation of the prospective bride. These tales are climaxed by the departure from the gold fields to the stability of a farm in Oregon or to the fruitful promise of a California rancho.

These categories group the bulk of the pioneer literature under study. Certain individual novels do not quite fit these categories because of one or another differentiating feature. The bulk of the action of Dale Van Every's *Westward the River* takes place on a Mississippi flatboat; it otherwise fits a mixed hunter-farmer type into a Revolutionary War intrigue. Emerson Hough's *Magnificent Adventure* chronicles the Lewis and Clark expedition; it might be a combination overland trail–forest frontier novel. *The Virginian* by Owen Wister recounts the early ranching days while *The Thundering Herd* uses the buffalo hunt as its background theme. These novels and several others like them follow the other plot structures, though they occasionally combine the features of two. This last is not so unusual when it is considered that many such features overlap among the novels from one category to another with the regional-occupational theme as the basic variant.

CONFLICTS

A discussion of the plot framework of the several groups of novels is not quite complete without at least a general analysis of the crosscurrents of themes and conflicts, which do not, however, present a uniform picture. There are a few themes which prevail in a general way in many of the novels regardless of the time written or the period written about; others reappear time and again but with less frequency. Still others are frequent for only a short period of time.

Perhaps the most repeated theme is the conflict between the wilderness ideal and the cult of progress as represented by the culture of civilized society. This theme appears in each of the groups of novels—with the exception of those of the overland trail—throughout the period of the study. It includes several ideas and conflicts: East against West, usually comparing members or attributes of each; wilderness ways in opposition to urban ways, usually pitting the frontiersman against the settler; a free wandering life versus marriage, responsibility, and settling down.

The presentation of the conflict between good and evil is related to this previous theme. The relationship is in the personification of good as the frontier ideal, while evil often emanates from civilization. In a few novels, notably the earlier ones, these concepts are manifested in particular characters in the melodrama of hero against villain. More subtle representations of this conflict are developed as pressures on individuals or as malignancies fostered by society. The symbols of this conflict take the form of opposing values: proper, respectful attitudes towards women compared with misbehavior and lust; honor and manliness compared with cowardly deceit; generosity and loyalty compared with materialism and faithlessness; and simplicity of life compared with the idolization of the fancy and the superficial.

The class theme, subtle and indirect as it is in any of the novels, is more pronounced in the pre-World War I period. Thereafter the tone is changed and the attitudes toward class are redirected. Similarly, the presentation of the pioneer's attitude toward the Indian alters.

A theme, which curiously enough is most pronounced during the decade of the nineteen thirties, presents the concept of hard work, diligence and occupation as opposed to easy, laborless

11

gains. The latter is often related to corruption or gambling, which usually has an association with evil. A correlated idea is the efficacy and virtue of marriage and accepted responsibilities. The solitary, aimless, independent life is frowned upon in these novels.

Novels within the specific frontier groups show some particular emphasis. However, there is not necessarily a limitation of such an emphasis to a group; there is some overlapping between groups.

The conflict between organized society and the wilderness is strongest in the novels of the forest and mountain frontiers. The fabric of these novels presents the individual who is faced with infringement on his territory and habits of life. The incipient settlement represents a final challenge to his code and his ideal. Other individuals, already caught up in the net of marriage and responsibility, wish to throw off the hold of the settlements.

The novels of the prairie emphasize man's conflict with nature. The elements of weather and land are the dual menaces to the survival of these pioneers. These novels also tend to discuss social and psychological conflicts as the characters grope between their desires to maintain their traditions and to foster progress and change. These adjustments of man form a clearer theme perhaps because these novels are less concerned with the other passions and trials of the frontier. In addition, they portray a later period in American history which may have given rise to problems of social orientation.

The mining novels' special emphasis evolves from the motif of hard work versus easy gains which develops directly from the availability of the gold. The easy-come, easy-go nature of the gold is contrasted with the more lasting values of the land, both materially and humanly. As a result of the mining environment, there is frequent reference to the theme of law and justice. The concept of frontier law and the problem of maintenance of order is here frequently in evidence; it appears in other novels as well but not with such regularity.

The progress of organized society, democracy, and opportunity for the individual form the basic theme and impulse behind the overland trail novels. Just as these ideas are presented in special circumstances in the novels based on the other frontier locales, so do these novels consider problems of work and justice and responsibility. However, a framework is created by their physical trials and idealistic goals.

It would be improperly facile not to clarify a possible misrepresentation derived from the construction of this discussion. Specific patterns of themes and conflicts are more apparent in given regions or with certain character types; others seem more common to books written contemporaneously. However, since the pioneer faced some relatively common situations and problems historically and socially, and since authors had some related consciousness about the pioneer, there is corresponding overlapping of themes and conflicts. The noted emphases do not contradict this relationship.

2

He Towered Above Them

In a roomful of people, he towered above them, singled out and remarkable.[1]

THE PIONEER: in a nation of people, he towers above them. Was this a special breed of men? Was there a special quality in the young Americans who blazed the trails and opened the West? The literature of the frontier creates a powerful figure in the pioneer hero, one who stands out from all others.

The physical image is not sufficiently consistent in its details to create the "young American type," but certain impressive qualities are developed:

> . . . the finest figure of a man . . . so now stood this young American type of a new race, splendid as the Greeks themselves in the immortal beauty of life. His white body shining in the sun, every rolling muscle plainly visible . . . so comely was he, so like a god in his clean youth.[2]

This description of Meriwether Lewis sets the tone and pace for what follows.

Several patterns are apparent in the physical portrayal of the pioneer. These patterns seem to fall into regional-environmental designs. There is overlapping in these designs, as shall be seen, but the basic discussion will concentrate on the development of the regional figure. Influences of environmental factors as well as a sense of historical application become apparent.

[1] Hervey Allen, *Bedford Village*, 50.
[2] Emerson Hough, *The Magnificent Adventure*, 136.

14

THE FRONTIERSMAN OF THE FOREST

The distant blue haze on the horizon drawing him onward over the low crests of the Appalachians was a promise of both adventure and bounty. He scouted the trails and followed the streams that led to the eastern tributaries of the Mississippi and their valleys. He was a hunter: the forest was rich. He ran the game, fought Indians, and relished his life as a free forester. He was a farmer: the land was rich. He carved the forest into clearings, fought Indians, and started a settlement.

The area covered by the forest frontier was broad and the forest pioneer was actually two men, each with a distinctive purpose. Yet, he is, in the novels, a man attuned to the requirements of his environment. In general physical prowess and skills, the two men—hunter and farmer—become one man. Variations occur and shall be related, but these are within the general framework of this figure.

The hero of the forest is a veritable giant of a man. Tall, ruggedly muscular and powerful, he stands taller and broader than those about him. His massiveness is carefully arrayed for literary inspection:

[John Bainbridge] was very tall. . . . But his shoulders were broad and his muscles bulging and hard under his butternut blouse.[3]

[Murfree Rinnard's] shoulder blades were big and humped with muscle; his back curved in and was furrowed deep between high hard muscles.[4]

[Keith Maitland] was handsome . . . full chested and sinewy. . . . Nature had molded him on noble proportions. His flat hips, his swelling shoulders, the symmetry of his arms and legs, lent him an air of distinction even in his frontiersman's costume.[5]

[3] S. Hargreaves, *The Cabin at the Trail's End*, 37.
[4] James Boyd, *Long Hunt*, 14.
[5] Mary Schumann, *Strife Before Dawn*, 25.

The general impression then is quite the same. There is some variation in the extent of bulk, some pioneers being of more slender build, but on the whole the forester is a well-built young man. Generally he is less than twenty-five years old although a few of the farmer heroes are older. Often enough his history is started early in his life so that the total impression is of youthful vigor and health.

In the analysis of these details, a point can be made about the presentation of these physical descriptions. The novels preceding the first world war, with the exception of those by Zane Grey, give a general account of height and breadth; however, in the successive decades, as seen in these examples, there is generally an increased emphasis upon photographic detail of muscularity.

There is greater variation in the general facial structure and in the total tone of the hero's appearance. The contrast is in type of handsomeness, ranging from prettiness to ruggedness, and the occasional plain hero. This variation is not merely at random. A chronological analysis of the novels reveals a general increase of rugged qualities with the passing years. The romantic heroes of the 1900–20 novels are evenly handsome; they are dashing and pleasing to the eye. In these early novels, a secondary figure, usually a pioneer of more common class,[6] is plain of face: D'ri in *D'ri and I* is given a nose like a shoemaker's thumb; Tom McChesney in *The Crossing* and Louis Wetzel in *The Spirit of the Border* are stolid or severe in appearance, heroic but not particularly handsome. Each of these plays second fiddle to the romantic, handsome hero.

The rugged pioneer begins to conquer the pages in the subsequent decades to the gradual exclusion of his smooth counterpart. A new sense of manliness, a hard strength, is in evidence, these being associated with less even features. Gabriel Sash, the hero of *The Limestone Tree* is described as having a face thin like a tomahawk between the fall of his hair. The details of Murfree Rinnard's features exemplify the trend:

[6] An analysis of class structure is found in Chapter VI.

16

[Murfree Rinnard's] hair, black and coarse like an Indian's, hung straight down to his shoulders. His face, faintly olive but otherwise pale from living in the woods, was like an Indian's. The bridge of the nose was high, the cheek-bones were high and the cheeks, flat and narrow, ran down to a long narrow jaw. His mouth was pale and straight and thin. His straight black eyebrows almost came together. Only his eyes gave him a look that no Indian could have. They were not large and brown and cruel, they were small and hard . . . deep blue-gray, almost lavender.[7]

Later, the hero of *Unconquered*, Chris Holden, is described as having a "useful face" with a mouth too wide and a facial structure too bony.

A marked preponderance of blue eyes, usually "bright and vivid," is noted despite the more common dark hair coloring. The remaining heroes are about evenly divided among eyes of gray—clear or steely; of brown—warm or deep; or black—inscrutable or cold and piercing.

These differences in facial appearance express in part some phase of character. An expectation is created of an unflinching quality and power in the rugged representation that is lacking in the more evenly drawn heroes. The chronological development, though not fully consistent, is apparent. Taken together with the detailed display of physical masculinity, it is revealing of an alteration of literary style. A similar social manifestation may be seen in the acceptance in recent years of the rugged-looking male as the idol of the motion picture. Like Chris Holden, the new screen idol has a useful face—not always an evenly handsome one.

A glimpse of the forest pioneer's manner of dress completes the outward portrayal. The dress of the woods is his uniform: deerskin hunting shirt and leggings, sometimes fringed and beaded; moccasins; with some, a coonskin cap. This is the logical costume to make from the materials at hand. Typically he carries a long

[7] Boyd, *op. cit.*, 7.

rifle and its accouterments; a few also carry Indian weapons—a scalping knife and a tomahawk.

The counterpart pioneer of the forest—the farmer—also favors the deerskins when he is tramping the woods either hunting or scouting. Deerskins are used for all garments when conditions made all else unavailable. A variation—homespun shirt and trousers, hob-nail boots—is made possible by better times and the work of his wife. But this dress is not preferred by all farmers, even though it spoke of some prosperity. They approve the moccasins and the deerskins as more comfortable and as symbols of the woods.

The forest frontiersman is not given merely a surface display of musculature whether he is a scout or farmer. In keeping with his frontier role and the needs of the situations he encounters, he is given the utmost of endurance and strength.

In many of the novels there arises some situation which calls upon the frontiersman to walk or run long distances, generally to give warning to some imperiled settlement or to conclude some timetabled task. Adam Helmer, a secondary character in *Drums Along the Mohawk*, runs some twenty-four miles to warn German Flats of impending attack; he outraces a pack of Indians on his heels and saves the populace.[8] Gil Martin, the less flamboyant hero of this same novel, along with Tom McChesney in *The Crossing* and Andrew Benton in *This Land Is Ours*, also manage long runs and forced marches as scouts and soldiers. In *Unconquered*, Chris Holden runs four hundred miles in just eight days; in *Look to the Mountain*, Whit Livingston walks fifty miles in one day including mountain trails; in *Free Forester*, Harley Boydley, his indolence notwithstanding, endures Indian torture and then escapes, managing a long trek through the woods, none the worse for wear. Generally, from Fitzhugh Beverley in *Alice of Old Vincennes* (1900) to Abner Gower in *Bridal Journey* (1950), the frontiersmen are able to run long distances

[8] Adam Helmer's feat is mentioned in history textbooks as is the saving of the village.

with a maximum of activity and a minimum of food and rest. In these respects, they are genuinely remarkable characters.

Other feats of endurance and strength are exhibited. A number of these frontiersmen seem to have a penchant and the strength for hurling their enemies. In *Thunder on the River*, apparently soft and green, Mark Elderidge is blistered and weary from an enforced trip into Indian country, yet is shortly able to pick up a molesting Indian and toss him through a wickiup. Sal Albine in *The Forest and the Fort* likewise tosses men about. Black Brond hurls a man bodily across a room, and his strength is again demonstrated in another passage:

> I seized her and threw her over my shoulder, holding her with one arm and carrying my own gun in my left hand. With a fine burst of speed, I covered several hundred yards.[9]

There are other indications of strength and endurance: Michael Beam, the hero of a novel so titled, lifts and guides a cannon up a cliff with only the slight aid of a pulley (his own gun is so heavy that no other man has the strength to shoot it). *Green Centuries'* Orion Outlaw, known as the strongest man in the community, chops down over a dozen grown trees one evening at the termination of a long tedious trip over the mountains. Angus McDermott in *Shadow of the Long Knives* wrestles with a grown bear and knifes him. John Wayland fights off a pack of Indians after the massacre of Fort Dearborn in *When Wilderness Was King*. Though wounded from a head blow and from knife and tomahawk wounds, he swims a relatively long distance to a boat to complete his rescue of 'Toinette.

Not all of the forest frontiersmen are given such superhuman strength or such trying activities. All of the scouts, however, prove their mettle and their stamina. Many of the farmers who are additionally hunters and scouts, as the heroes of *Drums Along the Mohawk* and *Green Centuries*, show similar capabilities in defense of their homes, in physical encounters, and in outlasting

---

[9] Hugh Pendexter, *The Red Road*, 236.

physical travail. The others show their endurance and strength in the clearing and planting of their lands and the building of their homes. These odds, too, were not easy to overcome. For very few does the reader lack a sense of the greatness of the task accomplished or for the efforts expended.

The frontiersman's skills are not limited to those of strength. From his easy, silent forest stride to his "woodman's sixth sense," he is every inch in tune with the forest through which he runs.

> At twelve the lad was doing a man's share of work, standing a short watch, handling a rifle, and above all developing that keen sight and memory. . . . The boy remembered with such startling clarity the "figuration" of the land through which they passed that he could at evening recount their progress yard by yard, recalling every blaze and mark. He had already acquired the tracker's walk, eyes scanning the trace, at regular intervals glancing up to sight ahead.[10]

As with Andrew Benton, some of the frontiersmen undertook their wilderness training from early youth from their fathers or from the Indians themselves; they were brought up with this constantly active "sixth sense." Others, coming to the frontier later in life, quickly picked up the necessary skills from associates.

The frontiersman displays instinctive reactions in the woods which sometimes seem to be an inherent aptitude. The secrets of the woods are his: he understands the language of the trees and brooks; the habits of wild creatures are known to him. His keen eyes and ears are aware of everything about him. Jonathan Zane in *The Last Trail*, for example, can hear distant snapping twigs, can recognize Wetzel's owl call though it sounds authentic to everyone else, can recognize the "grating noise of a deer-hoof striking a rock" by putting his ear to the ground, and hears sounds behind the barn that no one else hears.

He out-Indians the Indians. He walks nimbly, softly, silently. He is able to creep up to or into an Indian village without alarm-

[10] Louis Zara, *This Land is Ours*, 40.

ing their acute sensibilities. He tracks without comparison in trailing individuals and also in the reading of campfire signs: the remains of the fire tell him the type of Indian, his habits and activities. Not only is he frequently as good as or better than the Indians in the woods, but he also shows considerable—if not complete—understanding of the Indians' ways, their language, and the Indian mind. Their stealth in war and cunning in bargaining are no match for the frontiersman hero. This is so well known that he is called upon to advise generals in wartime in many of the novels.

His natural skill with weapons is imaginable only to the fans of Leatherstocking. His first weapon is the rifle. In his hands this is truly a fearsome and magnificent weapon. He is a dead shot. "Barking" squirrels, that is, shooting between the squirrel's body and the bark, is child's play. Even at twelve, Benton can drop a running squirrel at a hundred yards in *This Land Is Ours*. Murfree Rinnard in *Long Hunt* shoots an otter so that the bullet goes in one eye and out the other, while Wetzel in *The Spirit of the Border* calls his shot and shoots an Indian above his left eye at three hundred yards.

A number of the foresters exhibit similar accuracy with the tomahawk, the knife, and the bow. This is especially true of men like Abner Gower and Salathiel Albine, heroes respectively of *Bridal Journey* and *The Forest and the Fort*, who have been trained by the Indians, but it is not limited to them.

With these combined skills of weapon and knowledge of the woods, one sees as an understatement the comment made of Gabriel Sash, "He never failed to return with what he had gone out to shoot."[11] Proof of this, if more is needed, lies in the use of the forester hero as the hunter or "meat winner" of the beseiged fort or the winter-embattled community. He brings back some game where others have failed; if he comes back empty handed then there certainly is none to be had.

Other skills that the frontiersman evinces include such water

[11] J. Hergesheimer, *The Limestone Tree*, 27.

skills as canoeing—with strength, speed and dexterity—swim-
ming, and, occasionally, the handling and maneuvering of a
flatboat. He rides and is able to handle horses, subduing the wild
ones, and other animals. He traps. He is able to build things,
from fortifications to simple cooking utensils. In short, his survival prowess in the wilderness is unfathomable.

All this suggests the perfection of the frontiersman at his trade.
Most frequently the hero is superior to those about him. A master
scout, he can outrun them, outshoot them, outmaneuver them,
and outmatch them in the crafts of the woods. It is he who is
selected for the difficult, most dangerous missions. He is at least
equal to the renowned scouts; old professional woodsmen judge
him the best hunter ever seen. The hero's strength and agility is
touted as well. He is respected, admired, and feared.

This perfection is not universal, however. In a few novels the
hero is not particularly exceptional as compared with his contemporaries. It is suggested that they do not lack for skills and
may even exceed the hero in marksmanship. His position is
redeemed in his being chosen to lead a scouting venture or in
his being looked to for advice. In assuming leadership, he dispels
any lessening of his superior image.

As would be expected, the less gifted woodsman and marksman is found among the farmer frontiersmen. However, a number of these maintain a dual status resulting from dual skills.
While a few are classed in the preceding category as expert
shots and woodsmen, a more typical characterization of the
farmer frontiersman is found in *Drums Along the Mohawk* in its
hero Gil Martin. Martin eventually becomes sufficiently adept
and alert in the woods to be a member of scouting parties, but
experts like Adam Helmer initially considered him too noisy in
the woods and lacking an eye and ear for what animals would
reveal. His physical attributes and his marksmanship stand him
in good stead, but Martin—and others like him—is primarily a
husbandman. He fells trees, clears and tills the land, raises
houses, carves furniture and tools, and is proficient in all manner

of handicraft. In these respects, the farmer frontiersman is often superior to others of like occupation, who follow his example. That he can add to these numerous skills the advantages of forest lore is no mean accomplishment. Yet, he does.

The image so constructed is broken by occasional inconsistency that highlights the unconvincing tone of such perfection. The inconsistencies are more pronounced in the 1900–10 novels. The most outstanding occurs in *When Wilderness Was King*; here, John Wayland relates his own background and skill.

> I had grown up on the border, isolated from what men term civilization; and I could justly claim to know chiefly those secrets which the frontier teaches its children.[12]

Throughout the novel, his actions belie this self-appraisal and the appraisal of others, who also accept him as a knowledgeable woodsman. For example, while on the trail to Fort Dearborn, Wayland notes:

> What mysterious signs our guides followed, I was not sufficiently expert in woodcraft to determine. To my eyes,—and I sought to observe with care,—there was nowhere visible the slightest sign that others had preceded us.[13]

It is shortly revealed that some one hundred Indians had gone down that same trail before them. No self-respecting frontiersman would have been so sightless. In other episodes, Wayland goes charging through the woods on inane missions like a broken-field runner. Perhaps his fallibility is realistic, but it does seem that only an author could save this woodsman. A foppish Frenchman, against whom he is favorably contrasted, is used as a necessary foil.

Similarly Beverley and De Coubert, respectively the heroes of *Alice of Old Vincennes* and *A Sword of the Old Frontier*, are said to possess the "secrets of the woods" and extensive knowledge of

[12] Randall Parrish, *When Wilderness Was King*, 9.
[13] *Ibid.*, 45.

Indians. There is little display of these; some actions seem particularly careless and ill conceived in view of these skills and considering the threatening adversaries. Yet they manage to keep intact both their reputations and their lives.

The sense of unlikelihood is fostered also by the amazing ease with which some of the characters adjust to new roles in the woods. Unexplained is the learning process adhered to by John Lee, *The Wilderness Road*, who is respected as one of the best scouts and more courageous men on the frontier. Considering his arrival on the frontier after an apparently sheltered early life as a Philadelphia aristocrat and military officer, the extent of his frontier skill is remarkable. His teacher may have been his Indian friend, whom he surpasses, but the apparent duration of his training makes the results improbable. Several other neophyte foresters fall into this questionable category: Joe Downs, *The Spirit of the Border*, is given one month's training; Stewart Randolph, *The Heritage*, and Mark Elderidge, *Thunder on the River*, have two years of Indian captivity. Evidence to support this criticism can be found in other novels, in which latecomers to the forest do not attain the optimum of skill exhibited by those brought up in the trade.

Despite the questions of probability the reader might raise, the total picture of the forest pioneer—both average frontiersman and Herculean hero—leaves the impression that indeed he was a figure "singled out and remarkable."

THE MOUNTAIN MAN

Along the timbered streams that fed the western branches of the Mississippi, traveled the trapper. He wended his way into the mountain foothills, through the craggy canyons and grassed valleys into the higher passes. He crossed the Continental Divide and followed the rushing western rivers, sometimes to the north and sometimes to the south. This was the mountain man, following the beaver, the game, and some mysterious craving for the unknown canyon, the untrod park, the "big sky."

In the literature of the frontier, the trapper and the mountain man travel the same route. Their mode of life and livelihood are the same; their physical attributes similar. The trapper is slightly simpler in dress and manner than his exaggerated and wildly individualistic cousin, the mountain man, who is the most deliberately and proudly nonconformist figure on the frontier. In this discussion, they are treated as one.

We meet the mountain-man hero as a young man; he is often not yet twenty. Most novels carry his life forward at least ten years to the time of the decline of his special way of life. A secondary figure in these novels is an older, more experienced man who has been in the trade for a number of years. He takes the young neophyte under his wing, teaches him the ways of the wilderness and brings him into manhood. The mountain man also appears in the novels of the overland trail as a guide for the caravans. The overland crossings occurred after the heyday of the mountain man, so the figure in these novels is older. His personal decline coincident with that of his way of life is illustrated in these novels. Two A. B. Guthrie novels feature the same character, Dick Summers, as the mentor in *The Big Sky* and the guide in *The Way West*. Not all of the characters become guides, however; some fade into ranchers.

The line of descent from the free forester to the mountain man is direct. He seems to have inherited many of the qualities of the earlier hunter-scout. Distance and the resulting isolation, the longer periods away from organized society, seem to have enhanced certain primitive elements of his masculinity and thus create a distinctive image.

He is like his early counterpart in physical size and build, a giant in his own right, but comparatively leaner and more rawboned. Even the extra heaviness that comes with his maturing does not dispel the impression of long lankiness topped by broad shoulders. Typically Boone Caudill is at seventeen first seen in *The Big Sky* as big and straight but lean. As he matures he becomes

... heavier ... and even stronger, as strong as a buffalo bull. The muscles of his arms showed under his shirt and the thick column of his neck spread out along his shoulders and down the swell of his chest.[14]

The older man is not less of a man, though less muscular. In *Morning Light*, Dad Lamkin is "six feet six inches tall and straight as a ramrod."[15] Other equivalent figures are hard bodied and wiry, lean and leathery. The figure of the mountain man acting as a guide to the wagon trains, considerably older at this point, is faded and grizzled and not as rugged as the heroes of these novels, yet he is still lean and hard—a man to deal with.

In keeping with the rough, rawboned nature of his physique, the mountain-man hero has sharp or rugged features. He could be termed handsome but certainly not in the style of a Barrymore matinee idol. He is silent faced and unsmiling, dark eyed and inscrutable. Black eyes are more common to this frontiersman than to the other areas, possibly to convey this cold and deep aspect. If not black, they are cold gray. The older associates, who do not have this unemotional tone and are permitted an occasional warm glance or twinkle, are mostly gray eyed.

Another distinctive feature of the mountain man is the dress of his hair. Jed Cooper's is typical: "His dark hair hung thick and warm about his neck and mingled with the curling black hairs of his beard."[16] This loose-hung fashion was worn by the older men as well as the heroes, the one exception being Boone Caudill who favored the plaited Indian fashion.

The mountain man is an individualist in his dress. Variety and difference keynote each man's choice but a certain style is evident, a variant of the forest frontiersman. While he's in the hills, his dress is simple, subdued and completely functional: plain cotton shirt, buckskin leggings and breech clout. During rendezvous, he usually affects elaborate flamboyant display: leggings

[14] A. B. Guthrie, *The Big Sky*, 383.
[15] Frank Linderman, *Morning Light*, 37.
[16] Richard Roberts, *The Gilded Rooster*, 3.

ornamented with fringes, embroidered with beads, tufts of hair, and feathers dyed in brilliant colors; decorated mocassins. The younger heroes are generally less extreme, especially if they maintain a somber, silent aspect. Their weapons include the rifle, knives and a tomahawk. With these and his traps he is self-sufficient and ready for anything.

The mountain man, like the forest frontiersman, has tremendous resources of strength and endurance. He is able to withstand severe climatic situations with no apparent pain: intense cold, blizzards, heat, and drought. In *The Gilded Rooster*, Jed Cooper travels one hundred and fifty miles, fifty of them walking, in a blizzard to get help. In those stories in which he is given a canoe or a horse, he endures long hours of continuous activity. Daylong, weeklong, monthlong trapping, hunting, and open living are managed without pause or complaint. He is hardened and built up by such activity and seems, in total, tireless, alert, and agile in every situation.

As a battler he is able and unscrupulous. At seventeen, Boone Caudill in *The Big Sky* mangles an older, heavier opponent. Once he is matured, his punch is fantastic in its effect and earns him the the appellation "Strong Arm" among the Indians. On one occasion he snaps an enemy's arm out of joint during a battle. In *The Gilded Rooster*, Cooper breaks a man's neck with his brute force.

The older mountain men do not exhibit such feats of strength in direct battle or physical contact but are equally enduring; they frequently lead the way by their stoic acceptance of the inevitable hardships. To call them hardy would be a gross understatement. They withstand all manner of exertion and pain, including torture at the hands of Indians and a cruel environment. Beyond this, they are tireless in their efforts to assist others. As the leader of the trapping party, they undertake the protection and education of the neophyte; as the wagon train guide, they are everywhere at once: strong, alert, able, the epitome of the solid, dependable man.

Initially, the mountain-man hero is a novice on the frontier.

Having come from a semisettled area from the eastern side of the Mississippi, he knows only the rudimentary survival skills. Gradually, under the tutelage of necessity, environment, and experienced trappers, he learns. Like his forester counterpart he gains phenomenal skills.

As a scout he is among the best. Nothing eludes his practiced and restless eye.

> Little by little Johnny searched the line, the bald peaks, and the shimmering basin between. Had a campfire been burning, he would have seen it. Had a Mexican military patrol, or a Comanche war party, or even a single enemy been passing close by, he would have detected some sign.[17]

At nineteen, Johnny Christmas has not yet reached his prime, yet his skills are already at a high level. The older Dick Summers is not much better, if at all.

> Dick's eyes were never quiet. They ran to right and left and looked ahead and back, and what they missed, Evans imagined, wasn't much. When they crossed a trail that ran north and south, Dick gave it just a glance, but Evans had a notion that Dick knew from the one quick look just about when it had been travelled last.[18]

With ever-alert senses, a live instinct, and a well-practiced experience, the mountain man is able to estimate numbers of horses and riders on a trail, the elapsed time, the type of game. He is a superior rifleman, able to put the ball where he wants it. However, there is much less stress on this skill than with the forest pioneer. Extraordinary examples of marksmanship are not cited with the same frequency.

He is a trapper and hunter *extraordinaire*. This skill is only partly due to adeptness with the traps or weapons, or even in the skill of the trail. He also knows animals, can sense their moves

[17] Forrester Blake, *Johnny Christmas*, 3.
[18] A. B. Guthrie, *The Way West*, 86.

and reactions. This applies to his horse as well, resulting in superb horsemanship.

He compares favorably to the Indians in his own skills and can, at times, outwit them. Jed Cooper, in *The Gilded Rooster*, is able to crawl up to an Indian without discovery. Sam Lash, in *Wolf Song*, wounded, trails an Indian all night, outthinks him, waits motionlessly for him during the next night, and then he kills him. Others show like capabilities.

The only real difference in these terms between the hero and the older mountain man is his experience; the time spent in his occupation gives the older man the status of skilled elder statesman. He exhibits the constant alertness to sound and movements, the ease of reading signs and following trails. He knows Indians and animals—he's taught the neophyte. Greater stress is put on his skill with a rifle, especially during the education phase of the novel. In the overland trail novels, the prowess of the mountain man is signified by his indispensibility to the train, illustrated by the high regard and respect the pioneers have for his skills and by the results of those skills: meat, pasturage, direction, and safety.

Among themselves, the experience and worth of the maturer man is equally recognized and respected. In turn, as the neophyte fulfills his potential, finds his skill and grows into his strength, he too is acknowledged as a scout, a hunter, a warrior. With evidence of sureness and courage, the neophyte joins the inner circle. Respected, unmatched, unsurpassed, eventually he is top dog.

On the Overland Trail

The trail lay westward from the Mississippi, open. The drive was fearful and long. The country was unknown, unfriendly; the trail unbroken. This was different from the comparatively simple feat of breaking trail and clearing trees—space enough to let the sky in—out and away from the nearest settlement or over the near-distant mountain. The travelers heard accounts of the treachery of the trail but could not know the full store of misery they faced. They heard, but still they came: dreams of gold, dreams of land, dreams of new chance, dreams.

There is a special impact from this group of novels: this was a flow of ordinary people. The people of the wagon train are in the center of the stage. The activities of the train in the mile-by-mile odyssey create the drama. The many people of the train are reconstructed; the central character, the hero, is one of them. This scheme is more pronounced in such recent novels as *The Way West*, but it is evident in *The Covered Wagon*, the earliest one of this type. In contrast, the novels of the forest and the mountain frontiers spotlight the extraordinary man and the extraordinary situation. The general populace and the day-by-day routines are in half-focus in a blurred background.

The quality of the dream of the pioneers on the trail, the sense of their purpose, is not essentially different from their predecessors of the forest. However, the heroism and struggle of the caravan are detailed; the group is not overwhelmed by the concentration on the singular individual. The reader's total reaction grows out of a consciousness of the mass presence and not individual prowess. A few novels, like *Hickory Shirt*, accent a hero figure, but these are exceptions.

The word "ordinary" in describing the people of the trail is deceptive, for the fact of their presence on the frontier makes them not quite ordinary. And in a historical view, the events were quite extraordinary. The pioneers on the trail were ordinary in that they represented a cross section of all kinds of people. Although individuals among them have singular qualities, they do not seem particularly remarkable in a broad glance.

From out of this multitude comes the central pioneer figure, the hero, who is sometimes embodied as the leader of the train. If so, he is an older man, perhaps thirty-five; he is usually broad in build with a mature, arresting posture. He does not lack vigor or strength, but his strength is that of controlled power and steadiness rather than of brute force and agility. It is in unconscious display in the attendance upon the varied chores and emergencies of the caravan; it maintains him and others in the privations and toil of the trail.

A second variety of hero is younger. Though not the leader, he has qualities of leadership and, in some stories, takes on the leadership role—in fact if not in name—when the situation is desperate. More attention is given to his physical nature. He is a lean, lithe giant and exceptionally handsome: though slender, he is not without the necessary quota of muscle. *The Covered Wagon* presents Will Banion as

> . . . round and slender, thin of flank, a trace squarer and fuller of shoulder. His arms showed easily rippling bands of muscles, his body was hard in the natural vigor of youth and life in the open air.[19]

There is a preponderance of blond heroes in this group and their eyes—one of the few points of similarity between the younger and the more mature hero—are generally blue or gray-blue.

Two points are clear in analyzing this small number of novels. The younger hero is more minutely detailed in his physique and is more romantic. He is more dramatic and seems to descend in concept from the frontiersmen of the forest and mountain.

The level of endurance and hardihood of the pioneers is manifest. Unlike dramatic instances of such in the previous discussions, this endurance is made up of the endlessness of the drive and the hardships entailed. Much of the trip is made on foot to save the oxen or horses; crossing the desert or the mountains involves pushing and pulling and carrying. Streams and rivers, some placid and others deep and swift, have to be forded. Hunger, thirst, disease, and dullness and fatigue have to be overcome. The hero is tireless and of unfailing strength in meeting these challenges. He pulls through where others falter and fail; he manages to help others and is generally more concerned about

[19] Emerson Hough, *The Covered Wagon*, 68.

them than about himself. But his acts of strength and energy are masked by the ever-present tedium of daily work.

The younger heroes occasionally perform extraordinary feats in dramatic situations. While attempting to save the lost and close-to-starvation train in *Hickory Shirt*, a weakened "Hickory" successfully fights Luke to save the food they're carrying back; then he carries both loads as well as Luke the remaining miles. Before he gets there he has strength to save the train from a flash flood.

In keeping with the general presentation of this hero, it is rather the exception than the rule to find the kind of skills that are evident in the free forester and the mountain man. There is little emphasis on matters of marksmanship or trailing and the like, except for admiring glances upon the abilities of the mountain-men guides.

Several of the younger men—Case Ford of *The Land is Bright* and "Hickory" Galt of *Hickory Shirt*—develop certain of these skills. They go on scouting forays to find game or water or to look out for Indians; they are sent to sight out the advance trail. But few if any details of their abilities are given, and they are far from the class of the forest frontiersmen or their mountain-men guides. Other heroes, for example, Unwin Shaw and Martin Collins, of *The Far Country* and *Jornada*, clearly possess no such skills whatsoever.

As far as weapons are concerned, the impression of average accuracy but little proficiency is given. The adventurer-hero of *The Covered Wagon*, Will Banion, does show some dramatic gunmanship; he kills two buffaloes with simultaneous shots. For most others, Hickory's description as "a right sure shot" is the best comment. The shooting and hunting are usually left to the guides.

What skills does this hero possess? He is a farmer in search of a farm. The use of the aptitudes and abilities of his vocation is temporarily denied him, except in the care of animals and equipment. Their care and repair are no small task, but the glamor and adventure of the wandering frontiersman's abilities are lacking.

This hero of the wagon train is a mountain of strength, rising above the situation and his fellow pioneers. He has their respect, for he holds the group together and brings it through and is considered as the only man among them who could do it.

THE RANGER OF THE SOUTHWEST

The conquest of the eastern mountain foothills and the high plateaus of the Far West and Southwest had begun early. Colonization had proceeded from Mexico—cautiously and carefully—into Texas, New Mexico, and Arizona. The missions and adobe villages, the ranchos, the incipient trade centers were distant outposts of both the land claims and the culture of Mexico. But these hardly discouraged the infiltrating Anglo-Americans. They entered the trade; they took up land; eventually they made the country their own. The difficult terrain and the ferocious Indians also proved unequal to the tenacity of the trapper. He searched out the land, he opened the trails; he—and his weapons: guns, traps, whisky—began the final crumbling of the barriers.

Green and golden fields pulled the hordes of pioneers farther westward. Though the press to the Pacific at first overreached the eastern slopes of the Rockies, pioneers began entering the country. And then the tide flowed backwards in full force.

The novels cataloging the events of this frontier area rarely consider the earlier period described above. In the few instances when they do, the hero of the piece either joins a trapping party or strikes for the mountains as in *Wolf Song* and *Johnny Christmas*. These novels depict the wandering-trapping existence of their heroes (and have been discussed in the section on mountain men).

The great majority of the remaining novels develop the period after the California-Oregon stakes, the period when the ranch was initiated. There are two basic patterns in the construction

33

of the heroes. The first, obstensibly from an earlier historical period, develops the image of the enterprising trapper, hunter, or scout who, having settled down, turns to ranching. The second is that of the cowpuncher who was to become the cowboy of American life and literature.

Physically, although there is not complete uniformity, the earlier entrant is a heavier, more powerful man. The heroes of *Brothers in the West* are huge, stalwart men with bearlike physiques. Jard Pendleton, hero of *Conquest*, is described as barrel chested and heavy thighed.

These pioneers exhibit superhuman strength and great physical endurance. Long hours in the saddle or on foot in all kinds of weather are ordinary occurrences. Agility and power mark their encounters with the forces of nature as well as against antagonists. Paralleling his predecessors of the forest, Kirby in *The Last Frontier* throws someone across a room. But it is a scene from *Conquest* which displays the utmost in strength and endurance. Jard Pendleton—his head bashed, his thigh slashed, his arm broken—holds his own against a group of attacking Mexicans. Later, although weakened from loss of blood and lack of food and water, he unfalteringly fights off buzzards awaiting his demise. This exhibition of brute strength is extreme, but it illustrates the manner of their survival and the relationship to their literary forbears.

The cowpuncher, the second entrant on this frontier, who also appears as a secondary character in the mining novels, does not lack for ruggedness or strength either. Tall and broad shouldered like his fellow pioneer, he is, however, slim waisted and narrow hipped. His is a lean hardness, a lithe muscular development.

Generally, the cowpuncher's excellence of condition is illustrated by his endurance on the trail and the range. Occasional bouts with Indians or varments of the animal and rustler variety show both his strength and capability.

Tom Moonlight in *The Throwback* provides an example of crackling strength:

Suddenly a grip of steel closed over the wrist of Pedro the Knife. There was a twist, a sound of bones snapping.[20]

Tom Moonlight also breaks an opponent's arm and literally crushes an Indian in his arms. Although the other pioneers do not have similar experiences, their activities do indicate capabilities of power on a par with those of Moonlight.

In one respect there is similarity between these two types. This is in the silence of their faces—not an expressionlessness but a guarded watchfulness. Typical is Dan McMasters:

His eyes . . . were blue-grey, singularly keen and straight, his mouth keen and straight, unsmiling. He left the impression of a nature hard, cold; or at least much self-contained.[21]

In comparison to the wooden countenances of these men, the exception of the eager, boyish expression of Tom Kirby in *The Last Frontier* is almost startling. There is also general uniformity in the color of these pioneers' eyes: gray. Similarity of facial type ends there. To match their bulkier aspect, the trapper-ranchers have more rugged features. In contrast, the cowpuncher has a finer molded face.

In matters of dress, these differences are continued. As a carry-over of their original pursuit, the basic uniform of the trapper-rancher is buckskins. These are modified to a more appropriate style. The traditional outfit of the cowpuncher makes its appearance in *The Virginian* and is repeated: broad soft hat, leather chaps over his trousers, boots, a cotton shirt, and a handkerchief knotted around the neck. The quality of the dress does not basically alter, but the costume develops.

A continuity in the development between this figure and the pioneers of the forest and mountain is apparent in all these respects. This is logical, for the trapper-rancher is in reality the mountain man tamed or turned to another role. The cowpuncher

[20] Alfred H. Lewis, *The Throwback*, 150.
[21] Emerson Hough, *North of 36*, 16.

is a further refinement. It is not surprising to see a like relationship in the capabilities of these men and their earlier prototypes. The modifications that appear may be laid to changes in the terrain.

Like his counterpart, the ranger is a skilled scout, trapper and hunter, although the latter two are less evident in the activities of the cowpuncher.

> For Kirby was of the plains; he knew the trails . . . the call of wild things; he could trail a footprint from horseback, or align the sights of a rifle with a swift movement which almost equalled that of Wild Bill or Cody. He knew these things, knew them with the instinctiveness that came from the association of years.[22]

Their trailing is faultless, their marksmanship of the highest order. They appear equally adept with the rifle or the pistol, the latter being especially a skill of the cowpuncher. Tom Moonlight shows his skill with a rifle in *The Throwback* by picking off a raven at two hundred feet and with a pistol by hitting chips thrown into the air five out of five times. Spotting a rattler about eight feet away, the Virginian draws and shoots off its head. As this example illustrates, in addition to being accurate, they are quick on the draw.

This pioneer like his predecessors understands the habits of the Indian. He can sense one in the vicinity without having seen him and responds appropriately to avert tragedy. However, the Indian appears only sporadically in these novels and is not a constant menace.

The skill which separates this pioneer from his forest predecessor is his horsemanship. Following a continuum, the cowpuncher is particularly proficient in this respect, though the trapper-ranger is very able. Both sit their horses effortlessly and tirelessly as if they made a single unit; they know horses. The cowpuncher also knows the cattle and how they will react in all circumstances,

22 C. R. Cooper, *The Last Frontier*, 132.

general and special. His rope, another facet of his horsemanship, is a flowing extension of his arm.

There is no comparison between the hero of the range and his associates. His superiority is clearly evident; he stands head and shoulders above them. Kirby, as noted in a previous quotation, is favorably compared with Cody and Hickok and is highly thought of by them. The Virginian's skills with ropes, guns, and horses is shown to surpass his contemporaries'. McMasters is the best shot and the best hand on the drive. None can match the overall excellence of each hero. He is acclaimed by all for his merits and is respected for his fearlessness, his tenacity, his physical strength, and his strength of purpose.

THE MINER

The hard, golden honey of the mines drew men like flies. Some were land seekers detouring from the Oregon trail after the more glittering lure. Others came directly, alone and in groups, overland and by sea. Some few brought women; some women came on their own. They scraped the surface of the earth and filtered it in the mountain streams. At "good diggins" they built makeshift cabins. Shanty towns grew and into them came all manner of men and women, parasites of the fever.

The novels of the mining frontier do not create a distinct pioneer image. The heroes are a mixed lot drawn from multiple sources. Several of the books have two or three equally prominent characters, each different in origin, each apparently representing a type.

There are the Northeasterners: "Yank" Rogers in *Gold*; Noel "Yank" Peabody in *'Forty-Nine*. Rogers appears to be type-cast as a forest frontiersman and trapper who has wandered out of his element. Lank, leathery and slouched, his profile is completed by the long rifle, his constant companion and trademark. His cold gray eyes are frequently alluded to and help to develop his typically nonemotional and silently forceful presence. Peabody is "called Yank because his physical conformation to the type was so pronounced. Noel had a tightly-knit singularity that distinguished him . . . ."[23] He is tall and broad and stands out in a group.

Coming to the gold fields from farm country—either New York, Ohio, or Indiana—is a second type. Wakefield, though somewhat older than the average, typifies this physical type:

> . . . a fine specimen of the typical American, a well-nourished, farm-bred giant, over six feet in height, of big bone and hard muscle, trained by outdoor labor to the condition of an athlete, a blue-eyed, fair-haired Saxon, temperate in habit and clean in thought.[24]

A Southern type is represented by Rance Poole in *The City of Six* and Johnny Fairfax in *Gold*. This caricature of a gentleman type is rather loosely drawn to depict a slender, well-knit, and poised figure. In brawn, muscularity and strength, he is not the equal of his companions. His agility and alertness, however, compensate to some degree for his relative lack of strength.

Somewhat similar in origin but clearly not styled a gentleman is a Southwesterner, the classic cowboy: Tex Potter of *The City of Six* fully represents these in physique and character, paralleling the details already discussed.

The bulk and strength that dominate the physical attributes of other frontiersmen are not found in all of the mining pioneers. When the plot calls for a display of brute strength, it is the farmer or the "Yank" who produces it. Peabody, for example, singlehandedly routs four "Hounds"; in another episode, reminiscent of the forest frontiersman, he throws Buckeye out of a window. Similarly Wakefield destroys some marauders by himself.

This multi-faced hero is likewise presented with skills as various as his background. In keeping with his flavor of the forest, Yank demonstrates the range of woodsman skills, including pro-

[23] George Cronyn, *'Forty-Nine*, 34.
[24] C. L. Canfield, *The City of Six*, 20.

ficiency with the rifle. The others show little or no background in the secrets of the woods and generally exhibit no interest. Wakefield is fairly adept with a rifle as are the Southerners.

A comparison must necessarily be general. Since there is little in common among the several types, there is little to compare. Each character serves his purpose in the furtherance of the enterprise and the plot. However, the figure who gains most respect for his ability and fortitude is the wanderer from the forest. Second, by reason of strength and endurance, is the man of bulk, the ex-farmer. The Southerner, who is at times the romantic hero, does not have much prestige in terms of skills and hardihood, and the man of the range is a comparatively minor figure.

THE PRAIRIE FARMER

The pioneers of the prairie came from eastern cities and farms and from Europe. They were farmers, canallers, tavern keepers, businessmen and the wealthy nonemployed. They came to break the soil and live in sod huts. They fought the land until it was conquered; they fought the weather to an uneasy draw. They plowed and planted and built a whole world.

At first glance, this pioneer appears pale in comparison to his brother frontiersmen. He lacks the drama and color; he lacks, too, the situations to bring out sparkling action and striking courage. Some relationship to the group can be seen with these considerations kept in mind.

These are stalwart men, to be sure, of great perseverance and physical strength. The heroes of *Giants in the Earth* and *Cimarron*, Per Hansa and Yancey Cravat, exhibit great bulk and power. There is constant reference to their gigantic frames and the huge breadth of their shoulders. Aside from them, there is less emphasis on the men's physique in this group of novels. Wayne Lockwood, the hero of *Song of Years*, is briefly described as "a perspiring Adonis in buckskin breeches." Jacobus Vandemark, the hero of *Vandemark's Folly*, is stocky and well built

39

but has the dubious distinction of being the shortest hero—five feet seven inches—of any pioneer novel. Other figures are more generally described as stocky, lithe, or powerful.

Equally indistinct are the facial qualities, especially with respect to variation of tone and character. There is a great preponderance, nearly ninety-five per cent, of blue-eyed heroes. This is in keeping with the general trend in all the novels but is decidedly more pronounced.

These men have a boundless vitality which is expressed in their dawn-to-dark workday. Literally as strong as oxen, they pursue their backbreaking occupations with tireless fervor. Per Hansa, the epitome of energy, finds time between house building and prairie-sod breaking to develop his far-flung ideas. He bursts with zeal. The others, though they lack his degree of dynamic vitality, are certainly made of the same fiber. These strengths take them through blizzards which cover their sod huts with snow, hail storms and locust plagues which destroy their crops, prairie fires, sickness, and other disasters.

Upon occasion there is opportunity for these men to show a more obvious heroism, but such situations are rare in these novels. Mort Sturdevant battles two of the vicious Mobray gang in *Oklahoma*, singlehandedly beating them:

> . . . the lightning of Mort Sturdevant's upraised left arm, as with fist doubled into white tensity, it drove forth in a vicious left hook which caught the man at the side of the chin and sent him careening floorward.[25]

Pugilistic display of this sort compares with the forest frontiersman's proclivity for heaving his opponent bodily across the room. Sturdevant, a somewhat tamer pioneer, uses a finer but not less devastating technique.

The majority of the pioneers are farmers. Their exhibited skills are in this area: knowledge of animals and their care, planting, harvesting.

[25] C. R. Cooper, *Oklahoma*, 84.

Jesse Ellison, the hero of *Buckskin Breeches*, is unusual for his knowledge of the woods and his skill with weapons. He is able to trail and to move over unknown terrain soundlessly. His ability with the rifle and the knife matches the forest pioneer.

> His intention always preceded the bullet and showed the way. . . . When he aimed his rifle . . . in an instant a man would be dead—forever dead . . . brought back squirrels shot cleanly through the head. He never wounded game.[26]

The other pioneers of the prairie exhibit some skills with weapons. They supply their families with food for they also bring back game, but their ability in this respect is more general, and the delicate art of fine marksmanship is not practiced. Of course, the plot structures of these novels do not call for much self-defense of this nature.

Several of the novels, notably *Cimarron, Oklahoma*, and *Nebraska Coast*, are only briefly concerned with a farming frontier, if at all. In an incipient business settlement, their heroes are not called upon to display responses to environmental stimulus. Occupational developments move these novels away from a frontier setting.

Each of these heroes is outstanding in his own milieu. The pioneer hero is appreciably more dynamic than others in the area and his creative imagination works in high gear. Results can be measured by his rapid rate of advance and the high esteem that he gains as a pillar of the developing community.

[26] Phil Stong, *Buckskin Breeches*, 5.

41

3

Role and Character

A rifle, and an axe, and a hoe. There's something for you to have and to hold in the great peace of the Forest.[1]

THESE WERE the weapons that opened the forest. Some of the pioneers came with only the rifle; they held themselves fiercely aloof from the hoe. To others, the hoe and the axe were the primary weapons, the rifle secondary. But the necessities of the times and place forced the rifle into early prominence to the temporary neglect of the other tools.

The forest-runner, the hunter-scout, came first on the forest frontier, but he was indeed short lived. As he came over the trails, he might have figuratively looked over his shoulder to see the axing of his fresh-blazed tree by the closely following farmer. In the literature, the two types are coexistent, although individual novels usually accent one role and group of characteristics. The hero is primarily either a forest-runner or a forest-leveler. In some works, the line of demarcation is distinctly and sharply defined, usually by the attitudes of the former. However, the attributes of both are often melded into one character: the scout was perhaps a potential farmer; the husbandman also a hunter and scout.

The measure of a man may be estimated by his purposes. The hunter and the farmer, if they may be considered separately, were essentially motivated by different purposes, though these stemmed from a similar symptom. This common factor is stated in *Westward the River*. In response to a query about the westward movers and what they are looking for, the hero says that

[1] Meade Minnigerode, *Black Forest*, 330.

"they know what they want . . . they want a new country!" Most were not in rebellion against the old; they "just crave room—room to do what they want."[2] This includes a yen to go beyond the horizon, to track the wilderness. It involved an elemental independence, the will to pit individual strength and ingenuity in the designing of one's own way of life.

Unalloyed freedom from restraint and an absolute minimum of associations characterize the lone scout or hunter. He bases his life on a strict independence of thought and action. He maintains limited contact with society, if at all, and feels free to go his own way at any time, in any circumstance. His sense of himself emanates from this credo; it is the root of his pride and spirit. James Boyd's hero in *Long Hunt*, Murfree Rinnard, is the strongest conception of this figure:

> Anyway that was the way he was, and he was proud of it. He was prouder of that about himself than of anything else. He didn't think so much of his looks, and he reckoned there was meanness in his nature; he even admitted that there were some few better shots than he was; two anyhow. But there never was, and never would be anyone better able to live his own life without a "by your leave" from anybody.[3]

He is not interested in building things or settling down and raising a family. Rather, he values solitude and the silence of the woods.

This free forester is unconcerned about other people's reactions toward him. He holds their opinions in contempt.

> He had never cared what people thought of him and had, in fact, rather enjoyed his own way without regard for anyone's opinion.[4]

Abner Gower's self-dependency is echoed by other characters of like status. This contempt carries over in a distaste for the put-on and the fancy in manner and dress. His preference is for the

[2] Dale Van Every, *Westward the River*, 45.
[3] Page 153.
[4] Dale Van Every, *Bridal Journey*, 259.

simple and direct, the unencumbered life, as realized in the wilderness.

In keeping with these attitudes, the forest-runner feels hampered by responsibility, especially that involving the dependence of others. Marriage, by making him less able to act on his own, entails a distinct loss of his basic freedom. Significantly, a solid number of such free hunters who do marry falter in the traces. One after another these hunters break their vows and drift away from the tame life into the comforting void of the forest either permanently or for long periods.[5]

The forest farmer, too, has pride in a measure of independence. He feels the openness, the freedom; he knows his desire to be his own man, to develop in his own way, unfettered and unlimited by a closed society. He manages to maintain an individual identity indicative of his self-assurance, his inner strength, and his will for freedom of action.

His sense of purpose comes not from wanderlust alone; he has his roots in the land as well. Though a frontiersman of the woods, given to hunting, skilled at scouting, his basic purpose is to create a home, to construct a farm and a life out of the fallen timbers. He feels his primary responsibility to his family. Typical of the forest farmer are Gil Martin, *Drums Along the Mohawk*, Hugh Murray, *The Day Must Dawn*, and Orion Outlaw, *Green Centuries*. While they may be off into the woods to hunt or fight—in all manner like the free foresters—their eye remains on the land.

In many of the early novels, the characters are motivated by less prosaic purposes. They are searching for their lost honor and status, or trying to regain depleted fortunes, following the pattern of literary romanticism of that early period.

The total impression of the forest pioneer in these terms lies somewhere between these types. The image is modified, being less extreme than either the willful isolation of the hero of *Long Hunt* or the determined settling of *The Trees*. Generally, it is a

---

[5] The discussion of the wilderness ideal in Chapter VII analyzes this attribute and response more fully.

far less savage image than that evoked by the mountain man. Even the most extreme is less crude and less belligerent about his isolation. Indeed his isolation is more sporadic. While the mountain man's aloofness is complete, the forest-runner observes enough of the mores of the community and visits it often enough to be accepted, though not enough to become a member. He prefers the woods to the rudimentary settlements, but the existence of settlements in the near vicinity acts to modify this characteristic. As has been stated, the incipient farmer was close enough to his wilder counterpart to take on elements of his traits.

A number of the forest frontiersmen spend time with the Indians; less frequently than the mountain men is this from choice. Rinnard's preference for Indian life in *Long Hunt* is rather the exception than the rule. Several heroes, like Mark Elderidge in *Thunder on the River*, marry Indian women but neglect their wives, alternating between them and the white settlements. These men vacillate between the wilderness and semi-organized society, showing an eventual preference for the latter.

These several patterns create a modified impression of the forest pioneer. On the one hand, there is a slight tendency toward limited associations with community life coupled with a relatively infrequent adherence to the stricter borderman code. On the other hand there is included within the forest-leveler's construction the wilderness habits and codes, an outgrowth of which is the hero who attempts to live both lives. This pioneer becomes, then, a man of the wilderness with a strong concept of independence but with his face eventually turned away from lone wandering.

Further there is built up a tentative image of each type based upon secondary characterization. In many novels the hunter-scout appears in a lesser role. He is shown to be an honest and forthright person, confident and resourceful but also impetuous, ruthless, and somewhat coarse. He is not particularly dignified or humble or gentle, and his values seem two-dimensional. When

45

a reversed emphasis in the novels places the farmer in the background, his vague construction is of a frank and simple soul—unafraid, hearty, and generous but rather heavy handed, crude and insensitive. These are not totally unkind images, and though they have a various coloration their hue is similar.

However, a close scrutiny reveals that the pioneer hero is not only somewhat different in his qualities and in his general tone from the secondary figures, but also that the images of the two types of heroes have frequent areas of strong identity. Of course, some of the characteristics delineated above are applicable. All the positive qualities apply. The pioneer also has a streak of impetuosity, and a core of hardness, but these generally are revealed at times of extreme stress or necessity. Beyond these, the pioneers' characteristics evoke a man of understanding, sensitivity, modesty and of strong principles. He is not a two-dimensional character but one of depth of thought and action. These qualities are not conveyed by each novel but are formed in a totality of conception, with several exceptions emphasizing individuality of characterization.

Certain special emphases are apparent. The heroes of the early novels, 1900–20, generally have an aspect of dignity and sensitivity. There is little display about them; they tend to be modest in their relations with people. A quality of assurance and superiority sets the majority of these characters apart from a smaller secondary group, which is represented as humble and earthy. The former group stems from high cultural background while the latter is of backwoods quality. In keeping with these mild qualities, the heroes, although they are most often of the forest frontier, are not—with but wavering exception—adamantly free foresters.

The characters in the later novels, generally after 1920, are depicted in stronger tones. These are men of will and pride and possession. Theirs is not so much a dignity of culture or manner as it is one of strength, of character, and of purpose. Their humanity seems more compassionate, their manner more spirited and less patterned. The apparent differences between the hunter and the farmer are displayed in personal relations. Thoughtfulness, gentleness, and simplicity are more emphasized. However, the nature of the plots and personal relations is such that this emphasis is only one of degree.

Although the quantity and variety of the novels in the forest group spell a diversity in the general character structure of the pioneer, some aspects are fairly universal. The man's courage is indisputable, though it is sometimes modified by caution and a consciousness of danger. At times an utterly bold recklessness and fearlessness are displayed. These variations are rather evenly distributed, though there is a slight tendency for the greater caution to be manifested in the farmer. This courage usually springs from unlimited wells of loyalty—loyalty to companions, to family, to the white man, and to a chauvinistic fervor for the cause of the pioneer. Determinaton, trustworthiness, dependability: these are qualities which come to the fore. A sense of duty and of responsibility are key factors in the development of these attributes; for the forest frontiersman who is less duty bound, there is the sense of personal honor, which, of course, is not limited to him.

These attributes imply a certain selflessness, a willingness to put oneself at the disposal of others and of a cause. This inference is generally drawn from the heroes' readiness to risk their lives to help someone or to save a settlement. Jonathan Zane and Lewis Wetzel in the Zane Grey novels spend their days in the defense of the area; Jonathan Zane's sense of duty is so strong that he declines all personal life; John Lee and Abner Gower, frontiersmen in *The Wilderness Road* and *Bridal Journey* respectively, undertake the impossible task of rescuing a captive woman from tomahawk-sharpening Indians. The heroes generally, when the need arises, forget their personal pursuits for the needs of others.

This is not the case with all men on the frontier. In many novels the self-interest of certain negative characters is used to accent the selflessness of the hero. In *Unconquered*, Garth takes on this role: he aids the Indians in their war against the pioneers, and he kills peace messengers, all for his own advantage and wealth. Chris Holden, in comparison, represents the seeker of justice and fair dealings, humanity, and the saving of the settlers. Similar contrasts are given in various other works.

Nor are all of the heroes completely clean and blameless. A few have blemishes brought on by their egocentric concept of themselves or by their specific objectives. Before the impact of the frontier reforms him, Mark Elderidge in *Thunder on the River* is a conceited young braggart. He is thoughtless and cruel and concerned mainly with the fulfillment of his own desires. Another's suffering and expense do not occur to him. Young Noah in *Westward the River* presents a similar problem, though it is posed with greater depth.

> He had always taken it for granted that the first thing there was for a man to do was to get ahead. In the course of doing this he naturally built up his place and took care of his family, but the main question still was to amount to something himself.... But he knew now it could not be his only aim. Not unless he found some deep woods where he could stay forever by himself. His main aim had to be to figure out how to get along with all the other people who had the same natural desire to get ahead.[6]

Noah is not simply selfish. His built-in code had dictated a self-interest above others. He, too, changes with the realization that he cannot live alone, and he gains the attributes of other pioneers.

From these general constructions of the pioneer character, preliminary images can be drawn related to changing literary traditions. A residue of romanticism, apparent in the early novels, dictated that pioneer's gentler tone and noble motivations and did not permit the hero to be common or ordinary. He evinces all of the positive qualities and skills but remains unblemished by any crudeness. Whatever happens to the characters and whatever actions they take are honorable and acceptable by the most

[6] Van Every, 271.

48

stringent standards of propriety and gentility. The development of the plots of these novels—the coincidences, the disguises, the flavor of fantasy in the events—furthers this impression. The stronger tones in the depiction of the later heroes is a more realistic modification of this tradition. Although the concept of the pioneer may still be romantic, the characters have earthiness and virility. Manners are not permeated with a drawing-room aura, and situations do not rely upon the make-believe.

The value patterns exhibited by the pioneer reveal similar factors. The attitudes and actions of the early heroes in relation to women is impeccable. Neither thought nor act strays from the morally and socially legitimate in their relations with both white and Indian women. In the successive decades the moral barriers break down. The love-them-and-leave-them motto of Murfree Rinnard is introduced in *Long Hunt* while the concupiscent Harley Boydley in *Free Forester* is a far cry from the early borderman. There is a further variation other than the chronological one.[7] As compared with the free hunter, relatively few of the forest farmers carry on excessive illegitimate sexual activities, though a number show few inhibitions. This generally coincides with the patterns of the prairie pioneer.

Violence in various forms was a tool of the pioneer trade. In the novels of the frontier, there is a fairly constant assault on the sensibilities. The general portrait of the pioneer carving out his homestead or blazing a torturous trail in unwelcoming areas is one of constant threat, defense and reprisal. While the image conveys a fighter, sharp differences in attitudes about fighting and killing exist, these being related to both the chronology of the works and the hero's orientation.

The early novels, those which show residual influences of romanticism, present a muted attitude. The heroes kill Indians in combat; a number of them speak out for just vengeance and the necessity of fighting for one's rights and family. However, these

---

[7] The chronological variation in sexual mores of the literary pioneer is discussed in Chapter V.

men are not permitted to kill white men. When the time comes for Jonathan Zane to shoot the renegade in *The Last Trail*, someone else's bullet spares him this onerous task. Similarly is John Lee, the hero of *The Wilderness Road*, not openly permitted to kill his enemy.[8]

In the later, more realistic books, there are almost as many variations as there are characters. While Angus Drumlin is proud of never having killed a man in *Black Forest*, Geoffrey Ormandy in *Land of Tomorrow* appears to kill unhesitantly, even proudly. Between these extremes are heroes who kill, but with cause: patriotism, vengeance for personal wrongs, survival, prevention of war. Still others pose objections to the killing of women and children, though this does not seem to be troublesome to all. The revenge factor plays an influential role causing such heroes as Curt Fletcher, *Each Bright River*, Angus Drumlin, *Black Forest*, and Berk Jarvis, *The Great Meadow* (the last two otherwise quiet peaceable), to be ruthless and unswerving.

A key factor here is the code of independence and individuality of these heroes. When Hugh Murray in *The Day Must Dawn* willingly assists his best friend in avenging a rape by arranging an "accidental" shooting, he illustrates not only man's ultimate loyalties but a conception of individual man as an instrument of justice. The murder is not questioned, nor is the desire and need for vengeance. The strong implication is that individual man can be—perhaps should be—judge, jury, and executioner; he cannot wait for law. Actions which determine law and justice on the part of individual pioneers are frequent, especially in the more recent novels which emphasize a stronger hero. The men go out and do what they think has to be done. Orion Outlaw states this tenet simply enough: "But a man had to fight, one way or another, for everything he got."[9]

There is correlation between the orientation of the pioneer and the extent and strength of these attitudes. The free hunters,

[8] The various attitudes towards law and justice are discussed in Chapter VIII.
[9] Caroline Gordon, *Green Centuries*, 92.

though not without exception, more readily resort to killing and their own law; the farm forester's tendency is to apply more civilized codes. These attitudes prevalent in the novels of the last decade of this study complement the other and provide another view of people and life, another concept of justice. An underlying belief in and striving for peace and human dignity, different from the ineffectual pussyfooting of the romantic tradition, causes heroes to hesitate in killing, to attempt to prevent or mediate Indian quarrels, to preach justness and fairplay and the elimination of violence and treachery. They are sympathetic toward the Indians and strive for understanding, co-operation, and justice. These attitudes, held by such strong characters as Elmer Hale, *Mighty Mountain*, Hercules Dousman, *Bright Journey* and Andrew Benton, *This Land is Ours*, are not limited to the last decade, but they are rare in the earliest novels.

In the novels dealing with the forest farmer, the value of work is expressed mainly by work's omnipresence and the characters' eagerness and willingness to undertake constant and backbreaking chores. Some of the characters speak out in its favor, emphasizing its good, wholesome, honorable qualities as well as, in fewer instances, the profits resulting therefrom. On the other hand, the forest hunter's negative attitude is represented, at least indirectly, by his unwillingness to settle down to it, hunting and scouting being in the nature of easy, joyous living. This is particularly apparent with Murfree Rinnard and Harley Boydley, the vehemently anticivilization heroes of *Long Hunt* and *Free Forester*. The earliest heroes of this wandering type do not evince either reaction.

Exemplified through many of these novels is the spirit of the community, of helpfulness, of stubborn courage, and of humanity that made up the frontier. The pioneer's activity and perseverance, his honesty and directness, and his success are symbolic of the spirit of America. Rare indeed is the novel that does not call attention to the "few steady, stalwart pioneer citizens who put their roots down firmly . . . ."[10] But rarer still is the more delicate sense of vision suggested in the quotation from Elizabeth Roberts' *The Great Meadow*.

> Together, men and women they went slowly forward, the men to the fore, the man's strength being in the thrust, the drive, in action, the woman's lateral, in the plane, enduring, inactive but constant. They marched forward, taking a new world for themselves, possessing themselves of it by the power of their courage, their order and their endurance. They went forward without bigotry and without psalm singing to hide what they did. They went through the gateway into Kentucky. They walked quietly being subdued by the greatness about them in the great cliffs and the fine mountain rises that lifted upward from the pass.[11]

FURS AND FREEDOM

In the literature of the mountain man, there are indeed few things which can be taken intact, which can be isolated to form a consistent structure of the inner man. Changing modes in literature and changing values in society are evident in the development of the figure. However, with every advance wave of technique or ideal, there remains an eddy of the past. The traditions exemplified in the early literature appear to die slowly.

There is a general concept of the mountain man. In the mind's eye we can see the stalwart figure of the man breathing deeply, drinking in the heady vapor of his freedom. And it was a total freedom, total and deliberate:

> . . . this was the way to live, free and easy, with time all a man's own with none to say no to him. A body got so's he felt everything was kin to him, the earth and sky and buffalo and beaver and the yellow moon at night. It was better than being walled in by a house, better than breathing the spoiled air and feeling caged like a varmint, better than running after the law or having the law running after you and looking to rules all the time. . . . Here a man

[10] Agnes S. Turnbull, *The Day Must Dawn*, 149.
[11] Page 108.

52

lived natural. Some day, maybe it would end . . . not so soon a body had to look ahead and figure what to do with the beaver gone and churches and courthouses and such standing where he used to stand all alone.[12]

This credo fosters and dominates his way of life; in its expression he is the most extreme of all the pioneers.

This independence is expressed in two distinct ways. There is a strong negative reaction to organized society—to civilization, and a corollary glorification of the wilderness; there is also the negation of any straight-jacketing of freedom of action.

He could stay anywhere. He could stand anything but comfort. He could do anything but rest. He lived a life of starvation and liked it.[13]

The comforts of civilization are belittled. The mountain man finds the mass of people and houses claustrophobic, the "smell of huddled sheltered men" distasteful. The open country, a haven, provides release also from the forces that acted to curb his basic manhood, the pressures that lessened his individuality. After a brief sojourn within the walls, he has to flee to find himself.

Alone and miles from men, for the first time in weeks he sat safe and easy. *** Once more he was whole and alone. . . . He who had been caught and torn apart once more felt whole and free.[14]

The mountain man finds unending satisfaction in his work—in the times of starvation which he overcomes and the times of plenty. The lonely vigils and the exploration of the unknown combine the glory of being first into virgin lands with that of being his own man. This world was his in all its openness and bigness; nothing could compare with it.

His love of the wilderness is not made to seem a rebellious reaction only. Sensitive to his surroundings, the mountain man

[12] A. B. Guthrie, *The Big Sky*, 201.
[13] *Ibid.*, 143.
[14] Harvey Fergusson, *Wolf Song*, 38.

found beauty in nature. Frequent allusions express the character's consciousness of the natural life and beauty surrounding him. There is also a consciousness of comparison: the country of the East is tamed and torn by the plow and axe. And the West's splendor is allied to his own quest for freedom.

Best of all, he is his own man. The hired man, the worker, was at the nadir of society. Joe Crane in *The Long Rifle* vehemently expresses this feeling.

> "Hired flunkeys," he snorted disdainfully, "working for wages and takin' orders like a passel of sojers. Don't even get the value of the furs they ketch. Jist wages! Sp'ilin' the kentry fur a white man!"[15]

In *The Gilded Rooster*, Jed Cooper's contempt for the soldiers is complete. He sees them as slaves subject to restrictions and regimentation inappropriate to manhood. He sees his strength as deriving from his freedom of thought, his independence of action.

Anathema to the mountain man was organized society's regulation of life. Boone Caudill in the cited quotation from *The Big Sky* clearly rejects law and implies the efficacy of a man's individual action and thought. In the open country a man made his own laws and served himself better. This attitude is further established by the negative depiction of society.[16]

This, then, is the mountain man's sense of independence: a life untrammelled by law or custom or people. Each of them achieves it and is, in terms of that goal at least, satisfied.

Significant though it is, the creed of independence is only one facet of the total image of the mountain man. He may have searched for freedom and based his life upon it, but other concepts and attitudes also construct his experiences and develop the image of this pioneer. In these areas, however, there are variances between the novels that preclude a one-view formulation of the image of the mountain man.

In the earlier novels, the notion persists that the literary hero

[15] Stewart E. White, *The Long Rifle*, 127.
[16] The wilderness ideal vs. civilization is further discussed in Chapter VII.

must somehow represent all the clear-eyed ideals of society. Literary realism—for even the earliest novel of the mountain man is late enough to have been affected—is applied apparently to other characters and to those areas where there is no social issue. In the more recent novels, a lustier realism dominates and includes the hero.

Stewart Edward White's depiction of the mountain men in *The Long Rifle* (1930) is a prime example of literary cross-purposes. Superficially, the presentation is much like that of the other novels, but there are some crucial differences. The hero, Andy Burnett, grandson of a Kentucky pioneer and owner of the Boone Kentucky rifle, goes west eagerly, proudly; his going is a matter of heritage and destiny, the past in his blood swirling to the present. He pursues his new life with fervor, aping the exalted mountain men in almost every way. And he succeeds: he learns the skills; he takes on the outer mannerisms; he assumes leadership. He is accepted; he is one of them—on the surface.

He is not quite one with them, however. Beyond the acceptance of dress, habits and habitat, and generally philosophy—their disdain for organized society becomes his—he balks. At the annual rendezvous, Andy Burnett stands apart. He does not participate in the frenzied boisterous activity, the loud boasting, the hair-raising games which like Russian roulette eliminate some of the roisterers. Whereas other mountain men are likely to spend their year's profits in this single extravagant free-for-all—and have to borrow for next year's supplies—Burnett is frugal. He is modest and grave and calm, a steadying influence.

Nor does he partake of the liquor and debauchery. He sees the evil of liquor, its debilitating and demoralizing effects. While the others take Indian women freely, sometimes as wives, Burnett rejects this, too. In fact, except for a fleeting attraction for Estralita, a vague, quickening of an emotion which is never realized, he remains virgin pure in thought and deed.

The variation in these details can be seen in a comparison with other mountain-men heroes. As with Burnett, Lige Mounts in

Morning Light (1922) romantically looks forward to adventure, to discovery, to finding his place in life; he additionally—perhaps to satisfy standards of social acceptability—is determined to earn money to help a destitute aunt and uncle who raised him. Sam Lash's thoughts express the romantic but more modern flavor of these novels:

> He dreamed of wild country and of himself in buckskins on a horse, of fine fights and easy money and towns to blow it in.[17]

By comparison, Boone Caudill, the hero of Guthrie's *The Big Sky* (1947) is a runaway from a hard, intolerant father. Unwilling at seventeen to take parental orders, beatings, and surveillance, he moves out, having first fully repaid his father. Though he develops a similar purpose, though his essential strivings are like those of his earlier literary compatriots, the initial motivation is much less romantic.

The literary requirements which denied the earlier hero sexual freedom or marriage to an Indian changes completely in the later novels. Each of the mountain men fulfills his desires freely, the novels providing varying degrees of sensuous emphasis. Each becomes a "squaw man" at one point. Boone Caudill's code that a woman's role is to serve man and to wait upon his pleasure signifies the change as does his love for and marriage to Teal Eye. Further evidence is the way he rather ruthlessly takes advantage of a young white girl who mistakes his temporary physical passion for permanent agreement.

Following the Burnett example, the heroes of the Linderman novels, Mounts and Lamkin, do not drink or carouse. Indeed anti-liquor editorial remarks appear:

> Nothing on earth could suit me more than having our government put a stop to the whiskey trade with Injins. I'd seen what liquor could do on the plains, enough to turn any decent man against it.[18]

[17] Fergusson, *op. cit.*, 23.
[18] Frank Linderman, *Beyond Law*, 19.

In the novels of the forties, the impression is not given of easy drinking in the main characters, but neither is there a total abstinence. Caudill tends to be sober, though not in the same moral tone as Mounts or Burnett. His is an aloofness of his character—an inability to let himself go, rather than a sense of morality or law.

A sense of deep friendship pervades the novels. The close association formed between the hero and one or two close companions is built upon silent trust and understanding and highlights loyalty and brotherhood. Stressed is the idea that friends stand with each other in times of distress and danger no matter the personal cost. The general tone is of a relaxed, close male society.

A slight difference exists in this respect with some of the recent heroes. Although they develop a close affinity with an associate, it is unspoken and more restrained. More limited associations with other characters emphasize this and show the streak of proud independence. For example, Boone Caudill in *The Big Sky* withdraws; he is short of talk and is aloof, avoiding people whenever he can. Similarly is *The Gilded Rooster*'s Jed Cooper a loner. Johnny Christmas, bound in self-assurance, relates this conviction:

> Trusting no one, having faith in nothing but his own eyes and
> ears and in his fine Hawken rifle, he knew that he would work
> more swiftly alone.[19]

Friendship is not an open proposition. The mountain men are clannish with a prejudice that closes out strangers; they have close-knit cliques within their own family. In this respect, the broad and easy associations of the earlier novels is atypical.

The behavior patterns of these men parallel these attitudes and illustrate further the variations of time upon the image. Generally forthright and honest, the early heroes manifest a degree of self-effacement. They are proud but do not parade their skills or

[19] Forrester Blake, *Johnny Christmas*, 17.

manliness. They are trusting and calm and deliberate in their actions; they are not given to displays or bursts of anger. In keeping with this, they prefer not to fight if possible, though there is no lack of strength or courage on their part. They exhibit fierce courage when justifiably aroused and when fulfilling an obligation or code. The later heroes further develop these qualities. They are equally honest but their nature limits the degree of forthrightness and trust. They are extremely proud and easily flare into ferocity; the slightest suggestion of character defamation or physical assault creates heat which builds into destructive power and overpowering courage.

The variations are not abrupt in occurrence and not complete in each character. However, Jed Cooper, the hero of *The Gilded Rooster*, appears to represent the completed circuit as compared with Andy Burnett in *The Long Rifle*. He as a hero is the swaggering prototype against whom Burnett is compared; he maintains the very values from which Burnett holds himself aloof. He has no sense of responsibility, no loyalties. He is self-centered, selfish; his actions a reflection of pride and self-superiority. His behavior seems to accentuate the negative qualities of the mountain men. Only in his final acts does he redeem himself in a display of the unaccountable courage and strength that identifies the mountain man.

Replacing the romantic overtones of the early novels is a psychological orientation of the recent ones. An interior view shows them to be unsure of themselves and in their relations with people. An exterior hardness masks their sensitivity; an inner hurt causes their withdrawal. Unable to voice their feelings, unable to trust people fully, they live in their guarded world, poised for reaction. Their anger and action represent the build-up of their suppressed emotion. The mountains and open space protect their isolation and render them safe.

Circumstances work against this safety. The mountain man's way of life was doomed because he had been unconcerned about the future.

He was a mountain man . . . and traveled with hunters who never gave a thought to soil or timber and tricks to pile up money but went along day by day taking what came, each morning being good in itself, and tomorrow was time enough to think about tomorrow.[20]

He who had been impervious to his self-destructive ways began to see the writing on the wall. At least in the literature he sees the end of the dream: the dream of the good life never ending.

Few are able to translate this dream into the idyllic compromise envisioned by Dad Lamkin, not even he himself:

But some day I'm going to settle down in some pretty spot where the mountains meet the plains, an' where the clear cold streams are contributin' fresh snowwater to this here river. Then I'll hev 'em all with me, an' jest take what I want an' need out of the herds an' from the waters.[21]

Several do move in this direction; further, a number of novels of the ranch frontier present their hero as a former mountain man. The pull is toward the inevitable organized society—toward marriage and settling down.

The conclusion does not always bring such adjustment. Jed Cooper, defeated by civilization, makes a final heroic effort to maintain his pride and principles and brings on his own death in a more thorough escape than the one taken by Andy Burnett. With the destruction of all that he loves in the battle between his friends, the Blackfeet and the mountain men, Burnett leaves for California with its vision of seclusion and pastoral beauty. But his life is ruined and gone and California can only promise a brief reprieve.

At the close of *The Big Sky*, Boone Caudill and Dick Summers sadly reminisce on the past and the demise of a way of life. Another alternative, a preamble to the future, is offered as they gaze back and forward:

[20] A. B. Guthrie, *The Way West*, 52.
[21] Frank Linderman, *Morning Light*, 72.

Boone looked down. . . . "It's all sp'iled, I reckon, Dick. The whole caboodle."

"I don't guess we could help it," Summers answered, nodding. "There was beaver for us and free country and a big way of livin', and everything we done it looks like we done against ourselves and couldn't do different if we'd knowed. We went to get away and to enj'y ourselves free and easy, but folks was bound to foller and beaver to get scarce and Injuns to be killed or tamed, and all the time the country was getting safer and better known. We ain't seen the end of it yet, Boone. . . . Next thing is to hire out for guides and take parties acrost and spi'le the country more."[22]

THE TRAIL

The mountain man looked askance at the pioneers who came in wagons with plows and axes and a sense of transplanting civilization. He saw them as a menace to his freewheeling life; he saw them as the despoilers of his country. But Dick Summers' prophetic warning in *The Big Sky* is realized. The pioneers come and the mountain men serve as guides.

The mountain man serves still another literary purpose: an initial measure of comparison and insight. This symbol of glorious freedom is but an unclean, undisciplined—though a valuable and skilled—savage to the pioneers of the caravan. They welcomed his guidance and loyalty but withdrew from his manner of life. He, through occasionally recognizing the perseverance and solid strength of individual pioneers, could not accept their organized purposefulness. Only a few of the mountain men, like Dick Summers, who fulfills his own prophesy in *The Way West*, understood it.

Dick Summers thought lazily that these were different from mountain men. These couldn't enjoy life as it rolled by; they wanted to make something out of it, as if they could take it and shape it to their way if only they worked and figured hard enough. They didn't talk beaver and whiskey and squaws or let themselves

22 A. B. Guthrie, *The Big Sky*, 385.

60

soak in the weather; they talked crops and water power and business and maybe didn't even notice the sun or the pale green of new leaves except as something along the way to whatever it was they wanted to be or to have. . . .

Summers didn't guess his heart was as troubled as some. There wasn't any burr under his tail. He was a mountain man, or he had been, and traveled with hunters . . . but the movers were different. They traveled to get someplace . . . they looked ahead to farms and schools and government, to an ordered round of living.[23]

The chief difference lay in this sense of purpose. The mountain man had all that he wanted.

In moving West, these pioneers were not escaping from a repressing civilization. Their strivings are to build a replica—though perhaps not an exact one—of the society they left behind. They see in their move a revitalized future in new lands and bright opportunities for themselves and their children. Homes, schools, churches, government—these are part of their plan. They saw some injustices and inequalities in the old society to be corrected and are sure that they can do it. They will get something out of life, a life built around hope, ideals and trust, a life built by work.

Many of the movers are in need of a new chance to remove misfortunes of the past, so they grasped at the straw. This alone, however, does not account for their taking this drastic step, nor does it account for those who had comfortable situations in the East. Some additional impetus was needed. This is suggested by Wingate, a reasonably well-to-do farmer, in *The Covered Wagon*. He has an urge to move on.

Besides this country is too old, too long settled. My father killed his elk and his buffalo, too, in Kentucky; but that was before my day. I want the buffalo. I crave to see the plains, Molly. What real American does not?[24]

23 A. B. Guthrie, *The Way West*, 51.
24 Emerson Hough, *The Covered Wagon*, 35.

Indeed the American wants to pioneer, to partake of its spirit, to let his children live that adventure, as well. In *The Way West*, Lige Evans specifically makes this point for his son, adding to it the sharing in the golden harvest at the trail's end. Aside from the glory and the profit, pioneering was said to build men and character, which, too, was a reward.

A stronger reaction against the tameness of the East is expressed by some of the younger, romantic heroes:

> He'd put behind him . . . the starched and stuffy monotony of his old life. Let other men count the money in the tills back home, let them wrap up packages for fussy old women, let them grub patiently in the stony acres their fathers had dug before them, let them sleep soundly at night in soft beds and get up on Sunday morning to array themselves in broadcloth and walk soberly to church. He was done with all that.[25]

This strong sense of escape from drudgery is not typical in these novels since the pioneers are expressly building an organized society. This feeling of escape is more reminiscent of the yearnings of the mountain men, but it also conveys some of the spirit that carries these pioneers into and through their trials. They could not have left the sheltered lives without some call away from the prosaic. But the dominance of their practical approach and goal masks any sign to the contrary.

A spirit besides that of adventure is infused into these novels, that of being an American and of America's Manifest Destiny. With some modification of method, this idea is built into the framework of most of these novels from the first, *The Covered Wagon* (1922) to the last, *The Way West* (1949). These concentrate on the "saving of Oregon for America" issue; others raise the flag over California and over every wagon:

> The wagons came on, with slow inevitable motion . . . that no individual mattered much in this mighty movement, that no single caravan mattered much. . . . the wagons would still come rolling

[25] Robert L. Duffus, *Jornada*, 8.

on. . . . It was a nation, not a caravan, that was on the march. These wagons were a symbol . . . perhaps America was going at last to the Pacific. The soul of the boy who had played in the sands of Cape Cod thrilled at the thought. When the drums were beating how could one stop to think of justice, or ask by what right the armies marched.[26]

This frenzied patriotism justifies the conquest and instills into the pioneer a sense of destiny which transcends his prosaic problems. This, together with the urge for self-improvement, for adventure and distant places, separated these men from the sheep who kept to the protected folds of the East.

As has been suggested in the parallel discussion of the physical features of this group of pioneers, there are a multitude of types of people that made up the trains. The novels suggest their solid, earthy quality as well as developing insight into human frailty and human dignity in the face of great travail. There are weak characters to match the courageous and strong, characters who despair and those who hope, representation of greed as well as selflessness. The total makeup of the train creates the essential pioneer presence in these novels.

Superimposed in vivid relief is the hero. He is the leader or assumes some leadership functions usually in the face of impending disaster. Compared with the heroes of other frontiers who undertake leadership, he is a remarkably mild type. This is so for both the younger and the older figures, Ohio Jillson in *The Long Knives Walked* and Lige Evans in *The Way West*. (The major exceptions are Will Banion in *The Covered Wagon* and Joseph Hewlett in *The Proselyte*, who will be separately discussed.)

The older hero of the overland trail is a humble man. He is self-belittling, having protracted doubts about his ability to lead the train. When elected, he serves. No one questions his capability, but he is nonetheless haunted by fears of inadequacy. The younger men are equally nonassertive and hesitant about assuming leadership and seem to be pulled into it by sheer force of

[26] *Ibid.*, 71.

63

circumstance. Again, others seem to recognize their abilities for their advice is sought; in *Hickory Shirt*, for instance one old-timer has confidence that the train will get through if young Hickory sticks with the group. And it does, chiefly by his efforts.

A quiet nature, a general reserve in human relations, are natural counterparts of these qualities. He is a steady man, calm and controlled; from these much of his personal strength emanates. Like the mountain man, he has a high sense of loyalty and trust, but his is channeled into strict moral code of duty, responsibility, and selflessness. Kindness, justice and generosity typify his relations with the train personnel. His thoughts are for the safety and the maintenance of the train; all his people have to get to the destination. These traits, it can be seen, catalog a conscientious human being, honest and fearful of his responsibilities, who attempts to maintain personal honor in his difficult activities.

Needless to say, this pioneer also represents those elements of courage, determination, and resourcefulness which were necessary on any frontier. There is a difference in quality here, however, which is fostered by the peculiar circumstances of the train. His characteristics are not so much factors of fleet, fearless action. Rather, they are characterized by steadiness and stability in the face of overpowering natural phenomena and human misery.

Will Banion, the youthful hero of *The Covered Wagon*, strikes a different note. His greater self-confidence and his pride translate into a more decisive quality which, coupled with impetuosity, separate him from the general mold. Also, his particular sensitivity about a man's honor is a throwback to the earlier romantic writing.

The hero of *The Proselyte*, the Mormon zealot, Joseph Hewlett, stands out as well for his decisiveness, confidence and drive. His entire make-up is steeped with the fervor of his religion; when called upon by the cause, he marshals his forces and those about him and joyously undertakes the burdens of leadership.

The religious impact, of course, is quite pronounced in the

several Mormon novels, for their very life was dictated and driven by their precepts. That the pioneers in the other novels are carriers of religious and moral teachings is also clear, though the women are designated as the chief participants.

> Personally I believe in Sunday rest and Sunday services. We're taking church and state and home and law along with us, day by day, men, and we're not just trappers and adventurers.[27]

Following Will Banion's lead, the pioneers in *The Covered Wagon* and the other novels designate times for services. Stops along the way for prayer and Sunday rest are frequent. The comparative statement in the quotation differentiating these pioneers from others is significant.

A consciousness of moral teachings is immediately apparent in the concepts of love and marriage conveyed in these novels, so markedly different from the general code of the mountain man. The hero is not involved in premarital or extramarital sex. From the devoted husbands to the restrained lovers these are moral men.

Not all of the characters are virtuous, but the acceptance of morality as the status quo is justified in that those who fall from virtue are condemnable. Banion's stolen kiss in *The Covered Wagon* (1922) is shameful and unpardonable; Mack's seduction of young Mercy in *The Way West* (1949) is equally so. The designated degree of these sins is relative to the period in which the novel was written, illustrating the changed social morality. However, a suggestion of open-mindedness is apparent in the later books. The hero maintains his ethic but he does not necessarily judge his neighbor as harshly as he would have in earlier novels.

The relations between men and women are drawn on lines of respect and simplicity. Courtesy and manners hold a significant position. Even in the face of extreme situations, the men attempt to spare the women embarrassment and hardship. They are

[27] Hough, *op. cit.*, 29.

deemed the weaker sex in the early novels and excluded from men's affairs, like the management of the train. In the later novels, they are constructed with more character, and they exert significant attitudes. These differences notwithstanding, the basic codes still maintain.

In another aspect of morality, the justice of frontier law is questioned in these novels either directly or indirectly. The hero is shown to be a man of strong principles who is generally opposed to killing and fighting. Dan Johnson, the train leader in *Don't You Cry for Me*, speaks out strongly against the eye-for-eye punishment decreed by frontier practice. He argues for the spread of civilization and the need for disciplining more savage habits. Lige Evans agrees in *The Way West*, indicating that killing must be justified by more than fear or whim; he fights an adversary only as a last resort and after long abuse. Case Ford and Christopher Strange, younger heroes in *The Land is Bright* and *Christopher Strange* respectively, cite the brutality of killing. Strange feels great remorse over an Indian killing which circumstances force upon him and undertakes to save another dying Indian as part recompense. Will Banion's reaction, as is that of Hickory, is to spare his adversary the full reading of the frontier law. He does not take advantage of his victory, declining the right to put out his opponent's eyes.

Another issue of some consequence in the earlier novels derives from the land-gold conflict of the pioneering period.

> "Did ever you see a pick and shovel build a country? Did ever you see steel traps make or hold one? Oregon's ours because we went out five years ago with wagons and plows—we all know that. . . . To hold a country you need wheels, you need a plow. I'm for Oregon.
>
> "Do some thinking, men before you count your gold and drop your plow. Gold don't last, but the soil does."[28]

This impassioned speech by Leader Wingate attempts to stem

28 *Ibid.*, 326.

66

the pull of the gold fever which threatens to break down the train. The land is the symbol of stability and security; it represents work, home and country, the essential goals. The easy profits of the gold fields cannot bring ultimate happiness. The positive characters go to Oregon, but several—notably Will Banion (this fits in with the adventurous quality suggested in his makeup) and Ohio Jillson—are permitted a brief excursion to the mines to gain a nest egg before they, too, turn to the land. It is significant that this same concept is conveyed in the mining frontier novels.

The trail to Oregon is judged ultimately more heroic, more fulfilling. The pioneer who endures the hardship of the trail and succeeds in planting the seed of his civilization across the continent marks a finer destiny. In the previous quotation, the role of miner and trapper in building America is relegated to secondary importance. The farmer is given the superior purpose and the superior accomplishment.

This tone is further borne out by a final scene in *The Long Knives Walked*. The trapper guide, who had urged the route to gold, falls into the mud—useless, unknown, reaching back to past glories—"We war free trappers." At the moment of his demise, the Jillsons ride by, headed for land, fortune, and fame in their Conestoga wagon. Symbolically, the trappers' glorious role was short lived and of transient value, especially as compared with the more purposeful pioneer.

The essential variation within this group of novels is not the structure of the plots or even the basic lines of the characters, but merely the literary method. *The Covered Wagon* (1922) as compared with *The Way West* (1949) belongs in the romantic fiction of the pre-World War I period as far as pioneer novels go, and earlier as far as the general literary development is concerned. Will Banion, with his concern for honor, with his oversensitive pride, his sense of guilt for stealing a kiss, and his grand flamboyant reactions, is the dashing romantic hero. The other early books, *The Long Knives Walked* and *Jornada*, are similar in the romantic presentation of their themes and characters. The later books in their emphasis on the more solid citizens and their practical pursuits reveal the effects of the changes in literary approach.

Another aspect of these novels is their incomplete, paper-doll characterizations, the people and their emotions seeming word deep rather than actual. An exception is *The Way West*, in which the realization of character is practically unique.

STRONG, SILENT MEN

The succession of strong men who roam the land comes down at last to the men of the range. From appearances the line of succession stems directly from the mountain men. Indeed many of the heroes of these novels are reformed men who have come away from the mountain. There are some crucial differences between them, but on some levels the distance from the mountain to the range is not too great.

The similarity and the difference emerge from the same point. While the strength and character of the man of the range stems from his independence—as with the mountain man—he modifies this independence with a consciousness of stability. He is a loner. Whether he is in close association with people or not, he basically tends to rely on himself and to limit his relationships. Taciturn, self-possessed, he keeps within himself. Unlike the mountain man, however, he comes to recognize his need for some purpose. He sets about building a life—a home and family—while he keeps his basic code intact. By surrounding his spirit with the open range, he achieves some manner of compromise between the unconscious forces that drive him.

The literary manifestations of this idea vary over the course of the years. In the earlier novels, the ideal man, grand in his lonely existence, sees life as complete and meaningful. He meets the perfect woman; with her comes the sudden realization that life offers something more. Together they face the future. The pattern is essentially the same in the later novels, but gone is the romantic overtone. The men are less than ideal; their sense of themselves far from a comfortable satisfaction. The aloneness is sometimes lonely. Their search for stature, for the purpose of life is neither sudden nor cleanly resolved. A psychological paint-brush defines more realistic issues. Rather than ending with the happy couple facing into a beautiful sunset, the certainty of achievement is withheld.

. These men are scrupulously manly. This is conveyed in part by their unwillingness to give up their self-possession completely or easily. By this they affirm their essential control of themselves and their destiny. To give up self-possession would indicate a giving in to the forces which eat away at manhood. They go only part way towards establishing a secure place in the world, for, with exceptions, they remain basically aloof from the community of people. In some instances, the meeting ground with their wives and families is in a world outside themselves; the close knit development fostered in the pioneer homes of the prairie is not found here.

The sense of manliness is also established by the range hero's identity with masculine tasks and his creed that a man must prove himself a man. Ranching has the necessary attributes to fit these demands. It is wholesome, free, open. It necessitates strength and courage, endurance and decisiveness. He regards other work as unmanly and looks down on those who can not meet the requirements and challenges of the range. In this light, the Virginian initially finds little to be pleased about in his role of protector of the mild, refined Englishman, his attitude signify-ing a belief that a real man must and does take care of himself. He belittles the visitor for not being able to and resents the unmanly task asked of him. Only when the visitor proves himself is he accepted.

The portrait of the ranger includes hard work and directness. Not only does work pay off, but it develops and proves the man. One who uses chicanery to get ahead, or the disadvantage of others, is not showing his own ability, but the weakness of others.

The reliance on chance factors—such as finding gold—is also unacceptable. Out of these attitudes grow several associated characteristics: honesty, straightforwardness, honor, sincerity. His total strength grows out of these and the courage to carry out his convictions. Greed and deceit, are condemned, in keeping with his manliness and his directness. The sole exception to this is Jard Pendleton, the hero of *Conquest* who cheats freely and uses force to his own advantage.

Following the characterization of the earlier mountain man, the ranger also emphasizes the value of friendship. A strong relationship between men, calling for loyalty and helpfulness, is considered fine, clean, and wholesome. It develops out of mutual trust, builds upon understanding, and calls for an extension of the self. The Virginian is greatly hurt by Steve's failure to bid him farewell at the lynching and much relieved later to find him true to this code even before death. Such circumstances should not have changed friendship to enmity, for friendship does not question duty or depend upon fair weather. The quality of friendship is further emphasized by the attitude of Jard Pendleton in *Conquest*, who is otherwise the black sheep of the group; although he disregards all other laws, he feels bound by the law of friendship.

The uniform general construction of this pioneer is offset by an inconsistency in the presentation of individual rangers who differ in the tone of their personalities. The Virginian and Dan McMasters in *North of 36*, for example, are modest in demeanor, generally calm, dignified, and gentle with the addition of the proper dosage of virility, masterfulness, and a relentless pride and will in the maintenance of their masculine status. This inflexibility comes to the fore when a principle is at stake; then their determination overpowers any other tendency. To the contrary, Jard Pendleton is tough and hard; his approach is crude and borders on the cruel. Tom Moonlight in *The Throwback*, as befits the title and the theme, is an awkward combination of gentleness and brutality, as are the heroes of *Brothers in the West*. This inconsistency seems to be part of the literary patterns discussed previously in this section; the tradition of the ideal hero depicted in the mountain man section seems also to apply here. The early heroes, the Virginian, Dan McMasters, Tom Kirby and others of this type, can do nothing really unacceptable; Tom Moonlight's brutality turns out to be a masquerade which he repents and reforms.

This essence of the idyllic is further suggested by a comparative glance at the moral principles of the heroes. The early ones deport themselves with complete propriety and strict morality with women. A kiss and an embrace are permitted after the necessary commitments have been made. Sexual encounters for the later heroes are not unusual and are related as a commonplace. *Conquest* again is exceptional in its comparative emphasis on sex and its stress on the hard living, loose loving of its hero.

There is somewhat more uniformity in the concepts of law and justice but a similar pattern related to the key traits can be discerned. *The Virginian* is generally opposed to killing and filed-trigger justice. However, when the lynching tribunal makes its decision based upon the evidence and the previous warnings, he carries out the lynching of his friend. He cannot forego his role as trail leader, his manhood before his peers, or his sense of fair play and honesty. Similarly, McMasters disapproves of certain killing, like Indian women, but accepts and persists in his role as avenger of his father's murderers. After he has killed, however, he considers himself unworthy of the virtuous Taisie, despite his many-faceted rationalization: for the sake of Texas, for law and for the safety of women and children. Tom Moonlight, semi-brutal, antilaw—he sees it as a trap, a resort of weak, unscrupulous men—acts as becomes a man: directly, forcefully. To fight is man's right and obligation in the defense of self, of principles, of the weak, particularly when, as in this instance, the threat is not above board or honorable, not manly, though within the law. In contrast, the later heroes are not provided with either a moral opposition to killing or a rationalization of honorable vengeance.

They kill without fanfare or excuse when it is necessary to do so. Their killings are not excessive, especially as they mature, nor are they emphasized. Jard Pendleton, in keeping with his particular portrait, kills most freely and viciously to eliminate those in his way.

The degree of purpose varies with the novel and the character being represented. David and Charles, the *Brothers in the West*, emphatically deny for themselves and question the validity of purpose.

> "That's what's eating those folks in Omaha," he was sure. "They want to get some place so bad that there's nothing on the way but the hope of getting there, and when they get there it's all over; or if they don't make it in the end, it's just as bad to them as never having been alive at all."[29]

The brothers condemn much of society, its false gods and false ideals. The corruption of planning one's life away and missing life in the process is answered by these two by purposelessness. Love and marriage change them externally only: they build a home and ranch, carry life along, and leave when there is nothing to keep them.

More typical an attitude is revealed by the development of Gowd Skinner in *Diamond Wedding*:

> . . . his changed attitude toward what the world knows as "getting ahead." Gone was the mountain wanderer whose pride it had been that he needed little for today and nothing for tomorrow. . . . The items of his aspiration kept multiplying. . . . Substance, security, grace of living to benefit Hope's grace. . . . It is likely that all these strange new resolves sprang of a very simple new yearning. To be doing, earning, learning, as other women's men did.[30]

But Gowd maintains a strong desire "not to be cramped and elbow-tied" throughout the progress of his life. Just as the broth-

[29] R. Raynolds, *Brothers in the West*, 13.
[30] Wilbur D. Steele, *Diamond Wedding*, 130.

ers remain true to their ideal and to themselves, so does he. Progress fits into the scheme of existence but it is not the total essence of life. The essential code of independence is still there. The brothers return to their wandering in the mountains. Gowd and Hope Skinner pack up their gear, close their organized life behind them on their diamond wedding anniversary and head back to the simplicity and beauty of the mountains. That is where their spirit has been.

However, the road does not lead back to the open spaces for most of these men. Change of the old ways is inevitable, and the open life fast disappears. While they attempt to maintain a hold upon the ideal and the old way of life, the heroes gradually adjust. They do not accept the confinement of civilization but they do take on its organization. Even Jard Pendleton's hard living dies when he marries a cultured Easterner; he exchanges his old ways for new stability and social status.

GOLD IN THE HILLS

The old song of World War I vintage that tells of the difficulties of keeping the boys "down on the farm after they've seen Paree" might well have been written about the men at the gold fields. However, the conclusion would have to be reversed. The heroes of the California gold rush novels, all published before 1925, after having had their day in the gold fields, do return to the farm.

The initial lure to California is that of adventure and fortune. There is the vague element of breaking away from routine or of making a brilliant coup, after which a return home is contemplated by a few. Adventure and excitement abound; the hero joins the diggers and amasses gold, being caught up in the frenzy of the time. At this juncture of the plot the nature of this man begins to be felt. There are a series of reactions against the dominant patterns of the mines.

Among these is the consciousness of the illusion of the gold. It turns out not to be so easy to get or to hang on to. It does not bring the sense of achievement, peace and happiness for which the hero yearns. Wakefield recognizes that in the land and the simplicity of his life on the farm he had happiness. Gold is a false lure. In another novel, a character echoes his feelings:

> "Do you know," he said suddenly, "I believe we're on the right track. It isn't the gold. That is a bait . . . that attracts the world to these shores. It's the country. The gold brings them . . . some, like us, will stick. And after the gold is dug and scattered and all but forgotten, we will find that we have fallen heirs to an empire."[31]

This is the empire of land. The heroes take their winnings and go back to the land.

The future lies in the land. The land is also shown to signify stability and permanence. The miner can now develop a civilized society, where law and order, decency, and peace prevail. The land also stands for honest labor in which a man can reclaim himself from the loose and easy living of the mines. The virtue of work is most directly emphasized in *The City of Six*, which attempts to show the weakening of character resulting from shiftlessness and the corollary of personal accomplishment derived from work. Even the mine in this novel is highly organized and the resulting success is a symbol of what effort and labor can do.

Reactions against lawlessness, drink, and gambling are also strong. When drunkenness or banditry become rampant, when the miners who are generally honest and stable cannot feel safe because the land is ruled by the ruthless, then action to curb these evils is effected. The hero joins these vigilante committees to stamp out the lawless. There is vague discussion about the justice of such action and of the miners' courts, but the enforcement of some sort of law and order comes first. Drink is associated with lawlessness in its deteriorating influences. The hero usually remains detached from the gambling activities, which are generally depicted as evil and are coupled with waste and shiftlessness. The gambling does not usually bring rewards either, and if it does, such easy money is considered ill gotten. Exceptions

[31] Stewart E. White, *Gold*, 437.

are made in some novels to allow for special circumstances and selfless causes. In *The Splendid Road*, young Sandra Dehault, suddenly on her own with three orphans to support, assumes the attitudes and role of a man. She goes to the casinos to increase her funds so that she can get to Oregon—and land. Since there can be no question about Sandra's intentions, her actions are not put in a condemnable light.

The literary hero of the mining frontier exemplifies rather strict moral principles in keeping with the literary patterns of the earlier romantic novels. His attitudes towards immoral love follow the same patterns. Guided by a concept of true love, his reactions toward sex are strict and controlled. Actually, there are but few, quite hesitant accents of sex.

The small number of these novels and their plots which present several key characters limit the definition of the image of this pioneer. He evinces the general pioneer traits that are expected: strong individualism, self-reliance, honor, vigor, and courage. He is a loyal and trustworthy friend. These are general characteristics which are not especially emphasized, and this hero is not otherwise particularly outstanding.

THE PIONEER TAMED

The people who came to pioneer the prairie may not have had an essentially different character from their predecessor pioneers. However, the situation and the environment they faced cause an emphasis of special traits which seem tame in comparison. They are not, as it might seem, lesser men, and their particular problems are hardly tame. It is merely that their day-by-day struggle with nature seems less venturesome.

In general, the prairie pioneers are farmers. They come for land and to fulfill their special dream of prosperity. The prairie is the big factor. Not the prairie for itself—not at first—but the fact of free land, open land, land to build on. They want to amount to something, to get ahead, to build communities; they applaud every advance in culture and comfort. The prairie is both the big drawing card and the final ace in the hole. It creates the basic opportunity by permitting the poverty stricken from Norway and the Missouri newlyweds, with their hopes and tiny nest eggs, and the somewhat jaded son of a New York tycoon all to strike out on their own.

For they come West because they want to be on their own. They neither can be harnessed to someone else's fortune nor can they be trapped in a narrow existence that does not permit a man to be a man in his own right. It is this degree of independence which makes them pioneers. In search of this quality and a prosperity which may not have been available to them at home, they become missionaries to tame the prairie.

For these early settlers, the land is life's very symbol: it sustains life; it builds life; it is life. Alexandra, the immigrant heroine of *O Pioneers*, conveys both her devotion to the land and its stability in the following quotations:

> Her face was so radiant . . . [the land] seemed beautiful to her, rich and strong and glorious. Her eyes drank in the breadth of it, until her tears blinded her.

> Suppose I do will my land to their children, what difference will that make? The land belongs to the future, Carl. . . . We come and go, but the land is always here. And the people who love it and understand it are the people who own it—for a little while.[32]

Bess Streeter Aldrich in her three books avows a like principle. When all else fails or becomes false, when life has lost meaning, the land remains. Return to it, is her message, and be replenished.

> Never go depending on money alone . . . always own a piece of land and you can fall back on it for food and fire and shelter. The good land won't go back on you like gold or a piece o' paper that only says it's worth so much. Own a little land and you've got shelter and food and warmth and independence. You're a king in

[32] Willa Cather, *O Pioneers*, 65, 308.

your own kingdom. Nobody can tell a farmer what he can and can't do.[33]

The pioneer hungers for land; he accumulates more land and he grows with it. His descendants leave the land for what seem like greener fields but discover merely the desert of high life.

The frontier still represents a special consciousness in terms of civilization. The prairie pioneers do not see it so much as an escape, but rather as a chance to prove their manhood. They see positive features that will permit personal development: independence of life, freedom of thought, security of income. So Wade Cameron in *The Edge of Time* declines the job in the bank offered to him by his fiancée's father; Mort Sturdevant gives up the easy rank and duties of his father's New York office in *Oklahoma*; Will Dean, the hero of *Lantern in Her Hand*, automatically heads to the open country when he marries rather than stay on the folks' farm.

A reminiscent comment by old man Vandemark relates the essence of the pioneer experience which these men sought for themselves and their families.

> We went through some hardships, we suffered some ills to be pioneers in Iowa, but I would rather have my grandsons see what I saw and feel what I felt in the conquest of these prairies, than to get up by their radiators, step into their baths, whirl themselves away in their cars, and go to the universities. I am glad I had my share in those old, sweet, grand, beautiful things—the things which never can be again.[34]

A stronger dissatisfaction with existing mores is suggested in *Buckskin Breeches*. Before going West, Jesse Ellison notes the softness of his sons, his wife's fripperies and ostentation, the general degeneration of life's purpose and the prostitution of his values. He expects the frontier to recreate the life of his family and to raise it above the mud level of humanity—and it does. His

[33] *Song of Years*, 213.
[34] Herbert Quick, *Vandemark's Folly*, 362.

wife concentrates on raising her family. The older son develops self-reliance, skills, an honorable wholesome manhood; he loses his preoccupation with dalliance and ease and accepts life's challenge. His daughter forgets her requirements for fancy comforts to build a home and family.

Yancey Cravat, the tempestuous hero of *Cimarron*, is especially incensed with organized society. He is not satisfied with changing his own life but wants to recreate the entire social fabric:

> ... that here's a chance to start clean, right from scratch. Live and let live. Clean politics instead of skulduggery all around; a new way of living and thinking, because we've had a chance to see how rotten and narrow and bigoted the other way has been. ... We can make a model empire.[35]

As with the travelers to Oregon, the prairie pioneer sees a future society. He envisions well-ordered farms and neat communities, schools for his children, churches. The school house is provided for almost immediately; prior to this, education, highly valued, is carried on in the home. Equally significant to his life but less pronounced in most cases is his religion. The building of the church is often a crowning achievement, as justifiable measure of his progress. The pioneer constructs a society along traditional lines but with a stress upon personal development and human associations.

These are simple, direct, and humble people. They extol the elemental aspects of life and derogate the superficial, the false. Marriage, raising a family, building a happy home; these are primary, the sources of fulfillment. The beautiful and wholesome aspects of life are gained from love and selflessness in regard for others. The home is the center of their lives. It is instrumental in the formation of positive values and culture traits, the elimination of crudeness, and the strengthening of the moral verities.

Along with these in importance is the value of work. Whether this value grew out of necessity is not clear. But their vigorous,

[35] Edna Ferber, *Cimarron*, 116.

continuous activity, their industry and energy, their ambition clearly spell their willingness. They believe in hard work and say so. In many of the novels, notably those of Bess Streeter Aldrich, a significant conflict arises when the initial work in developing the frontier has been accomplished. The superficial creeps into their lives to take the place of honest labor, permitting their attentions to focus on nonessentials:

> He went back often in his mind to the first of Myrtie's pleadings to change things. Pasting a cheap stucco over the good old stones of the house had been almost prophetic in its covering up the real issues of life, the things that were vital. Work? Why should he have lessened his activities because there had seemed enough to live on. Work was good. Work was man's portion in life. He had grown soft,—under fifty yet, and he was flabby.[36]

The raising of the living standard—simple comforts, security in the necessities—is important, but this should not take precedence over basic values. This is emphasized by the stark comparison between the life of the pioneer and the fast and fancy living of some of the second and third generations. Where the former finds happiness and stability in work and love and simple pleasures, their descendants have lost sight of real life and follow hollow pursuits. Aldrich sees the problem in symbolic terms.

> There was something symbolic about [the old soap kettle]. . . . His grandmother had made soap in it every spring and fall,—. His mother with her lessening activities had dispensed with it. . . . His wife had planted flowers in it,—typical of the way they had grown to look at life,—flowers, no work, but plenty of income. Flowers over all the harsh facts of life.

> Well, the flowers in the soap kettle were dead and rotted now. So were the fancy notions of life.[37]

The simplicity and lack of pretense direct the pioneers' interpersonal relations. They maintain strong loyalties and feel sym-

[36] Bess Streeter Aldrich, *Spring Came On Forever*, 264.
[37] *Ibid.*, 265.

pathetic neighborliness to be a necessity of human conduct. A friend or stranger needing help cannot be turned away. Per Hansa in *Giants in the Earth*, for example, naturally extends this code to help an injured, wayfaring Indian, even when the Indian spelled terror in the pioneers' hearts. They give of themselves freely and are generous with their possessions.

As would be expected from the foregoing, these pioneers are people of high moral principle. The majority of them reject illegitimate relations out of hand. Others who have "sinned" recognize it as such and feel remorse; their actions are disapproved. Alexandra experiences shock and disbelief when she learns of Maria's extramarital relations with Emil in *O Pioneers*; Beret, the wife in *Giants in the Earth*, is sure she is being punished through her prairie travail and isolation for her sin of premarital relations. While her husband, Per Hansa, does not react in this way, he is nonetheless a devoted, strictly moral husband. Sexual escapades are in decidely minor key in these works.

The moral fiber is also spun out of justice, honesty, and fair play. The preservation of these ideals is more important than personal desires. Per Hansa faces a real conflict when he must choose between the justice of saving his friend's land and the dishonesty of destroying another's stakes. Honor loses to greater justice but he continues to be secretly troubled for some time for his deed. The defense of these principles is not taken lightly, nor is the safeguarding of home and country. One fights; one is responsible to duty; one does not give up either to man or nature. Men who do not uphold their principles are weaklings; men who stand for things they cannot uphold are fools.

There is courage here and strength of purpose. The fighting qualities, the confidence and pride in self, the unassuming tenaciousness are built upon a supreme human dignity. Man's spirit can transcend his own frailties and the natural forces that thwart his way through life. The pioneer of the prairie exemplified this spirit with his big dream, his independence, and his determination for progress.

One other gift remains, one other thing handed down from those early settlers. . . . It is something typically and sturdily American which has not yet been entirely extinguished—a bit of the old pioneers' independence, practical philosophy, ingenuity, and propensity to pull on through.[38]

[38] Bess Streeter Aldrich, *Song of Years*, 490.

4

Silks and Calico

Together, men and women, they went slowly forward, the men to the fore, the man's strength being in the thrust, the drive, in action, the woman's lateral, in the plane, enduring, inactive but constant.[1]

THE WOMAN of the frontier stands with the man through fortune and adversity. She is in her own right a character of consequence, and often she is credited with strength and heroism on a par with that of the frontiersman. The plot may unfold around the activities of the male pioneer, but it circles and encompasses her as well. Indeed, in almost twenty per cent of the novels, she shares equal billing with the hero or is the heroine of the piece. In this latter case, the frontiersman—usually her husband—is in a secondary role. A somewhat smaller proportion of the novels—principally those of the free hunter and free trapper—do not concern women in any major role.

Even when she does not figure prominently, comments woven into the dialogue or the description suggest qualities in the pioneer woman that are at once essential and heroic. Eleanor Atkinson in *Johnny Appleseed* alludes frequently to ". . . the bright bravery that in pioneer woman was one of God's miracles."[2] and John Terrell's hero in *Plume Rouge* remarks with awe,

> . . . these are women of a kind I have never known. . . . I wonder if there have ever been women like them before. Has our country created a new kind? If anything, they have more spirit than the

[1] Elizabeth M. Roberts, *The Great Meadow,* 168.
[2] Lois Atkinson, *Johnny Appleseed,* 13.

men, nor can I see fear in them . . . only the fear that they will not succeed or may appear weak in the eyes of others.[3]

These flattering bits of dialogue and description, though they create an ubiquitous quality of spirit and strength of the pioneer woman, do not necessarily portray the pioneer heroine. Her character develops out of her specific roles and manners. From an analysis of these in the literature, we can see if "our country has created a new kind" of woman.

Basically, there are two pioneer heroines which, with some minor modifications, dominate the literature: one is the product of a romantic ideal and the other of the current realistic image. Key segments of the two quotations could apply to each, for both types of heroines were created to express bravery and spirit and heroism. However, the two types are quite distinct from each other. One type dominates in the earlier novels and the other in the later ones, and a parallelism, which will become apparent, also exists with certain elements of the characteristics of the frontiersmen.

PROPRIETY AND FEMININITY

In each of the novels between 1900 and 1910 and in a sprinkling of the novels of the subsequent decade can be found an example of what seems to be the romantic female ideal. With but one exception she is the novel's heroine, though rarely the central character. Invariably, the machinations of the plot revolve around her: certainly, the hero's attentions focus upon her while he is enacting his particular frontier drama. The novels preserve a uniform pattern in their presentation.

In *When Wilderness Was King*, 'Toinette expresses a key element of this female ideal in a remark to John Wayland.

> "I have known many men such as you are, men of the border, and have always felt free to trust them; they are far more true to helpless womanhood than many a perfumed cavalier."[4]

[3] John Terrel, *Plume Rouge*, 365.
[4] Randall Parrish, *When Wilderness Was King*, 64.

"Helpless womanhood," says 'Toinette. This phrase, along with its implications of expectant protection and innocence, is echoed in the behavior and attitudes of all the early heroines. Fragile femininity, delicacy, gentility, purity: like layers of tissue carefully enveloping an exquisite porcelain doll, these make up the aura that surrounds her.

Around this heroine is spun a gossamer web of refinement and gentility. Delicacy defines her manner; there is no harshness or roughness. She demonstrates a sensitivity to beauty in nature, a beauty which others do not see or do not have time for. The sense of refinement is enhanced by her apparent education and her interest in literature. Her opposition to force and bloodshed, her advocacy of forgiveness and peace in the face of the terrors of the frontier further establish her fine, civilized sensibilities. She is like a cultivated garden flower somehow transplanted in surrounding thickets.

The heroine is completely a lady, conscious of and observing the social niceties and proprieties. Her speech is correct, her manners cultured. Innocence and purity are her standards, which she wears like a glowing crest which is at once a symbol of identification and a medallion of protection. It is not clear in the novels just how this purity is represented, but it is always immediately recognizable to the hero. The result is his protection of her person and her virtue, a protection which she leans upon and clearly expects.

These characteristics derive from her aristocratic background. She comes from a world of ease, comfort, and bountiful security. She is used to care and, in some instances, luxury. Generally, she is a dependent creature. This dependency is expressed in her expectation of being looked after. She does not seem to do things for herself nor try to help herself. She looks to the hero or others for assistance, again with an underlying air of expectation as of a right rather than a privilege. The plot develops a large measure of this helplessness. Invariably, the heroine falls into grave danger. In such situations this pacific and tranquil person merely waits for rescue. No act of self-help is indicated. The assumption in the novels is that this kind of woman must be served and protected.

Fittingly, the heroine does not seem to do much work; she does not labor though she may fulfill at times a useful role. This usefulness seems to be developed for the sake of appearances as the several ladies so occupied are not shown at their work. Dorothea Wakefield, the rapturous maiden in *City of Six*, sporadically nurses her ailing father between strolls among the beauties of the forest; Molly Wood in *The Virginian* is supposed to teach school between the readings and the long conversational rides on the range. More typical is Betty Zane, who rides her handsome mare of an afternoon, sews, and is able to keep to her room for long spells, a room which hardly sounds rough. Helen Sheppard in *The Last Trail* seems to spend much of her time wandering through the forest gathering nuts, bright leaves, and flowers. Otherwise she is like 'Toinette and Alice, heroines of *When Wilderness Was King* and *Alice of Old Vincennes*, who seem to have few occupations other than running about, frolicking, and teasing the men.

Of course, these women may have performed their tasks before they enter the scenes. The authors do not make this evident as in later novels. The romantic, dramatic episodes are presented while the simple realities of life are rarely depicted.

Normally, then, the heroine exhibits a personal reserve and dignity which is buttressed with her ladylike propriety and assurance. This tone of femininity is increased by her occasional resort to flightiness and mild coquettishness. These womanly arts are practiced to apparent advantage by 'Toinette and Alice, as suggested above. They are a bit flirtatious, glib, and demanding of masculine attention. At the outset of *The Virginian*, Molly Wood is both proper and coy. In *Betty Zane*, the heroine adds an element of spoiled imperiousness and sophistication as does Theodosia Burr in *The Magnificent Adventure*. Although sincerity and simplicity seem to be lacking, these wiles are accepted as admirable by the male characters. Their reaction is that this is Woman: unpredictable, saucy, alluring. This drawing-room behavior does not detract from the sense of helplessness but only projects an additional essence of femininity.

The dress of the heroines is also indicative of their background and porcelain-doll role. Both in the text and the illustrations, the ladies are found in attire that seems unsuitable to the scene as well as quite unlike that of later frontierswomen. In *A Sword of the Old Frontier*, Alene and René wander along the trails in long gowns adorned with laces and shawls. In *The Throwback*, Ethel's outfits seem suited for a fox-hunt, while the Zane heroines seem constantly ready for afternoon tea rather than the rigors and tasks of the frontier.

An occasional display of heroics from these women only barely offsets the tone and pattern established. Betty Zane's daring run under the hail of Indian bullets to bring aid to a beleaguered force is unusual in its action and flavor. It is a streak of the Zane vitality and courage superimposed on the femininity. Molly Wood, however, decidedly preserves her feminine status, in the midst of her heroic act of rescuing the wounded Virginian. Coming upon his motionless body, she catches sight of his blood. Then:

> She held tight by two rocks, sitting straight beside him, staring and murmuring aloud, "I must not faint; I will not faint."[5]

She doesn't. Nor does she let him bleed to death. She proceeds to half drag, half carry him to his horse and to lead him to safety; but when he is safely back, she reverts fully to type.

Although it may not be clearly revealed, there is under the innocence and helplessness, the gentility and decorum of the heroine, a strong and sweeping influence over the men and society. Some of this influence is exerted by her very presence on the frontier, for it is change she stands for. Some of her power is fostered by her desirability and her purposes and codes.

[5] Owen Wister, *The Virginian*, 280.

A comment made in *The Last Trail* represents the attitudes expressed in the novels on the role and influence of the women.

> "Women make trouble anyways; an' when they're winsome and pretty they cause more; but if they're beautiful and fiery, bent on having their own way . . . all hell couldn't hold a candle to them."[6]

The individual or composite image of these heroines could hardly be described as "fiery," but there can be little question of their maintaining control of situations, especially in the male-female relationships, and of directing the future course of the hero and of the frontier.

The heroine's control of the male-female relationships is most apparent in those novels where there is some contest involved. In *The Last Trail* Helen Sheppard early decides that Jonathan Zane is the man for her. He is permitted to elude her for awhile, but in keeping with the above quotation and the tone of inevitability of progress, he does succumb. In *The Crossing*, it is Polly who leads Tom McChesney into a proposal; she clearly commands the scene while he fumbles for words and status. The characteristic male behavior of strength and dominance is also sublimated in *The Virginian*. This hero waits patiently and humbly like a lap dog for Molly Wood's decision to grant him her favor; he is in the palm of her hand. Although it is in keeping with their image to appear reluctant and delicate, these and other heroines call the signals in these situations.

The woman symbolizes culture and civilization and carries these into the wilderness. As such she epitomizes the change of the frontier world from the wild, rough, sometimes crude man's world to one in which the social graces are observed and in which the basic culture is advanced. She brings stability and civilized values. A major instance of her effect is the actual change in the hero's ideals, attitudes, and purposes; his allegiance to independence crumbles before her influence and charm. She succeeds in

[6] Zane Grey, *The Last Trail*, 99.

reclaiming the exiled males to a more positive way of life—in the eyes of the period. As she represents the sinking of roots and the curbing of the wandering impulse, she stands for settling down and growth. She is the spur and impulse of building: Polly McChesney in *The Crossing* is responsible for the development of the homestead; Molly Wood in *The Virginian* causes this hero to consider for the first time that his current situation lacks substantial rewards and that he needs to aim higher and strive mightily to assure a future worthy of a bride. Education is considered the forte of the woman. In *When Wilderness Was King*, it is noted that John Wayland has been educated by his mother from her treasured store of books. More than reading and writing is involved. Molly Wood serves beyond this simple school-teaching role, for example, in introducing the Virginian to such poets as Shakespeare, Tennyson, and Scott. She is associated with the transplanting and development of culture.

The heroines also manifest value patterns that are indicative of greater humanity and culture. In her disapproval of killing, Alene in *A Sword of the Old Frontier* represents the spirit of kindness and good. In portraying and forcing adherence to high codes of manners, she preserves these and advances the frontier away from barbarism. The impression is that if the men were left to themselves, all would be crudity and brutality.

In total, the woman's influence is profound. Her insight and knowledge are supreme; her presence is ennobling. She is at once the inspiration and strength of the hero and the developing spirit of the culture. So, though she may have undermined the hero's way of life and certain of his values, hers is a positive role. It must be remembered that this influence is only a facet of the greater image of helpless womanhood. How these two aspects are joined may be illustrated in this quotation:

> Her experience had been almost too terrible for belief . . . she had passed through scenes of incredible horror and suffering, but her nature had not been chilled, stunted or hardened. . . . It was even thus that our great-grandmothers triumphed over adversity,

hardship, indescribable danger. . . . Few of us who have inherited the faded portraits of our revolutionary forbears can doubt that beauty, wit and great lovableness flourished in the cabins of pioneers.[7]

The characterization of helpless womanhood is not without exception. There is one major female character of the first decade's novels who does not fit this picture. Polly McChesney in *The Crossing* is a strong, direct, and practical woman who manages and works the frontier homestead. She is a part of a working world, toiling and struggling with crude and insufficient materials in a raw environment. Although she is the sympathetic female character in this novel, she is distinctly not in the same class as the genteel heroine and does not rate the same regard or attitude. She is complemented in the novel by the aristocratic, pampered Mrs. Temple who, though negatively characterized, has the respect and prestige of her class as well as its cultural attributes.

In several of the other novels, there are women similar to Polly McChesney who form part of the background or are featured in some minor capacity. They take charge in times of stress and manage the affairs at hand: directing certain operations at a mining camp, ministering to the wounded hero, and the like. The chorus of women in the background are stereotyped as plain, reliable, matronly neighbors. Usually described as grave or sober faced, they are strong and hard in the face of danger. They exemplify the stoic spirit suggested in the opening quotations to this chapter. In these novels, they rarely leave the background; however, it is their traits which form the foundation of the pioneer woman's image in the later novels.

STRENGTH AND SIMPLICITY

The frontier women depicted in the novels from 1920 to 1950, as well as those of Willa Cather in the preceding decade, are cut from a different cloth than their earlier sisters. The cloth is not

[7] Maurice Thompson, *Alice of Old Vincennes*, 184.

entirely of one design to be sure, but the several patterns have a unity of construction. Some of the women, in addition to being the heroines, are the central characters of the novels. The drama and events revolve around them directly. In the other novels that contain major female characters, they are closely involved in the events. As with the selections in the preceding discussion, there is also a background of female figures; in these works, however, the portrayal of these women serves to reinforce the general portrait of the heroine.

Certainly, the change in characterization from the early group of novels is not abrupt. Some of the dominant qualities are carried over; they linger in the literature but decrease in frequency and strength with the passing years. This extension of certain aspects of the romantic image is essentially the basic variation in the design of the later heroine.

Whereas the heroine of the first group of novels was primarily found on the forest frontier, in this group she is not so limited. In addition to helping open the woods, she travels with the overland caravans, she helps to conquer the prairie and tame the range, and she joins the rush for California gold. With but minor exception, her milieu is the farm. Her background and knowledge is usually of a plain or reasonably prosperous farm existence rather than of the luxurious plantation or town house.

Like the earlier heroine she is an attractive woman, with a beauty of face based upon healthy coloring as well as fine features. In keeping with her more active life, the lithe slenderness of her figure is accented, it being no less attractive for these qualities. As befits her station and occupation, she dresses in calico, or homespun linsey-woolsey, or in buckskins which she herself has treated and stitched. Gone are the silks and laces.

This heroine is a worker. And she does not engage merely in semi-laboring tasks that meet a minimal requirement of usefulness. She is a housewife, child-rearer, doctor, nurse, weaver, seamstress, butcher, food preserver. Housework itself is no simplified mechanical chore. Primitive tools and materials, crude

methods, and frequent scarcity of supplies made cooking, wash-
ing, and such duties major tasks in themselves. From Cather's
Alexandra in *O Pioneers* to Richter's Sayward in *The Trees*, she
is also a farmer: she clears the land and breaks the soil; she plows,
seeds, and harvests. Certainly she does a man's share of work.
Exceptionally, Aldrich draws the line for the heroine at farming.
Women toiling in the fields is an anathema to her, and she belittles those women in her works who stoop to this low state. She
denounces their husbands as weak to need and to permit such
help. Her heroines, Abbie in *Lantern in Her Hand* and Amalia
in *Spring Came on Forever* frown upon such farming. They are
permitted vegetable gardens, but their husbands handle the
heavy work. This particular ethic seems to grow out of and enforce Aldrich's somewhat sentimentalized concept of the frontierswoman, for it is rather isolated. The heroine who assists her
husband in the fields as well as managing the household work is
more common in the literature, and this routine is common to
the non-heroine woman as well.

On the overland trail, the farm woman is by no means at rest.
If possible, her household work is more complicated, for the
materials and methods are more rudimentary. She stoops to cook
in the evening over an open fire; she does the wash on the banks
of streams; she drives the wagon during the tedious day. At
times she is forced to walk to ease the burden of the oxen. The
heroine is usually the wife of the wagon leader and, in this capacity, is often called upon to nurse and comfort the ill and weary.
Her day is rarely done before it begins anew.

In several of these novels, the heroine is younger—the daughter of the leader, perhaps, or a stray aristocratic lady. Typical of
these are Molly Wingate in *The Covered Wagon* and Nancy
Greenfield in *The Land Is Bright*. Significantly, work is not
denied this heroine either. In the earlier novels especially, a
breath of the romantic tradition spares the daughter-heroines
of some of the more onerous tasks, but their duties cannot be
described as completely superficial. However, they do have op-

portunities for interludes that seem more to belong in the earlier novels.

Another minor variation in these terms is the heroine who takes on the skills and role of the male. In *Debby Barnes, Trader*, the heroine learns the secrets and skills of the woods and trails in the pursuit of her sister's rescue from Indian captivity. Sandra De-hault in *The Splendid Road* learns to shoot and throw a knife with deadly accuracy. She is alone with several orphans in the gold fields and requires these skills for self-protection. She also displays other manly attitudes. When the proper man comes along, both of these heroines revert to their female capacities and turn to housewifely chores. Other heroines do not manifest these masculine skills to any special degree.

An occasional comparison with nonpioneer women in this group of novels serves to emphasize the breadth of the heroines' skill as well as the quantity of work she performs. The nonpioneer women are simply unable to take on the burdens of the frontier. They are ill equipped; they lack the knowledge and skills for the job.

Aside from these skills, basic equipment for the role of pioneer heroine is an enduring strength, a strength which rarely falters before pain, grief, or hardship. This is not only a physical endurance and sturdiness, which she also exhibits. She is maintained by a strong will, a confidence and courage, a determination to prevail. These characteristics also dominate her husband, the hero, but in her they are less obvious. She is not quite as aggressive—perhaps she does not need to be—although she is certainly more so than the earlier heroine. She is generally self-contained, deceptively so, but her energy, her persistence and resourcefulness define her elemental strength.

As with the ladylike heroine, it is possible to describe this frontierswoman as reserved and dignified. But it is not reserve or dignity that come from decorum and gentility, or feelings of superiority. Rather they derive from her steadiness, her quiet assurance and independence. There is little frivolity about her.

She is humble and proud, the salt of the earth. She is a bulwark of spirit and faith in a wild, unfriendly world.

She is also relentless as the tides but more successful in gaining her objective: the eroding of the wilderness. Progress of home, progress of family, progress of society: these are the basic goals that she pursues. She is credited in many of the novels for basic achievements, often at the expense of the heroes.

"Arter all's said an' done, with men a braggin' an' sech, hit's Marthie an' her kind that makes a kentry. Men livin' alone air no better'n Injuns, but bring wimmen onto a frontier an' see whut happens. . . .

"Yes, jist bring wimmin ter a frontier . . . an' in a few years hit hain't a frontier no more. Hit's a peaceful, law abidin' community with schools an' churches, an' men a-actin' decent an' a-pervidin' fer their families. Men brag aroun' a power about subduin' o' a frontier, but, arter all, hit's the Marthies . . . thet actually do the subduin'."[8]

Once woman reaches the frontier, it thrives and prospers. Basically, as in the earlier novels, she is the wedge that opened up the man's world and permitted changes to be effected. The temper of the man's world is the first victim. Structural changes and revised values and interests come next. At the core of these is the development of the home, the land, and the community. High on the list are schools and churches. The home and family are at center of life's achievements. Motherhood is often praised, sometimes glorified; the raising of children to a better life is the truest gratification.

These goals are seen as far more valid than the superficial fancies of an ultra-sophisticated world. The women oppose a gaudy and frivolous display while they steadily move towards improvement and security. Sympathy and honor are with Debby Barnes when she elects a life in the wilderness over a return to the Tidelands. Rose, her sister, who chooses the latter, is portrayed as shallow.

[8] Sheba Hargreaves, *The Cabin at the Trail's End*, 341.

Rose's amazed and indignant outcries claimed all her attentions for some time. What was Darling Debby thinking about? Did she really *want* to wear ugly deerskins and coarse homespun all her life—and work hard, and live in fear—and never *have* anything— never have *anything*?[9]

Debby's choice of work over luxury involves love and an awareness of the honest, direct nature of frontier life as compared with the make-believe false trappings of the East. Life's fulfillment lies in work and love; well-being will come later. The eventuality of well-being is the lamplight gleam in the surrounding blackness, but she struggles toward it.

This goal identifies one of the significant conflicts that the women face. As they move steadily ahead in their strivings for progress, it is evident that the goal is overreached in the eyes of some heroines. They see about them the very things which had been left behind—perhaps not specifically by them, but by the pioneer heroine in general. These heroines urge the return to the simplicities that had marked the early days on the frontier; they decry the false treadmill ways of their children's children. In other novels, notably *Cimarron*, it is quite evident that the virtuous women, including the heroine, are set upon making the new frontier community as much like the old as speedily as possible. Their success is complete, social shortcomings included. In many works, this issue is not present as this degree of progress is not achieved.

The heroine is not wholly a drudge or a steadfast Rock of Gibraltar. A deep core of love and compassion is the basis for her relations with her family and for humanity in general. She is known as a "good woman." She is selfless in her dealings with them, freely giving all she has. This is her way and she sees it her duty as well—clearly and unquestionably. She is sensitive to other's needs and grief and responds with thoughtfulness and kindness. Her loyalty is unlimited in both its scope and depth. Sayward Luckett unalterably struggles for progress against the

[9] Constance L. Skinner, *Debby Barnes, Trader*, 207.

94

forces of the wilderness in *The Trees*. Yet, she is able to recognize that her father and brother seek opposite goals and to commiserate with them for the loss of their woods. Hers is not an idle sympathy, an empty grief. She works to ease their distress though her success in that direction only increases her own difficulties in maintaining the rest of the family and forging ahead.

Ladylike qualities are also part of the heroine's make-up, although she cannot be described as a lady in the manner of the genteel heroines. The difference lies in the flavor of simplicity in her actions and the wholesome sincerity that motivates her. Symbolic are her open door and welcoming hearth. These are not simply politeness. The fixings may be rough, but the intent is warm and complete. She is respectful and eager to please and comfort though her crude materials are limited. Her speech is sometimes slurred in the backwoods idiom, for often enough her education is limited, but she never speaks as brokenly as many around her; sometimes she speaks unaccountably well. Her words are neither harsh nor crude and "rough talk" is not permitted in her presence, though the definition of what this includes is appreciably broader in the nineteen fifties than the nineteen twenties.

The stress on innocence and purity is somewhat lost in the shift from romantic to realistic traditions. However, the inroads of looser attitudes are not immediately felt, the heroines of the twenties and thirties being rigidly pure though perhaps less innocent. The comment, "A spotless character was a woman's dearest possession,"[10] expresses a prevalent attitude. By the forties both the purity and the innocence are less apparent. She is still concerned about being compromised but less strongly.[11]

Certain other values are associated with the heroine. Some of these have already been suggested in the discussion of her purposefulness and her goals. Churches, schools, family—these are

[10] Sheba Hargreaves, *Heroine of the Prairies*, 151.

[11] Chapter V studies the treatment and changes in moral attitudes and behavior.

the basic values. There is some opposition to liquor, but this is not pronounced in the later novels. The heroines are repelled by brutality and killing and occasionally speak out for understanding and peace. The literary approach to these ideas alters the effect of the heroine's beliefs. The genteel heroine in the early works seemed to sermonize; the simple heroine seems to represent these attitudes in her conversation and actions rather than in her speeches.

Another variant in the presentation of the heroine is her attitude towards herself. Her concept of her role in the group, and her acceptance of herself change in the passing years; a completely clear and unified expression of this concept does not emerge, since there is considerable overlapping, but a trend is apparent. An immediate comparison between *The Covered Wagon* (1922), *The Land Is Bright* (1939), and *The Way West* (1949) is possible since they each deal with the overland trail and since the role of the women is identical: they play featured parts. In *The Covered Wagon*, women are not welcomed to certain activities which are considered the province of the men; they are told not to meddle in men's affairs such as making decisions. The women accept this passive role and form a solid but silent backbone to the caravan. The heroine of *The Land Is Bright*, however, does not remain silent; she expresses righteous indignation to the leader at some of the activities of the train. The other women do not really respond; it is still not their place. In *The Way West*, the women do more than suffer and be led by the men. They exert influence, foster decisions and change. The portrait of the delicate unthinking woman which lingers from the earliest novel comes in for attack through this characterization.

Similar though less unified chronological evidence of this gradual shift in attitudes is found. Cean Smith, the heroine of *Lamb in His Bosom* (1933), faithfully enacts the credo that a woman's place is to follow her husband meekly and honestly and without question. Upon his death this alters to a new view of the strong, self-reliant female. Rose Wilder Lane and Bess Streeter

Aldrich's heroines convey quite strongly their agreement with this first principle. Amalia in *Spring Came on Forever* (1935) decidedly denounces Myrtie who raises her son to take a secondary role in the family circle. Only when he reasserts his dominance does he regain honor and self-esteem. In *Strife Before Dawn* (1939), the women define their role as a waiting one, a role in which they act to strengthen the man's spirit. In these novels the women generally follow the men, easing his burden, filling in the chinks while he builds the structure. These are all extensions of the expectancy of protection and service so clearly evident in the character of the genteel women but are modified by the stronger role of the woman in determining the structure and effecting its completion.

The contrary attitude also develops. The women, especially those like Sayward Luckett in *The Trees* (1946), best exemplify the change. It is she who is the builder, the creator, the vital strength. She has counterparts in Gerda, the heroine in *Foundation Stone* and Sabra in *Cimarron*. They, like the heroines of *The Way West*, are integral parts of the whole if not the prime movers of progress. The actual verbalization of the female equality idea comes in two chronologically separate books, *The Splendid Road* (1925) and *Each Bright River* (1950). Says Sandra Dehault,

> . . . a woman is a human, same as a man. Shall any deny her right to virtue—to fortune and the way of life she chooses?[12]

And Kitty Gatewood declares,

> There was more to living than comfort and security. . . . A woman, too, had the right to seek, to know. A woman had the right to live; she was not just a minor episode in the life of some man.[13]

The antagonism of the women to the men's concepts of their role is simple proof of their attitude. In 1900, such an attitude could not have been possible.

[12] Vingie E. Roe, *The Splendid Road*, 166.
[13] M. M. McNeilly, *Each Bright River*, 86.

The pioneer heroine is definitely not a static figure either in the chronological sequence of the novels nor in many of the individual novels. She has developed in the literature from a two-dimensional doll to a heroine who is full of life and a large enough figure to meet its challenges.

Aside from the individual values and traits and the evidence of change, there is a stereotyped portrait of the pioneer woman that persists in the literature. The frontier woman who formed the background of humanity in the novels of the first decade is still in the background in these later novels, but certain of her practical qualities and earthy values have been elevated to heroine level. She has accepted these; they have become part of her strength and purposefulness. Although she fits that part of the following quotation, she had not become the wasted woman of *Cimarron*:

> A gaunt woman, with a weather-beaten face; the terribly neg-lected skin . . . that means alkali water and sun and dust and wind. Rough hair, and unlovely hands, and boots with the mud caked on them. It's women like her who've made this country what it is. You can't read the history of the United States . . . without learning the great story of those thousands of unnamed women . . . in mud-caked boots and calico dresses and sunbonnets, crossing the prairie and the desert and the mountains enduring hardship and priva-tion. Good women, with a terrible and rigid goodness that comes of work and self-denial. Nothing picturesque or romantic about them. . . . You'll know it's the sunbonnet and not the sombrero that has settled this country.[14]

Whether this unlovely image will ever fully become that of the pioneer heroine remains to be seen.

[14] Edna Ferber, *Cimarron*, 19.

5

The Moral Fiber

CLOSE RESEMBLANCE between novels is not particularly surprising in a series of works limited by the watchful eye of historical accuracy. Within the groups of regional novels, similarity of events exists rather frequently. In fact, the plots of several novels are identical. But the similarity in plot structure is not always transferred to the literary method and social mores displayed. Usually, the more widely separated the works in time of publication, the more diverse are the elements that distinguish these factors.

Two such novels widely separated by time evince strongly similar plots: *The Wilderness Road* by J. A. Altsheler published in 1901 and *Bridal Journey* by Dale Van Every published in 1950. Close scrutiny reveals similarity in the direction and the evolution of the plot, parallel events, and an identity in role and status of the hero. However, they are far from the same book, for the differences in social mores represented in the behavior of the characters and the literary method are evident. Especially pronounced are the attitudes of the hero towards the heroine, and his relationship with her. In these respects, an introductory comparison of the parallel attributes is revealing.

Both heroes are sometime officers in the American Army who are in a state of semidisgrace and social ostracism. John Lee in *The Wilderness Road* has left the service as a result of an unjust accusation which has defamed his character; his sense of honor forces him to withdraw from polite society and to escape to a frontier exile. Abner Gower in *Bridal Journey* is on leave from the service, but in his capacity as double spy, his good name is under a cloud. Considered the black sheep of the respectable Gower family because of his dubious connections and asocial actions, he, too, is not quite acceptable to polite society. From time to time, each serves the Army in some capacity, usually scouting, for both have ability in woods skills and friendship with numerous Indians.

Against this background are enacted the various frontier incidents. Chief among them is a daring rescue of the heroine from Indian captivity. The behavior and attitudes that distinguish each of the heroes in this like situation establish the codes in the relationship of the male and female and illustrate the changes in literary technique that are used in these chronologically separated novels.

John Lee had already become secretly enamored of Rose Carew prior to her capture and goes on his rescue mission most willingly. Assisted by his Indian companion, he discovers Rose's whereabouts; he enters the Indian village with a trader under a flag of truce and attempts to bargain for Rose's freedom. At first all efforts are refused, for Rose is fated to marry her captor, until Lee agrees to exchange himself for her, facing torture and death, to save her. In tribute to his bravery, the Indian chief offers him an honored place in the tribe with Rose as his wife if he will renounce his white heritage, but Lee cannot think of placing his secretly beloved in this position either. He sees himself, a social outcast, as unworthy of her; even in these circumstances and despite his love such an act would be dishonorable. In the ensuing scenes, Rose, who has not been harmed or mistreated, is shown in noble courageous demeanor; she unwillingly accepts Lee's bargain for an exchange and finally leaves with the trader. Her final act is to kiss him on the forehead with "her face aflame." Lee escapes by acting the part of a Frenchman who wanders about the woods and village playing a flute, seemingly unaware of his surroundings; the Frenchman is considered a madman by the Indians and thus sacred and untouchable. During his passage out of the village Lee meets and talks with a renegade and an Indian acquaintance, with whom he had held conversations in the past hours, but unaccountably no one recognizes him. He meets his Indian friend in the woods, they catch up to Rose and her escort, and they guide them to safety.

Similarly, Abner Gower sets out to rescue Marah, his cousin's fiancée. His danger is heightened by evidence in the Indians' hands which questions his allegiance to them and suggests his double role. His known close relationship to Marah also makes him suspect. Upon arrival at the camp Abner learns that Marah is to be burned at the stake in a few days. She has been treated as a slave—forced to do menial chores, and has been ridiculed and beaten; her life is in constant jeopardy. An immediate rescue is necessary. To allay suspicions about his motives and to seem to pledge his allegiance to the Indians, Gower proposes to so compromise himself that he could not possibly return to the pioneer's cause. His plan: to pretend indifference to her fate; to openly express his desire to seduce her prior to her burning, thus presumably sealing his renegade status, but actually opening an avenue of escape. Willing to test him, the Indians permit Marah to go to his cabin. Although Gower had intended only to simulate the seduction, it takes place, aided by his willingness and her rationalizations. Having thus seen his sincerity, the Indians remove the guards. At first light, according to the next phase of the plan, Marah leaves the cabin heading for the lake, ostensibly to bathe. She is naked but is clutching her dress wrapped around various tools and food and his loincloth. She pretends to drown, whereupon Gower, also naked, runs from the cabin, jumps into a canoe, pulls her in, and then paddles furiously toward safety. The nudity, intended to throw off any possible suspicion, serves its purpose, and they manage a fair head start. The chase is on but the Indians are eluded. After a harrowing, rigorous journey, they arrive at the settlements.

Both men develop greater admiration and love for the lady

during the trip. Lee does not permit himself to acknowledge affection, for he realizes the immense barrier that separates him from his beloved; a severe moral code keeps him distant. Gower is not unwilling at first to continue the affair, as evidenced by his admiring glances and comments, but these are ineffective before Marah's belated determination to keep him distant. He comes to respect this, and his developing love puts a new coloration on his intentions.

After various meanderings of the plot—including battles and the like, the couples are united. Rose recognizes the strong and noble character hidden under the pioneer's disguise and behind the façade of impersonal dignity. She also has proved his innocence and removed the slander from his name, so all barriers are removed. Marah compares Abner with her fiancé and decides that Abner is the man for her. She goes off to intercept him in the woods and to leave with him.

The not-so-subtle addition of sex to the plot is an obvious indication of the less rigid moral standards in literature comparable to those of society. Not as readily apparent are the pertinent attitudes and basic assumptions that underlie these events and motivate the characters. These will be analyzed in this chapter along with the extent of the change of the social mores in the literature. The discussion will concentrate on the first and last decades of the fifty-year period to show the extremes. However, evolution of the standards during the transition period will also be discussed.

PROTECTION AND PRUDERY—1900–10

Presented with the genteel image of femininity that dominated the literature of these years, how does the hero react? He puts the heroine on a pedestal and asserts his role as protector. He recognizes her innocence and purity and idealizes her; he sees her delicacy and is gallant, courteous, gentle; he accepts her dignity, recognizes her status and is respectful and deferential. All the social graces are observed from the French courtliness of

Raoul de Coubert in *A Sword of the Old Frontier* to the Southern gentlemanliness of the hero in *The Virginian*. Even the more rustic types like John Wayland and Jonathan Zane, respectively heroes of *When Wilderness Was King* and *The Last Trail*, are wholesomely attentive with seemingly inherent grace and courtesy.

The reactions and occasional statements of these frontiersmen reflect their acceptance of the refined and helpless female. She is made to seem the male ideal. In reacting to some lack of reserve on the part of the heroine in *Alice of Old Vincennes*, Beverley expresses his disapproval. He admires decorous behavior and demands purity and innocence. Behavior and manners must evoke social graces and good breeding. In this and other novels, the heroine ideal represents honor, dignity, and decorum. Disdain is expressed of those women who are forward in social or personal situations, particularly in the pursuit of men.

Protection of the female at all costs and above all else becomes a keynote of the plot and a primary responsibility of the male. Like John Lee in *The Wilderness Road*, the other heroes also leap to the rescue of an abducted heroine. They do this not merely for the sake of love or humanity—as is the case in the novels of the later decades. Rather, the tone is that of a sacred mission which cannot be put aside if honor and self-respect are to be maintained. The unreal and overdramatic aspects are illustrated in *When Wilderness Was King* when John Wayland thrusts sense, care, and duty aside to achieve the liberation of 'Toinette. He seems to act without considered thought, and he will let nothing deter him. When DeCroix loses courage and vacillates, John berates him and accuses him of not acting the part of a man, though, in terms of the Indian situation and Wayland's ill-conceived plans, DeCroix's hesitancy seems the more realistic reaction. Similar situations produce similar attitudes toward the defense of the heroine in the Grey and Parrish novels.

The strength of this attitude is even more apparent when it comes in conflict with patriotic allegiance and military duty, both of which are particularly positive values. In *When Wilderness Was King*, Lieutenant Helm, a strong, favorable character, declines to volunteer for a mission with these words:

> "I have a young wife . . . to her I owe allegiance, as well as to the flag I serve . . . as a soldier I will obey any command you give, and will go forth upon this mission if ordered . . . but I cannot volunteer for such service. I believe it too foolhardy . . . and certain death."[1]

Lieutenant Helm is not judged a coward. His impulse to serve his wife is considered worthy and just by the characters present, including the hero.

This protective guardianship attitude is not limited to the heroine. A man must also defend the honor and reputation of all women. The hero acts quickly when such an occasion presents itself. The clearest expression of this inviolability of a woman's honor and dignity is stated by the Virginian. Early in the novel, he ringingly calls the villain Trampas to task for daring to malign a lady. Many pages later, he reflects on this episode:

> ". . . Trampas thought I had no call to stop him sayin' what he pleased about a woman who was nothin' to me—then. But all women ought to be somethin' to a man.[2]

This emphatic statement of the Virginian's code and attitude exemplifies the credo of all of the pioneers. Even D'ri, the comparatively lowly frontiersman in *D'ri and I*, who has no contact with women and voices his own unsuitability for such associations, asserts this point of view.

Thus, the behavior and speech of the pioneer hero expresses his image of the heroine as a fragile flower and details his protective attitude. It is an attitude which emanates from a vision of her as something sacred.

However, the frontiersman is not limited to this flattering respect and care, for the heroine ideal is also to be sought and

[1] Randall Parrish, *When Wilderness Was King*, 286.
[2] Owen Wister, *The Virginian*, 459.

cherished. Woman and love become everything. In time the heroine becomes indispensable to the frontiersman's existence. This attitude is not immediate and is remarkable considering the almost complete and extreme negativeness that forms the core of his initial response to woman and what she stands for.

At the outset, the hero and his companions seem happy with their lot. They may have secret yearnings, but these are not expressed. The atmosphere in *The Virginian*, for example, is permeated with a sense of glad fellowship and of freedom. Life is zestful, hearty, and masculine. The hero views with distinct misgivings any signs—like the occasional fenced-in house and its tethered cowpuncher—that spell the demise of his way of life. He derides and mocks and resists such changes. Insofar as woman is considered the instrument and symbol of such changes, he resists her. A like partiality for the free way of life causes similar reactions in *The Throwback* among Tom Moonlight and his men.

Some slight modification in the Zane Gray novels, caused by a positive view of the forest leveler as well as the free forester, develops in the heroes a live-and-let-live approach. As long as they can maintain their independence, they remain impartial towards the incipient settlements. In view of this goal they keep clear of entanglements with women. In *The Last Trail*, Jonathan Zane's comparative values are stated:

> Loneliness was to him a passion. Other men loved home, the light of women's eyes, the rattle of dice or the lust of hoarding; but to him this wild remote promontory with its limitless view, stretching away to the dim horizon, was more than all the aching joys of civilization.[3]

These are strong convictions but they are respected only for a time. This frontiersman had simply not yet been affected by "the light of women's eyes."

Jonathan Zane values something more than personal fulfillment and passion.

[3] Zane Grey, *The Last Trail*, 86.

> Duty commanded that he resist all charm other than that pertaining to his life in the woods. Years ago he had accepted a borderman's destiny, well content to be recompensed by its untamed freedom from restraint; to be always under the trees he loved so well; to lend his cunning and woodcraft in the pioneer's cause; to haunt the savage trails; to live from day to day a menace to the foes of civilization. That was the life he had chosen; it was all he could ever have.[4]

Throughout the novel, this point is reiterated; Jonathan Zane's sense of duty in the protection of the frontier coupled with his unbound love of the wilderness are insurmountable obstacles. His life has been pledged as strictly and severely as the most devout monk. Yet "a woman with all a woman's charm to bewitch . . . [with her] willful burning love, and . . . mystery"[5] changes all this. Duty, independence, a way of life are exchanged for love, the wilderness for the hearth.

These reservations on the part of the heroes break down and he is caught in the mesh of desire and progress. Woman, a particular woman's love, is sought and with this an acknowledgment of change. Within two pages after his strict assurance of duty—a rapidity which is not unusual in these novels, Jonathan Zane expresses new insights and a complete change of view:

> At last so much of life was intelligible to him. The renegade committed his worst crimes because even in his outlawed, homeless state, he could not exist without the companionship, if not the love of a woman. The pioneer's toil and privation were for a woman, and the joy of loving her and living for her. The Indian . . . birds and beasts . . . all nature sang that love made life worth living. Love, then, was everything.[6]

Love of woman surpassed all odds. In *Alice of Old Vincennes* it surmounts class barriers and a touted sense of responsibility. Beverley, the hero, courts Alice despite strong misgivings about

[4] *Ibid.*, 147.
[5] *Ibid.*
[6] *Ibid.*, 149.

her lower class background; he also neglects specific duties. He goes daily to visit Alice while his express duty of seeing to the rebuilding of the fort is neglected. This is not a conscious decision on the part of the trusted lieutenant. He simply cannot resist the attraction of Alice. Direct attention is never called to his neglect in the novel; perhaps it is significant enough that the author develops the course of action as he does, without apparent consciousness of the contradiction between the hero's stated sense of responsibility and his romantic impulses. A more obvious manipulation of the action in *When Wilderness Was King* and *A Sword of the Old Frontier* again covers up for the contradiction in the hero.

The impulse towards the fulfillment of love seems undeniable. The outward signs of the hero's great emotion, however, are restricted by an interplay of values and customs. Thus the behavior of the impassioned male is strictly patterned. The patterns serve in addition to reinforce the concept of male protectiveness and adoration, as well as those of female delicacy, propriety, and innocence.

The signs of love are usually immediate; upon first sight the male is smitten. This love grows under the most negative conditions and despite all barriers; it is fed by dreams and sentiment. In the case of Tom Moonlight in *The Throwback*, it grows without the exchange of words; the other heroes are not quite so handicapped. Nevertheless, rare is the hero who speaks of his love or voices his admiration or aspirations. The majority of the women also fall in love immediately, but, in keeping with their delicacy, their reactions are subtle and silent. They, too, give no immediate evidence of their affection, and several of them do not reveal their feelings until the final chapter.

The first expression of the hero's love announces his adoration and his weakness before the woman. When they first meet and subsequently, the controlled, self-possessed male, image of strength and self-sufficiency, falters. His assurance is lost. He becomes hesitant; often he stammers. Of course, he cannot resist.

But his concept of proper relations—as well as his sense of rank in some instances—forbids his acting upon his emotion. His adoration is silent and sentimental.

These reactions might be understandable, even expected, of John Wayland in *When Wilderness Was King* or Stewart Randolph in *The Heritage*—theirs is youth's first contact with a new emotion. Their love lights upon ladies who seem more worldly wise or understanding of the ways of the heart. The similar initial bashfulness of Tom McChesney towards Polly may be laid to a backwoods upbringing, the inability to communicate emotion being a typical stereotype of the backwoodsman. (Tom's bashfulness rather rapidly changes upon Polly's acceptance.)

However, similar behavior is not easily rationalized on the part of such men as John Lee, the Virginian, Raoul de Coubert, and Tom Moonlight. They are adult men of the world who have been depicted as men of experience, purposefulness, and will. Yet when the latter finally comes in contact with his distantly beloved Ethel, he is at such a loss that the author remarks,

> Could this individual, whose voice broke, whose tongue stammered, whose agitation was almost aspen—could this be the unshakable Captain Moonlight?[7]

This inability of the hero to communicate emotion immobilizes him in his meetings with the heroine.

The hero is, in addition, hobbled by his sense of chivalric ethic and protective respect which make him unable and unwilling to be open and direct. The codes of the day did not permit the intimacy of first names. Typically, John Wayland thinks of, refers to, and addresses his adored 'Toinette as "Mademoiselle" throughout the novel. He has not only pursued her fairly obviously, if youthfully, but has been in almost constant company with her. He has rescued her several times, once from drowning, twice from Indians. Only after they have admitted their mutual love in the final chapter does 'Toinette finally say, " 'I wish you

[7] Alfred H. Lewis, *The Throwback*, 300.

would not call me Mademoiselle. . . . It is as if we were still strangers. . . .' "[8] It seems necessary for propriety's sake for the woman to break this final barrier to intimacy. Within pages they are married.

The same pattern is seen with the mature, experienced heroes. After numerous avowals of intentions and countless meetings and discussions, the Virginian still addresses his beloved in a letter as "My dear Miss Wood"; he is always equally correct in person. This barrier is not surmounted until after Molly has capitulated and given him her avowal.

Love develops not from communicated intimacies nor from physical contacts but from the secret flowering of the love image. It feeds upon sentiment—sentiment which appears rather cloying to the modern view. The men often spend much time in daydreaming over a mental picture of their beloved in a heart-smoldering fashion.

The hero's attentions, if they may be so called, are the epitome of propriety, dignity, and purity. He would never be forward, and rare is the instance when he acts impetuously. Yet, he is certainly not devoid of feeling. When he does chance to touch the heroine's hand, he burns from the sensation. This is not only the usual reaction but seems also to be the expected one. The author of *The Last Trail*, and presumably the reader, is somewhat amazed when Jonathan Zane fails to respond to Helen Sheppard's charms and seems impervious to her touch:

> . . . one of his hands touched Helen's. If he had taken heed of the contact, as any ordinary man might have . . . .[9]

The passing phrase carries the assumption that such contact should ordinarily have raised a marked degree of excitation. But Jonathan Zane, who does not notice or react to his liberty, is not at this time an ordinary man. He is still married to duty and sworn to loneliness.

[8] Parrish, *op. cit.*, 286.
[9] Grey, *op. cit.*, 30.

Impetuous conduct, rare as it is in the novels—and mild by modern standards, illustrates the definition of undue liberty in these relations. The extreme reaction to such an instance further defines the expected conduct. Alfred Clarke, in a moment of thoughtless abandon and passion, kisses Betty Zane in the moonlight. It is difficult to say who is more upset. She immediately shows her displeasure and flees to her room; she is sure that she had misjudged his character and that he deserves the worst. Clark, thunderstruck and humiliated by his action, sends a remorseful note begging for forgiveness. When he gets no reply—for Betty does not receive it—Clarke absents himself from the settlement. He takes his just punishment in exile.

From this example and from the actions of the other heroines, we see that the heroines' ideas coincide with this view of the hero's role in the pursuit of love. These sterile attentions are just what any proper lady would expect. The sense of innocence prevails. The romantic image of love is conveyed while elements of sex are at a minimum.

In those presentations that contain a shadow of sex, it is vague, unemphasized, barely implied, and usually condemned in some way. The strongest suggestion of sex is in *The Throwback*. In a singular scene, Ethel watches the pitched battle between the Indians and the man she loves. Her love is unrevealed to him; he has barely spoken to her. The drama and heat of battle and the glory of Tom Moonlight's heroism translate her mood into passion. She becomes savagelike: "She had slipped off her civilization . . . ." While she is in this state, with the battle still raging, she and Tom are brought together. Only eleven pages after his initial stumbling, stammering agitation (cited earlier), they gaze into each other's eyes and passion overcomes them.

> His eyes met hers, and their souls surveyed each other. The war raged outside; they minded it not. Without word, and as one who claims his right, he drew her close to his bosom and kissed her lips. . . . He kissed her again and again . . . .[10]

[10] Lewis, *op. cit.*, 311.

A kiss is rare indeed in these novels; rarer still is the removal of the conventional guise of innocence of the female. This is rationalized here by her reversal to a savagelike state. Three pages later there is a further attempt to avert deep social indelicacies in Ethel's behavior by reverting to tradition.

"Ethel," said he. Then pausing, he faltered. "I may call you Ethel, may I not?"[11]

Ethel having given her permission, betrothal is immediate. Marriage follows shortly thereafter and the novel closes.

Other manifestations of sex are rare and so slight as to merit attention only as measures of contrast. An alluring Spanish dancer briefly attempts to charm Tom Moonlight; though he dances a torrid Spanish number with her, the sight of beauteous Ethel apparently causes him to lose interest. The wife of a railroad engineer, about whom there is whispered talk, seems dazzled by the Virginian; her eyes constantly on him contain admiration and vague hints of welcome. He is unresponsive. Thus the heroes represent manly dignity, proper aloofness and moral behavior.

The attitudes and behavior patterns of the other heroes, their sense of morality and duty, mark a refusal of sex. They show a reserve and purity to match the innocence of the heroines. In some cases the sense of duty, discussed earlier, enforces a code of celibacy. This is the case of Jonathan Zane in *The Last Trail*, who claims gravely, "I do not wait on the girls. . . . I am a borderman."[12] His resolve is later broken, but up to that time he permits neither overt action nor reaction to a woman.

Romantic associations and eventual marriage were apparently valued; the hero therefore adheres to the requirements, though secondary figures, like Wetzel in this same work, may remain celibate—powerful but sexless figures. The novels bring fulfillment of love. Love leads to marriage and rather devastating changes to the hero's life. He who had been so contrary to any infringement of his freedom is brought to a re-evaluation of his

[11] *Ibid.*, 314.　　　　[12] Zane Grey, *The Last Trail*, 43.

direction and purpose. For example, strictly on the strength of his emotion, for he has yet to speak to Ethel, Tom Moonlight undergoes fitful self-examination:

> "I have based myself," he said in a tone wherein contempt and regret mingled, "I have based myself on myself . . . and I look about to find mere loneliness and desolation." . . .
>
> "From this treasure . . . I might . . . fashion freedom for myself. I had thought I owned the wilderness. I now see that the wilderness owns me. This treasure would be my liberation."[13]

Freedom is fashioned of different materials. Now, liberation will come from love and marriage. Love at first sight has opened his eyes. Similarly, the Virginian, lightning-struck by Molly, catches a sense of progress, of need for status and education—for change.

Sweeping reform is uniform. In *City of Six* the coming of Dorothea Wakefield into his life gives Rance a sense of purpose. He drops his studied unwillingness to apply himself and ends his casual wanderings. Vigorous, enthusiastic, filled with dreams, he joins a ranching enterprise. In the same novel, marriage dramatically changes Tex. Of a shy, silent, and backward nature, he blossoms into an outspoken man, wise in the ways of women and life. Rose Carew reawakens John Lee's trust in himself as well as his ambition. Helen Sheppard brings Jonathan Zane out of the woods. Thus the hero is married and saved from unending loneliness and wandering.

The core of the hero's reaction to the heroine is seen to consist of three seeds: protection, idealization, and desire. But his desire is shaped by the other two and is channeled by a strict social code so that the purity of neither image is violated. An equally strong code designates the "happy ending": marriage and withdrawal to an organized existence.

TRANSITION—1911–39

The introduction to this chapter showed that a great change in the attitude toward love occurred in the novels between 1901

[13] Lewis, *op. cit.*, 70, 75.

and 1950. The lack of restraint of the recent novels, as compared to the early ones, develops gradually and unevenly over the course of the years. Harbingers of the modern trends appear as early as 1913; vestiges of the old delay their total departure from the scene, cropping up now and then into the thirties though in somewhat modified form. Traces of the extravagant—written perhaps as stark realism—mingle with a more subdued acknowledgment of the physical aspect of love and passion.

The great exceptions to the early novels are those written by Willa Cather, a pioneer author of rare stature. They are exceptional not only for their depth of characterization but also for their glowing and faithful reality. They stand apart from the other novels before 1925 in their plain unstudied presentation of sex and morality. For the first time in these novels we have an unembellished view of love. It is not surrounded by an aura of the "ideal." The straightforward is not without its morality, however. Love becomes a part of life's drama and not a lace-edged valentine accidentally found on the trail.

Love and morality take on new definition. Alexandra, the heroine of *O Pioneers*, seems untouched by romantic notions and unaware of desire or weakness in body or spirit. She is disbelieving and shocked upon the revelation of her brother Emil's affair with Marie, a married woman. Her own codes do not permit such a betrayal of the moral fiber. She is more concerned with this than with social impropriety. Alexandra draws life's meaning from an inner source. She looks for fulfillment of the spirit as well as the mind and the body. Similarly, in *My Antonia* we are told of Antonia's determined independence of the small-minded village social codes. In this novel, the sordid strikes the heroine. Her elopement does not lead to the marriage she expects; deserted by her lover, she returns home with her illegitimate baby. She is both shamed by her experience and proud of her infant. She withdraws to her brother's farm, bowed but not broken by her sin. Eventually she rebuilds her life into one that is glowing and vital.

These novels display an idealistic faith through these values but do not evade basic facts or mask them with sentiment or romantic incidents. The reaction to and revelation of love are quite different from those considered in the other novels of this period. These illicit relationships in the Cather novels are underexposed; they are alluded to briefly, in a manner plain and without fanfare. There are no moralizing sermons. The reaction to immorality in the novels is negative, but neither character is flogged or outcast. Alexandra is not without compassion for Emil; the narrator of Antonia's story is sympathetic rather than outraged. The incidents are shown as falls from the slippery stepping-stones of life. This generous attitude and moderate tone are remarkable in a body of literature in which extreme propriety of conduct is still the keynote in the relationships of the men and women. In fact, aside from the reactions, the inclusion of such incidents at all in this group of novels—and certainly when compared to the literature of the preceding decade—is quite remarkable.

The other books of the second decade and through 1925 are in these terms generally replicas of the romances already discussed. These novels have a greater variety of locale—including the mountains, the plains, the overland trail as well as the forest, but the conventions of love and passion observed in the novels of 1900–10 are amply represented. However, there is a slight moderation of the strict codes of social behavior. Within the conventional framework, the departures from the strict codes raise signposts of a less rigid society.

In Hough's novels, *The Magnificent Adventure* (1916) and *The Covered Wagon* (1922), there is a reproduction of the scene from Zane Grey's *Betty Zane* in which the hero steals a kiss. The ardor of the heroes shows more passion in these novels but the shame and self-castigation are at least as pronounced. Lewis, the hero of *The Magnificent Adventure* could easily be speaking for both. He sees himself "accused and convicted of sacrilege . . . he had left his own creed . . . had lifted his hand to what was another's. He had sinned against the law."[14] Lewis' sin is all the

[14] Emerson Hough, *The Magnificent Adventure*, 163.

greater since the object of his love is already married. Both men go into exile of a sort.

The free trapper hero, Lige Mounts, in Linderman's *Morning Light* (1922) is moral by any standards. One of the major conflicts in this novel develops out of Lige's growing love for an Indian maiden. It is a gentle, warm, companionate love, building neither on sex nor on distant adoration. However, the threat of social disapproval hovers over the relationship. The ostracism is spelled out fairly directly rather than citing the abstract need to observe cultural and racial heritages, as was the case in a similar conflict in *The Heritage*, a novel of 1902. Lige withdraws to civilization but, repelled, returns to marry Bluebird. It is the first Indian marriage of the hero in this body of literature, though it happens off stage. It is a significant forward step in the literary acceptance of broader mores and a more open appraisal of them.

The morality of most other heroes is unquestionable. Yet within the several novels there is suggestive evidence in the background, evidence that could not have appeared earlier. In *Vandemark's Folly* (1922), the hero comes in contact with bold girls who cause him to blush and canalmen who curse. In *The Able McLaughlins* (1923) the hero is confronted with the rape of his fiancée and an illegitimate child when he returns from the war. In *The Thundering Herd* (1925), a Zane Grey novel which offers direct comparison with his earlier works, the hero and heroine are permitted reciprocal caresses—kisses and fond words. In *'Forty-Nine* (1925), Noel Peabody, shown as extremely attractive to women, is kissed by a married woman with a questionable reputation and a gambling-hall background. His interest is aroused as is his desire for more kisses; he forgets the plain girl he left back home but apparently retains his virtuous nature. This recognition and relative acceptance of physical contacts—the very use of the kiss as a romantic stimulus as compared to the hand's touch—are evidence of change in the social-literary fabric.

Interspersed in these novels are some of the attitudes found in the earlier novel, although they are presented in diminished strength. The idea of the man as the woman's protector is still quite strong. This encompasses the protection of her person as in *Erskine Dale, Pioneer* (1920), of her honor as in *The Able McLaughlins* (1923), and of her sensitivities as in *The Last Frontier* (1923). An extreme example of protection is seen in *North of '36* (1923). The entire ranch crew sets out to save the fortunes of the beautiful, twenty-two-year-old orphan who has been left destitute with nothing but her Eastern education, her ranch and cattle, and her fighting spirit. The men's devotion is laudable for they go all out to help her, but they also expect all sorts of allowances from rustlers, from lawmen, who are searching for strays, and from other ranchers. Such expectations are founded in an attitude of assumed male protection of the hapless female.

Of somewhat lesser emphasis is the idea noted earlier of the power of love and the power of the woman to influence change. Generally where this exists it is not direct. The strongest incidence is in *The Thundering Herd* (1925), in which Milly causes a reversal in Tom's cold-blooded attitude toward the killing of the buffalo. Love itself is still expressed as a soul-searing but vapid emotion, supposedly meaningful but lacking much depth in its evocation.

Much the same patterns are evoked after 1925 in the remaining novels of this decade. But the tide is beginning to run out. The somewhat rougher handling of women in *The Red Road* (1927), the background of premarital relations in *Giants in the Earth* (1927), the free show of affection in *The Cabin at the Trail's End* (1928), the defense of the prostitutes as victims of society by the hero in *Cimarron* (1930), the loose and loud behavior of the mountain men in *The Long Rifle* (1930)—all show the advance of the new freedom. In *The Great Meadow* (1930), the unintentioned bigamy of Diony Jarvis during the long absence of her husband also presents a situation which builds upon the reality of the life situation. Love is not a romance but a need for security and fulfillment as well as affection. These signs are in the same

116

developmental pattern as those in the earlier novels of this decade but are stronger in emphasis and in their outspoken quality.

There is, however, some balance presented by the extremely moral behavior of the mountain man hero in *The Long Rifle* (1930), who not only does not participate in the sexual escapades with the Crow women as do his companions but also disapproves of this wild behavior. Romantically, he has a fleeting mirage-like emotional involvement with Estralita, whom he never really gets to know or to see again. By way of balance, too, are the several novels that present a portrait of a pioneer couple, happily and loyally married. In Aldrich's *Lantern in Her Hand* (1928) there is no hint whatsoever of passion or physical needs; the love depicted is highminded. Hargreaves contrasts the virtue and honor of John Bainbridge with the cruelty and relative lasciviousness of McDermott in *The Cabin at the Trail's End* (1928); a good name, virtue, are still valued; a woman whose reputation is ruined has no future.

The other side of the coin is fully revealed for the first time. Three novels of this time are frank in their depiction of sex. Even more significant than this is the reversal in the value structure that grows out of the change, for sex in these novels is no accident nor is it shown in subdued hues as a normal part of life. The heroes of *Wolf Song* (1927), *Long Hunt* (1930), and *Conquest* (1930) proudly relate their sexual achievements; such encounters with women are in the natural course of life. Gone is the taboo against sex in this literature. The heroes do not hesitate to act freely and frequently on their desires. The descriptions of their feelings and their experiences is also comparatively open. Murfree Rinnard, the hero of *Long Hunt*, cites his lack of prejudice toward either white, Indian or half-blood women for sexual purposes. He feels no qualms against possessing his friend's fiancée, though he has no thought of a permanent relationship even after she becomes pregnant. He makes no excuses for his action. It is clear that he feels a physical need for her and responds to her love for him. As a known non-marrying kind, the risk is not his. This is sufficient excuse for him. His value structure is revealed in this thought:

> He was a king amongst women, too, and all because he set no store by any. . . . He just traveled his own trail, satisfied to be free, never tangled nor tied, and they followed after. He liked some men, and had come to like this dog, but he never liked them so much as he did his freedom. Women he did not like. They were troublesome and clinging. They were more winning, even the worst of them, and often suddenly dowered with soft and secret power. Except for this power against his freedom, he would like them best of all.[15]

The avid lustiness of Jard Pendleton, *Conquest*'s hero, relates the same values but without any gentle overtones that are part of Rinnard's character. He has numerous premarital and extramarital affairs and lives with three women. Sam Lash's awe and hesitancy when he first meets the rich and beautiful Lola in *Wolf Song* make him seem boyish and tame in comparison. This reaction to her is incongruous in view of his previous experiences but his inhibitions are short lived. He remains passionately true to her.

These novels do not limit their discussion to the sexual prowess of the heroes but are permeated with a sensuous tone. Blatant frankness and detail are basic to the descriptions of the activities and the characters. In *Conquest*, the nymphomaniac history of Pendleton's first wife is detailed. The major male characters each have at least one scene in which they are found nude by women or present themselves so; one character, wearing only a blue sash, faces an angered crowd from the steps of a bordello which he had rented for the exclusive use of his friends. Lola is portrayed with voluptuous word pictures in *Wolf Song*, and the passion of Lash's love is not underplayed. His recollections of her body are graphic and frequent; he even envisions it in wide-screen proportions as he kneels in church trying to convert from wild mountain man to Christian husband.

[15] James Boyd, *Long Hunt*, 232.

In this conversion, it is clear that progress is not a consideration. Lash's reactions to marriage and settling down, unlike
earlier pioneer heroes, are decidedly negative.

> Go where he will a man comes back to a woman. She pulls him
> down, she holds him down. . . . She sucks out of him power and
> longing to go. . . .
> She makes him plow and build who would rather wander and
> fight.[16]

He is converted by the image of Lola's body; his passion for her
brings about the negation of his old attitude. Progress is recognized as a vague future possibility only towards the close of the
novel.

Going, too, are the prim heroines. Lola in *Wolf Song* is shown
taking the initiative in her affair with Lash. She is not brazen,
however, merely passionate and loving. These proclivities appear
in the other novels as well, though not so obviously.

The contrast of these revelations to the attitudes represented
in the earlier works is strong not only in general effect but also
in terms of the assumptions that are inherent in the presentations.
The writers now assume the naturalness and driving force of sexual expression and make it a power in the lives of the characters.

The novels of the thirties express and reinforce the attitudes
developed in the novels of the preceding decades. Greatly diminished and modified but not entirely disappeared are the romantic
structure and attitudes of the first decade, 1900–10. The hero of
All Ye People (1931) might have been lifted straight out of that
period as regards his physical reactions to women. He makes no
ungentlemanly advances, though there is a greater accent of
passion in his emotions. *The Land Is Bright* (1939) by Archie
Binns could have been written by Emerson Hough for its similarity to his *The Covered Wagon* both in plot and characterization.
In the more recent version of the overland trail story, however,
Case is able to kiss Nancy without being ostracized. A kiss is

[16] Harvey Fergusson, *Wolf Song*, 202.

119

considered a comfort for the lovers in the troubled times rather than a danger to virtue. A rare kiss, a caress of the hand: these are the extent of this hero's daring.

The image of the respectable, home-loving, morally-straight pioneer is frequently exemplified in the novels of the thirties. Traveling the trail or working the land, this pioneer is generally direct and honest, but circumspect in his dealings with the opposite sex. In *The Man of the Storm* (1936), John Colter expresses this morality as a national attitude:

> "We [Americans] do not do that [take women] as much as the French. We most generally come home to settle. To take a wife is not the same as takin' a woman."[17]

John Colter is himself unwilling to take on the loose habits of a few of his countrymen and the Frenchmen. He is not, however, devoid of desire for women. An admission that such activities exist would have been unacceptable in the early literature, but by 1936 is not particularly surprising.

As in the previous novels, there are occasional characters who evince looser behavior and morals. In the more straight-laced novels such as *Spring Came on Forever*, such behavior is barely tolerable to the hero. In others, the hero or heroine show understanding or sympathy, or no reaction; the individual involved is not unwelcome because of such activities. In *Drums Along the Mohawk*, allusions are made to Adam Helmer's amorous activities but he remains a close and welcome friend of the Martins.

Along with the pioneers with strict moral standards, there are several who, though generally faithful to their wives, get involved in an extramarital escapade. Lonzo, the married hero in Caroline Miller's *Lamb in His Bosom* (1933), has an affair with another woman. Gil Martin in Edmond's *Drums Along the Mohawk* (1935) almost lets himself fall prey to desire during the period of his wife's rejection of him. The oldest son in Stong's *Buckskin Breeches* (1937), a boy just becoming a man, is fully

17 Ethel Hueston, *The Man of the Storm*, 187.

initiated into sex, an experience which is described with detail, before the father takes the family West. Driven by desire, the young man almost breaks away to return to the arms of his paramour.

Relations with Indians are still fraught with taboo, but a modification is evident. Lige Mounts has married his Indian sweetheart in *Beyond Law* (1933), a sequel novel to *Morning Light*, but she dies. The passionate hero in *Michael Beam* (1939) at first refuses to buy a lovely Indian girl, Red Bloom, as his mistress. However, he senses his desire and is later overcome by it when he is seduced by her. Unwilling to marry an Indian, he wishes not to deceive her, yet he is drawn and cannot resist her. She, too, dies at the novel's end, so releasing him. In *The Invasion* (1932), however, John Johnson marries the Indian woman he comes to love and they live together happily.[18]

The broadening attitudes of this period are evident in the open discussion of several pioneer women who become wives of Indians. A slight hint of this possibility was first seen in *Erskine Dale, Pioneer* (1920). Hidden among the literary niceties just as she remains hidden by shame among the Indians is a white woman (Dale's mother as it turns out) with a half-blood daughter. While its inclusion in the plot suggests a broader outlook, the overdelicate, cloaked and semiembarrassed handling is a throwback to the previous decade's views. Far different is the open treatment of such incidents in the novels of the thirties. Delia, the captured heroine of *In the Hands of the Senecas* (1937), is admired by a warrior-chief. Ignorant of Indian language and customs, the victim of a deception-seduction, she unwittingly marries him. She is horrified by this, not solely because it is at the hands of an Indian but because any such seduction would be humiliating. She, too, bears a child and until its death feels she cannot return to her home and husband. In *Strife Before Dawn* (1939), Hope is wooed by her captor. At last she assents to an

[18] Changing attitudes toward the Indian are more fully analyzed in Chapter VIII.

Indian marriage, having come to admire him and thinking her rescue impossible. When she is repatriated she returns only half-willingly with her child. Her white husband is repelled; he cannot understand Hope's "easy bedding with a savage." The author conveys sympathy for Hope in her plight. The complexity of these relationships, the impression of deeper attitudes and fuller interaction, the multi-valued orientation, and the relatively non-romantic assumption about these life forces are indicative of changes in attitude toward human relationships, love and sex, as well as toward the Indian.

The thirties have their share of free-loving heroes on a par with the twenties. The antisocial heroes of *Brothers in the West* (1931) actively reject society's moral codes. They take women whenever they want them; they do not profess to believe in marriage and would steal any man's woman if she were willing. Yet, they are depicted as good men. These men, for all their free ways, are mildly presented in this regard, especially when compared with the libidinous Harley Boydley, the hunter hero of *Free Forester* (1935). There is great stress in this novel on natural, fierce, and unhampered love. Rose, Harley's sister-in-law, advises Harley to love but to have "strength to resist marriage."

> She thought with relief of her brother's love affairs . . . and how, their passions once over, they gave themselves to the pleasure of the chase, wrestling, shooting, and pure idleness with never a thought of love.[19]

Harley takes Rose's advice to heart and adopts the ways of her brother but with frequent thoughts of love. Harley deliberately pursues Madeline and succeeds in her seduction despite the watchful eyes of her brothers. Though he loves Madeline in his own fashion, he is attracted to Esther, a nymphomaniac who surrounds herself with a harem of men to whom she doles out her favors with her husband's knowledge and approval, and he frequents her house and bed. Harley feels no guilt or remorse in

[19] Horatio Colony, *Free Forester*, 15.

this relationship; nor is there any expression of the braggart in his activities. He accepts his active desires, his sexual proclivities, as natural to his manhood and life. He feels no guilt or remorse in his extramarital relationship. In fact he returns to Madeline and sensuously woos her in turn, almost making it seem as if any fault in their marriage was hers. The visual descriptions of these various experiences are portrayed with detail and heightened by suggestion.

The lack of uniformity in the presentation of sex, as between the sexual excesses of *Free Forester* (1935) and sexual inhibition of *Spring Came on Forever* (1935), is amply related by the dually suggestive and antiseptic quality of *Jornada* (1935). Martin Collins comes to the Southwest via the Santa Fe trail. He is of Massachusetts derivation and, typifying the supposedly cold Puritan strain of New England, exhibits strict moral conduct. In an atmosphere heavily accented with a love consciousness—the lascivious habits of Mexican men, the eager willingness of the women to be loved by Americans—Martin becomes enamored of Mercedes, a lovely married woman. He is greatly inhibited by her married status, especially since she is trusted by her husband, but he is nonetheless romantically inclined. Martin comes to appreciate the life of the Mexican, which is not bound by stringent moralities but which seeks joy and happiness—the fulfillment of sex and love. Even though Martin remains true to his values and waits for the husband's timely death, the novel clearly signifies the attitude that "a man must have women, at all events."[20] Man's very essential values are torn asunder by desire. It is also shown that women assume that men "take women," and they do not seem to object particularly.

The general pattern of the novels of the thirties is similar to those of the twenties. Many attitudes toward the woman are represented. Infrequently is emphasis placed upon his protective role, though he often enough acts in this capacity. This code is balanced by the several heroes who do not accept responsibility

[20] Robert L. Duffus, *Jornada*, 144.

for their wives but leave them to their own devices and a neighbor's protection—at best. Where the protective attitude exists, it is a more simplified responsibility, not a pursuit of a sacred duty bound in honor. Keith Maitland, upon the capture of his wife Hope in *Strife Before Dawn*, does all he can to rescue her. He scouts; he joins an advance party; he does not, however, attempt single-handedly an impossible rescue.

The high esteem of the woman as an object to love and adore falters somewhat. Though she has not fallen from this pedestal, it has begun to tarnish. There are several allusions to her malicious and deceitful nature, to the fact that she cannot be trusted. There is a continued representation of the woman as the bringer of change but the heroes are less pleased and less apt to adjust immediately to these changes as were the earliest heroes. Harley Boydley states and lives up to this doctrine: " 'I like a place where there are men that come and go when they please without having to bother 'bout women.' "[21] Others, as has been indicated, simply pick up and leave. But the greatest alteration in the woman as an object of adoration is the nature of the love itself. Here it is less the tarnishing of the pedestal than the bringing of it closer to earth. She has become an object of sex as well; the body is not taboo. Of course there are distinctions made as to which women receive such attentions: all too often they are common Mexicans, hot-blooded Spanish ladies, Indian women, prostitutes. However, the heroine has been brought into this circle, though not always as directly. Certainly, sex is more openly dealt with and the values have come to include physical desire as a need to be fulfilled. Rigid morality is in disrepute. The works that manifest the strict moral codes are in small minority; they hang on in the image of wholesome relations in the family novels. Prudery and propriety have almost disappeared.

PRACTICALITY AND PASSION

A sense of sexual freedom dominates the pioneer novels of the

[21] Colony, *op. cit.*, 111.

forties. Rapid and vast inroads seem to have been made by the doctrines of full sexual participation and the pursuit of passion. However, it is a comparative rather than a complete dominance. Although there are few novels in which the older traditions prevail altogether, there are some in which the hero exhibits vestiges of the moral codes of the past. However, even in these books the looser sexual mores are not ignored, for they are part of the background of the novel. Often enough they are relatively insignificant incidents to the basic structure of the plot; at other times an important aspect of the plot hinges upon these factors. In either case, the presence in the novel of these incidents is a sign of shifted values.

The decline of the romantic image of the ideal woman and her re-embodiment as a figure of strength, assurance and purpose paralleled and necessitated the fall of the pedestal upon which she had been placed. The heroine who symbolized fragility, gentility and helplessness required gallantry and manly protection. The heroine whose stature approaches equality, who travels and works with her man, whose endurance and strength of character seem limitless can not be treated with the same courtliness and deference. The male is not indifferent to her needs. As she is physically weak and unskilled in matters of defense, she is protected, but her protection is a natural role, not a sacred trust. It is not the sole *raison d'être* of the man. The woman is respected not for her status but for herself. She is not an ideal; she is human.

There are still a few characters who attempt to maintain the older elevated tradition. These are not only in the minority but are generally set to rights by more realistic characters.

> It struck him that Byrd and some of the others, for all that they knew better, stuck to queer ideas about women, not liking to think of them as flesh and blood and stomach and guts, but as something different, something a cut above earthy things, so that no one should let on to them that critters had hind ends . . . women had harder heads than men liked to believe.[22]

[22] A. B. Guthrie, *The Way West*, 90.

The author's position is certainly clear in this statement.

The emotional force of love, in the early novels, recreated the hero into a more civilized image, an image more acceptable to the heroine—and presumably the reader. This triumph and climactic change, as well as the ethereal qualities of their romance, emphasize the over-powering, heady nature of that love. By direct comparison the development of love in these novels seems rather mundane and matter of fact. The love situation seems to take a less significant role in the course of the denouement. The relationships have a practical overtone. Love is nonetheless a compelling emotion; the woman is powerful in her attraction as an object of love. With or without love, there is a strong consciousness of sex. This is a crucial factor in the changed aspect of romance.

Several changes in the hero's image come into play. The current hero is not so addicted to aloneness; he is not in isolation, nor are his views towards women initially couched in extreme negativeness. Therefore his realignment towards marriage is less astounding. His reaction to the woman on a human rather than an ideal level lessens the visionary qualities and keeps his reactions and attitudes earthbound. His purposes are not for the most part antagonistic to hers; his purposes become hers rather than the reverse. The drama as a result of these qualifications seems tamer and perhaps places the love situation in a more realistic perspective but with the sexual aspects dominating.

The attitudes and behavior of a large proportion of the heroes reveal the dominance of sex and sexual love. Basically, the attitude expresses the idea that sex is natural to life. As such it is not questioned or denied; rather it is sought and enjoyed. The hero of *Westward the River* calls attention to the new perspective:

> . . . he felt no more personal pride in his success with women than in his superior marksmanship with a rifle. They were equal talents a man had or did not have. It was merely one of the facts of life that whenever he returned from the enforced celibacy of a long hunt or a war party, fathers and husbands became watchful. He

liked young widows best, but he could not persuade himself that discontented wives were not fair game.[23]

This is not stated with an excess of lust or braggadocio. It is a matter-of-fact demonstration of masculinity and an equating of potency with virility. Perhaps the man is proving his masculinity through such successes (now that he no longer has his ultra-protective role). The significant value which is represented makes sexual relations not only a natural desire but also a need to be fulfilled with no limitation regarding who is "fair game."

The development of the hero of *Perilous Journey* from a naive youngster to a knowledgeable manhood extends this point of view. At the outset, Jim Dalyrymple laughs off his companion's constant talk of women; Jim is but a boy. Then he meets Natchez Kate, a voluptuous, endearing prostitute who is attracted by his clean, young manhood. Jim is attracted too, although he doesn't know quite why—at first. However, his physical responses are on a natural level. Jim readily enough falls into her embrace and is overcome by the power and pleasure of physical contact. Passion and desire haunt him; he complies with his new sense of need although a conflict with his moral training results when he falls in love. The impression remains that his initiation into the rite of sex dispels his youth, defines his masculinity, and establishes his manhood.

Many of these novels convey an impression of sexual desire as a desire unabated by time or circumstance and barely affected by the conventions of society. Fulfillment of these feelings is not only natural but unavoidable—sometimes uncontrollable—a drive which takes precedence over other emotions and values. Hero after hero represents these pressures. The instances of references to sex apart from love are frequent and for these men a natural extension of their relationships with women. Heroes such as Salathiel Albine in *The Forest and the Fort* and Orion Outlaw in

[23] Dale Van Every, *Westward the River*, 95.

Green Centuries frankly express their yearnings, their assumptions that such pleasure is available for the asking and with little limitation: little awareness of social restriction, personal responsibility or hindrance. They also fulfill their desires easily with women of short acquaintance, whom they do not love, as well as those they love—not always with the benefit of marriage. There is exception made, the love object being sacred and untouchable to several heroes. This signifies a double standard in sexual practices as well as a somewhat romantic moral value that insists on the virtue of the loved woman.

Boone Caudill illustrates the lack of restriction and a selfish regard for his own needs in *The Big Sky*. During a brief visit to his former home, he casually seduces a young, apparently inexperienced neighbor and thinks nothing of it. That she had interpreted his actions as some sort of pledge and thus permitted him to have his way with her is not his concern. In his eyes, fornication does not necessitate marriage; he is used to buying Indian women readily enough; this girl should not have shown a spark of willingness. Besides a man wasn't owned by a woman; he could take what he wanted and then go off on his own pursuits.

Other heroes are equally deliberate about flouting conventional attitudes. Jed Cooper's neglect of duty and irresponsible actions in *The Gilded Rooster* are motivated by his desire for the major's wife. Mark Elderidge in *Thunder on the River* with premeditation seduces Jeanne the first time he gets her alone. These men seem unconcerned about any consequences of their actions, exemplifying the notion that this is what women are for; they take what they can get. Other heroes—Yarborough Whetstone in *Foundation Stone*, Curt Fletcher in *Each Bright River*, Nathan Hart in *Genesee Fever*—exert freely and frequently their abundant sexual desires.

This behavior and these attitudes are particularly embodied in the hero's premarital experiences but there is carry-over in the married hero's activities. Indeed, as shall be seen, the texture and codes of marriage as displayed have been affected.

However, there is first a minority report. As has been indicated in the introduction to this section, not every hero of the forties is given these excesses of sexual freedom, the sense of insatiable sexual appetite and uncontrolled passion. There are unmarried heroes whose sense of morality is more traditional and novels which de-emphasize sex.

Those heroes who "do not know much about women"[24] and those who practice sexual abstinence are in the minority in the novels of the forties. Johnny Christmas, whom the quotation describes, actually knows little and cares less about people in general. His antisocial patterns of life lead him into the desolate mountains away from the settlements, away from a strange, uncommunicative liaison with an Indian woman.

Others include several of the young heroes. Of these, Dick Mounts, the youngster who is hurtled into adulthood in *Wilderness Clearing*, is most believable. Left destitute by an Indian raid, initially unsure of himself, he is seen as groping toward a definition of his status and his life. His emotions toward Maggie Gordon are based upon love but his relationship with her is no more than affectionate. This hesitancy seems appropriate to their age and circumstances.

A number of older heroes exhibit traditional moral virtues in their behavior and values in that sex does not play a role in their premarital activities or emotions. Several of these, as those in *Mighty Mountain* or *Edge of Time*, are seen as ordinary young men developing toward marriage and love similarly to the youth just discussed. Romantic attitudes are expressed in the hero's actions and hesitations in Furnas' *The Far Country* against a background suggesting sexual realism. Two others—*Long Meadows* and *A High Wind Rising*—in which the heroes wait patiently for the girl of their dreams—suggest a sentimentalized pure view of love reminiscent of the romantic novels, but somewhat modified by a more realistic tone of the work.

Marriage is accepted as the basic pattern of life by most of the

[24] Forrester Blake, *Johnny Christmas*, 111.

heroes. This is certainly so of the settling-down variety of pioneer. It is true also of the independent roamer: freedom to roam at will does not entail being alone. The mountain men and free foresters do associate with people. Particularly are they not immune to or unaware of women. Johnny Christmas is atypical in this respect and even he—like other extremists—marries an Indian. Only very few heroes remain single at the end of the novels. For most of these, the intent if not the fact of marriage is present. The greater proportion of the heroes are either married at the outset or before much of the plot is under way. This is quite different from the novels of the first decade in which only one hero was married, the others being strictly independent, although all but one has proposed by the end of the novels.

The concept of marriage is also altered. It is more earth bound in keeping with the altered status and role of the woman and the image of love. Passion and practicality have replaced the ethereal nature of the earlier unions. Not being on a pedestal, the woman is seen in a functional capacity; through marriage she fulfills her function. Indeed, circumstances and practical need determine some of the marriages, quite the antithesis of the romantic touches already noted. Wade Cameron needs a wife to help on his western land claim in *Edge of Time*. Rather than go west alone, he accepts Bethany after his fiancée breaks their engagement. Elmer Hale similarly needs a wife in order to claim an additional portion of land in *Mighty Mountain*. He marries the first girl who accepts him after he has asked three.

A consciousness of physical as well as emotional love and the new codes of masculinity, described in the preceding discussion, have further altered the romantic image of marriage. The strict moral codes observed by implication or fact in the marriages of the early novels are undermined. While some heroes keep their marriage vows, others stray from their moral obligations. Virtue does not necessarily derive from marriage. The sexual consciousness may be less extreme than in the novels of the single hero, but it is present, for some of the attitudes carry over.

Fidelity in marriage is the natural course of events to some heroes. Those who display romantic sentiments are consistent in their high moral standards. Family men like Lige Evans in *The Way West*, who live realistically and practically, keep their vows unquestioningly. Steady young men like Whit Livingston in *Look to the Mountain*, who had premarital relations with his beloved Melissa—and apparently no one else—remains true to her. A few heroes who had participated freely in sex experiences before marriage settle down without straying. Sam Dabney, the breathtaking hero of *Oh, Promised Land* captures many a woman prior to his marriage. Once married, Dabney only goes so far as to admire other women.

Other heroes display looser moral standards, paralleling the single heroes; temptations of the flesh are yielded to with varying frequency. In *Green Centuries*, when Cassy becomes withdrawn after the death of their children, Orion Outlaw gains solace from a neighbor who offers herself. He is flattered and enjoys this brief liaison. However, he later feels guilty over this lapse. In *This Land Is Ours*, Benton warmly responds to another woman though he is apparently happily married; and this does not spoil anything at home. Both of these heroes had participated in premarital sexual relations but limit their extramarital activities. On the other extreme in this respect is Yarbrough Whetstone, the concupiscent hero of *Foundation Stone*. He is unable to control his passions and apparently must have a woman. Away from his equally amorous wife but a short time on a land-scouting trip, he sleeps with a willing household semiservant. There are only minor guilt feelings for his vows to his wife; he rationalizes his behavior in terms of his passions. There are many other occasions. On one of these he yields to his desire in the face of severe Indian laws and seduces the lovely wife of an Indian chief, who is also a friend. When war results, his guilt is short lived and easily turned from himself:

... Yarbrough stood with the burden not only of the betrayal of a woman who had put herself in his hands and a fair dealing man who had treated with him peaceably, but, above and beyond all, of the knowledge that he had placed in danger those of his own blood to whom he was unalterably bound. Grim grew his face at his own treachery. But there was no bending to fear in him; he had no faintest idea of how a white man would go about backing down.[25]

There was no thought to the bending of passion—not before his act in full knowledge of the consequences nor afterward. His driving desire is foremost. Interestingly, no thought is given to his wife.

Paralleling the virtue undertaken by a few of the married heroes is a double standard manifested by a number of promiscuous heroes. This shows an awareness of some moral convention. Although these men adopt an attitude of sexual license generally, when it comes to the woman they love, they draw the line. The sophisticated, experienced John Frazier in *Red Morning* because he intends to marry Jane will go no further than passionate kisses and caresses. Noah, the hero of *Westward the River*, usually so sexually direct and proudly uninhibited, does not molest the heroine, although he has ample opportunity to ply her with his masculinity. When he catches her bathing in the river, he becomes unexpectedly proper; when his rival kisses her against her will, Noah is enraged by this audacity and disturbed by Sarah's calm. The inconsistency of these reactions with his own code does not occur to him. Beyond a kiss, Salathiel Albine will not touch Phoebe, his true love in *Bedford Village*: he asserts, "I love her *right!*"[26] Equally strong in his usual appetites, Sam Dabney nevertheless will not approach his betrothed in *Oh, Promised Land*; he even offers a little resistance when she comes to him. Certainly these heroes desire these women. But their usual expression of passion is blocked by a special response to love. Needless to say, this special view is not universal, for there are a like number of heroes who are not so blocked.

[25] Lella Warren, *Foundation Stone*, 177.
[26] Hervey Allen, *Bedford Village*, 198.

Although there is little consistency in the value and observance of the moral conventions—in or out of marriage, the general criss-cross pattern shows recognition of their existence if not the will or desire to adhere to them. Such knowledge and lack of willingness is overtly betrayed in *Bridal Journey* (as seen in the comparative plot discussion which introduces this chapter) and is illustrative of the complex social fabric on which the hero is tracing his own design. He is not particularly influenced in his own behavior by the moral code, for it is not the code which causes him initially to consider Marah inviolate. The extent of his limitations is seen in his remark to Marah when she refuses him. " 'You're safe from me as long as you really want to be. Before I was fifteen I'd found out it was more fun that way.' "[27]

The evidence of change in attitudes toward the codes and of reformulated conventions does not depend solely upon the central activities of the heroes. Incidents are presented in a way to show a shift of focus; attitudes that develop out of such incidents emphasize this shift. These incidents are not limited to the novels which spotlight a libidinous hero but appear in those novels which promulgate a doctrine of virtue and fidelity. It is the attitudes in these latter books which emphasize the change.

A key change is revealed in the attitude toward premarital intercourse. In *Look to the Mountain* none of the characters seem particularly surprised or upset by Melissa's premarital pregnancy; it is taken rather for granted except for Whit Livingston's delayed return. In *The Far Country*, the hero's sister is unashamed of expecting the guide's child without benefit of marriage; she had come to love him and realized that time would not wait their pleasure. The hero, himself quite conventional, is shocked at first but becomes understanding. This is a decided shift in acceptable activities.

Extramarital relations receive an equally soft treatment. When Elmer Hale in *The Mighty Mountain* realizes that he has unwittingly been deceived into spending the night with his friend's

[27] Dale Van Every, *Bridal Journey*, 188.

wife instead of his own, he is quite distraught. His realization that she used him because she desperately wants a child—her husband is apparently sterile—changes his dismay to subdued compassion. Clearly her act, her frank explanation, and his understanding would not have appeared in the early novels. When Sayward Wheeler realizes her husband's secret infidelity in *The Fields*, she does not condemn him. She blames herself for denying him her bed, for failing to see his desires as well as her own needs. In *The Way West*, Mack, the seducer of young Mercy, receives a degree of compassion; his frustrations with his frigid wife place him within the scope of understanding. Mercy's need for love and affection, her naïveté, her sweetness despite her hard life, raise sympathy rather than condemnation toward her. The hero, highly virtuous himself, finds he cannot condemn either; he lets his son marry Mercy, and he questions the caravan's rule against fornication as an unnatural one.

The undercurrents in these novels contrast the central character's fidelity to moral values and break down the strict moral structure otherwise exemplified. The current of sex serves to intensify the hero's virtue on the one hand and to identify an alteration in the conventions which permits understanding and acceptance of a values system that does not include this virtue.

Other signs of the broadened base of morality can be seen. In the novels of 1900–10, the signs of love were immediate. They included hesitant speech and "burning" from brief touches. These signs are replaced but the immediacy of reaction is often still present.

> "I'm not denying what's been on my mind. From the moment you walked in the door." . . . [Marah] could tell now what he was thinking and it was far more urgent than his matter-of-fact words. The discovery gave her a thrill of harsh triumph.[28]

Abner Gower's frank admission of the attraction of Marah's body and his stated desire are spoken during their first meeting. Their

[28] *Ibid.*

expression is direct. Marah's sense of appreciation—as a girl who scowls at wolf whistles but is secretly pleased—is equally significant. John Lee in *The Wilderness Road* would never have had such thoughts; what Rose Carew's reaction would be is inconceivable.

Other heroes display an equal rapidity of reaction, a like facility and charm. In *The Forest and the Fort*, Salathiel Albine just meets a young woman and before long he has his blanket on the forest floor. Nor does it take long for the hitherto unaware hero of *Perilous Journey* to go from first vague reaction towards a woman, so new he cannot quite identify it or stop a hint of shame, to the woman's generous arms.

The initial meetings are not always so abruptly sexual. They range from this immediate enactment of desire to youthful tentativeness. In *Mighty Mountain*, Elmer Hale's practical marriage is fraught with embarrassment and flavored with solicitude and tenderness. Some of the older heroes, as has been described, wait out their passion with kisses and caresses or live a double life.

The depiction of the heroine is another element of change. The new heroine is by no means altogether passive nor does she attempt to resist the hero. In some of the novels she throws herself upon the male and initiates the affair. This type of action is not limited to harlots, gambling ladies or Indian women who are eager for money. A few are innocents like Ginny in *The Trees* who want their man at any cost. In *Oh, Promised Land*, Donna knows what she is doing when she induces Sam to possess her before their wedding; she wants him to; she cannot and does not want to resist him. Cassy in *Green Centuries*, contemplating her surrender to Orion Outlaw, admits to herself that she has subtly pursued him and directly called his attention to her. She determines to resist him, but when he appears moments later she finds herself willingly in his arms.

Marah's decision to go to Abner's bed in *Bridal Journey* reveals the full circle of the women's attitudes. She knows that he will not molest her. She rationalizes that she ought to keep part of their strange bargain, a bargain in which he seemed to be risking his life to save hers and she risking nothing; she knows that no one would hold her to this bargain. She thinks she hates him, yet she is drawn irresistibly to his bed. And he is waiting for her.

For the heroine has grown in passion to match the hero. She is not ignorant or naïve: Marah notes that she has had suitors who have wooed her, not without some forward behavior. Nor is she indifferent to passion:

> The wave of memory rushed over her, swept her back into the previous hours of darkness. The night had left her no single defense—not even the fiction that her surrender had been merely the payment of a just debt. For her sharpest memory was of the guilty and terrible pleasure which, once detected, she had sought so desperately to deny but to which eventually she had yielded in helpless abandon.[29]

But this heroine's admission of pleasure does not end here. She further suggests the necessity of her own fulfillment, an experience not to be missed. Gerda Whetstone is portrayed as a passionate woman who responds fully to her husband's desires. It is a proud portrait, an image of power and earthiness. Although all of the heroines do not respond so actively, a good proportion of them show a strong consciousness of sex and willingness to love.

As their willingness becomes apparent in their surrender, so their consciousness is further evidenced in their awareness of the hero's masculinity and their response to his virility. Sam Dabney in *Oh, Promised Land* is particularly irresistible. Wherever he goes he causes gasps of delight and excitement. Admiring women preen themselves before him, attempt to lure him; even in the circumstance of impending Indian attack do they take time to draw his attention. It is clear, though left more to the imagination of the reader, that other heroes so inspire the women about them. The heroes' successes among them would attest to this even if

[29] *Ibid.*, 194.

there were no other evidence. Such general and specific reactions did not exist in the earlier works.

The impact of sex is further increased in the vivid descriptions of the physical aspects of the characters. Details of both the male and female body are extensive, as are the reactions to them. The naked body is displayed from time to time with varying reactions. In *Mighty Mountain,* an otherwise conservative work, Elmer Hale encourages his upset wife, jealous of his admiration of the body of a young lithe Indian, to display hers without shame. He indicates his appreciation of it and under this urging she comes naked to sit near him by the evening fire. None of the novels go so far as *Bridal Journey* in such display. During their escape, Marah and Abner spend a long scene together naked in a canoe while they are being hotly pursued by Indians. Abner takes time to study Marah by daylight, and—lest the reader have missed the point—he blatantly states his appreciation, without self-consciousness, modesty, or shame.

These descriptions and incidents, the frequency of sexual experiences of many of the heroes, and the extensive evidence of looser moral practices in the backgrounds of the majority of the novels, including those which do not portray moral license, amply demonstrate the wide acceptance of a less rigid moral code in these novels. The reality of sex has reached the pioneer; sex is seen as natural to life and is not always related to love and marriage. This is heightened by the absorption of some characters in sexual experiences—in the fulfillment of physical needs as well as love. The pioneer is no longer a sexless wanderer who happens upon love and marriage but one for whom marriage is the accepted pattern. The incidence of marriage is frequent, but for the most part, it has lost its ethereal qualities. Love is still a factor in many of the relationships, but it is rarely sentimentalized; the relationships are characterized by devotion, passion and practicality, an outlook founded upon mutual concerns and understandings in a day-by-day existence. There is a diminishing adherence to faithfulness and fidelity in marriage. A few heroes practice a strict morality; a few more stray from the straight and narrow path only infrequently. A few others, like a great proportion of single heroes, exhibit few, if any, moral restrictions.

The image of the pioneer hero as a Victorian romantic has disappeared to be replaced by a hero of vitality and virility who is conscious of desire and its fulfillment. The extent to which he adheres to the traditional moral codes varies according to both the man and the situation, but there is individual as well as total recognition of a less rigid morality. More heroes are less bound by codes and conventions than in the novels of the previous decades.

The level of moral freedom generally effected in this group of novels results to a large extent from the tone of the writing. In at least half of the novels, principally those which portray the lusty hero, the incidents and descriptions are presented in a blatantly frank style. There is no subtlety in the language and the general development of the situations. Fine emotional overtones that would convey the essential feelings and deeper reactions are ignored. Surface aspects of relationships and superficial emotions are displayed. The style is realistic in the direct expression and revelation of incident and feeling; however, the tone of the presentation borders on the sensational. The choice of materials—the frequent display of overt sexuality in the incidents and descriptions—itself reveals this orientation.

These patterns in the writing and the choice of materials suggest that a new set of symbols is being manifested in these recent works, replacing the sentimental symbols of the romantic, genteel tradition of the 1900–10 novels. These new symbols represent an aggressive, abundant sexuality and moral freedom as illustrated in the previous discussion. These are prevalent in much of the popular fiction of this period—the thrillers and bawdy adventures, both historical and contemporary, which seems to require a minimum quota of raw sex and revealing display in its pages and, for paperback books, on its covers. In this respect the pioneer novel has evolved toward this tradition of adventure and sex, the realism taking on ramifications of modern romance. The trend is only somewhat modified by the more controlled expression of these patterns—in both style and choice of material—in the works which display less consciousness of sex and, generally, a corollary awareness of traditional morality. However, the evidence of less rigid standards in even these books, taken with the more extreme expression in the others, testify to the great influence of the modern popular tradition on the pioneer in the novel.

6

Class on the Frontier

The aristocrat was certainly not aloof from the frontier. Many pioneering enterprises were sponsored in early American history by the landed gentry of the Tidelands region; men of the upper class, since the time of George Washington and Thomas Jefferson, are known to have traveled, organized, and otherwise participated in the opening of the trans-Appalachian areas and points west. They were part of the pioneer movement but not the entire movement, and a general reconstruction of the frontier does not usually envision the pioneer as an aristocrat.

Yet, a striking recurrent theme in the early novel is the emphasis on class structure and on various high-class–high-culture attributes of the key characters. In the successive decades this emphasis fades rapidly and is counteracted in part with an anti-aristocrat doctrine. Even so the aristocrat is not completely removed from the scene although his role and his image change. Also altered is the interaction between the man and the frontier.

The Aristocratic Ascendancy

In the novels of the 1900–10 period, the presentation of the aristocratic aspect is of more than slight impact. In each of the novels of the period, one or both of the key characters is presented as of aristocratic breed or of superior cultural origin. In almost every instance an imagined or actual difference in class level between the central characters constitutes a basic ingredient of the plot. There is a distinction made of the characters' social backgrounds; frequently this is made evident in a comparative way by contrasting the hero or heroine with more "common" types. In addition the central, positive values represented in the novels emanate from the aristocratic milieu. The frequency and extensiveness of these concepts, though there are subtle variations, indicate that they were requirements of the plot structure of the period.

The aristocracy of the key characters is expressed in several ways: they are designated as of higher class status in terms of ancestry and wealth; their behavior patterns with regard to social graces and manners, speech, values, and activities are distinctly "cultured"; they are educated; they represent certain refined and socially acceptable occupations. Some expressions of these attributes are direct; others are implied through the characters' value assumptions and general activities, and their reactions to each other. In each novel, however, some element—or elements—of superiority of the key characters is made apparent, either in their own demeanor or in comparison with those about them.

The plot situations also serve to construct the general aristocratic milieu. These aristocrats find themselves in the wilderness. Sometimes they are merely passing through, but usually at least one of them—most often the male—has been living there. Generally, the reasons or causes that have enforced this situation are somewhat exaggerated in the romantic tradition as compared with the novels of the succeeding decades (when the search for land is a primary cause).

The hero, acting the role of the pioneer, is basically the central character. Occasionally he has exiled himself to the wilderness; some mysterious incident in his past, or some defamation of character, has declassed him and forced him to live away from his more usual surroundings. Other heroes are brought to the frontier by war; in such cases they combine the skills and status of both scout and officer. For others, a collapse of the family fortunes causes the hero to go west, either to recoup his fortunes or because there is little else for him to do.

Usually the women are more foreign to the frontier atmosphere. But at times the causes that act upon the men affect them as well. Often they are traveling to join their colonel-fathers who are stationed at some frontier post. Otherwise, some family mishap—death, bankruptcy, destitution, war—has forced them to leave comfort and security behind. They venture into the forbidding frontier country where they meet the hero, and the story unfolds. There are variations to these themes, but these patterns are predominant.

Most of the heroes are distinctly aristocratic—upper class in origin. Although many of them are in disguise concerning their past and their heritage, they cannot, however, mask the essentially aristocratic values and patterns of behavior. Those heroes who are not specifically of upper-class background are imbued with special traits which set them apart from the other characters and create for them a special rank; they are superior to the common people but not quite equal to the aristocrats.

The birthright of the aristocrat hero can be traced to a prominent, wealthy family. The background is frequently Southern. Fitzhugh Beverley, hero of *Alice of Old Vincennes*, is of old Virginia lineage, as are the aristocratic Randolphs, whose son Thomas Stewart is the prominent figure in *The Heritage*. In *The Crossing*, David Ritchie runs away from rich, tidewater Carolina relatives, while Alan Gordon likewise escapes a Maryland plantation in *The Throwback* to become Tom Moonlight. In a sense, Alfred Clarke, in *Betty Zane*, typifies the whole group. He is introduced as "a Southerner and from one of those old families."[1] Clarke's specific background remains shrouded by secrecy, but, as in all these novels, the stereotype of the gentility of the Old South is strong. Traditions of Southern aristocracy suffice to create an aura of refinement and culture.

Not all the aristocratic heroes hail from the Old South. John Lee of *The Wilderness Road*, his name notwithstanding, is a cultured, rich Philadelphian. Raoul de Coubert, swashbuckling

[1] Zane Grey, *Betty Zane*, 23.

hero of *A Sword of the Old Frontier* and the only hero with immediate non-American ancestry, is no less than a French nobleman. Ramon Bell, the "I" of *D'ri and I,* is a wealthy, upper-class New Yorker.

Several heroes do not fit directly into this class pattern. The authors appear to straddle the issue of class partly by avoiding the matter and partly by indirect or vague suggestions of inherent nobility of character, of gentility, or superiority of background. In this group is the Virginian, hero of the novel of the same name. An aura of mystery blurs the details of his early life, but, like the majority of the heroes, the Virginian also comes from the South, this fact being constantly reiterated in the text. Although the man is generally and determinedly reticent about his past, the author rather frequently calls the reader's attention to the fact of regional background by noting the man's Southern drawl—which isn't constant—and by citing the reactions of other characters to this background. Their reactions—positive in quality—fit the stereotyped notion about Southern gentility; the Virginian represents personal dignity, grace, and gentility. At a crucial point in the plot the Virginian does reveal this much in a private letter to the mother of his beloved:

> I am of old stock in Virginia English and one Scotch-Irish grand-mother my father's father brought back from Kentucky. We have always stayed in the same place farmers and hunters not bettering our lot and very plain.[2]

Thus the Virginian maintains status in the tradition of his literary contemporaries. At the same time he establishes an association with an earthy, direct image which is important to the symbolic aspects of this novel.

The Zanes in the Zane Grey novels present an unusual front, somewhat in the tone of a neo-aristocracy of the frontier. A patriarchal situation is developed in which the entire border community looks to the Zanes for leadership. They are presented

2 Owen Wister, *The Virginian,* 320.

as somewhat superior in status to the neighbors, having more education, general culture, and finances. Their way of life, their manners and speech testify to greater education and breadth of background.

Outstanding examples of aristocratic heritage are the heroines. Alene and René in *A Sword of the Old Frontier* are English noblewomen whose immediate relation on the frontier is a colonel who has command of a frontier fort. Similarly, 'Toinette in *When Wilderness Was King* is daughter to an English colonel. There are also several daughters of the Old South: Ethel, in *The Throwback*, of Maryland; Alice, in *Alice of Old Vincennes*, is actually of Virginia though her background is kept hidden throughout the novel; Ruth, in *The Heritage*, of Virginia; Mrs. Temple, in *The Crossing*, of Carolina.

The other heroines differ in the presentation only in their aristocratic ancestry. As with a comparable group of heroes, they are given distinctive attributes that fit the prevalent design of superiority. Rose Carew, *The Wilderness Road*, daughter of a wealthy land speculator, apparently comes from the Philadelphia elite; she is close to her sisters from the South. Others are alike in their cultured gentility, their superiority. The most explicit statement of heritage concerns the background of Molly Wood. Her lineage is traced directly to Molly Stark of Revolutionary War repute, and the reader is carefully informed of the numbers of patriotic associations to which Molly could belong, these being status symbols of high order. In discussing her family, we are told,

> Their possessions had never been great ones, but they had sufficed. From generation to generation the family had gone to school like gentlefolk, dressed like gentlefolk, used the speech and ways of gentlefolk, and as gentlefolk lived and died.[3]

Assuredly this passage identifies the superiority of Molly, especially since her new situation in the Southwest does not include "gentlefolk."

[3] Wister, *op. cit.*, 78.

144

A general superiority is also indicated in the early passage from *The Last Trail* concerning Helen Sheppard:

> She knew that on the border there was no distinction of rank. Though she came from an old family, and . . . been surrounded by refinement, even luxury . . . [she] was determined to curb [her] pride. . . . If she didn't find good true friends, the fault would be her own. She saw at a glance that the colonel's widowed sister [Betty Zane] was her equal, perhaps her superior in education and breeding.[4]

Even though a specific denial is made, we are made conscious of Helen's distinction, and the immediate comparison with those on the frontier assures this. In *Betty Zane* the "widowed sister" had already been similarly distinguished so it does not lower Helen's status to say that Betty was perhaps superior to her. Of course, as in the case of all the others, it is an "old family" from which origin is claimed. The old family name combined with a Southern background produces a strong stereotyped image of high class.

Aside from the stated origin, which is sometimes unrevealed as part of the plot structure, each of the heroes and heroines gives evidence of high breeding and background. This is so with the exiles and the nonaristocrats as well. The nature of the evidence is at times obvious, at times subtle; as with the representation of the background of Molly Wood and Helen Sheppard, some evidence is comparative in nature.

One indication of class is the officer mold into which the hero is often poured in addition to his frontiersman-scout role. Since officers in their role and rank depict higher status, the implications of such a portrayal are direct. It is also significant that such ranks were held primarily by the rich, the educated—the aristocrat. The expectation of deference and respect to the officer heightens the existing class structure. Evidence of the social aspect is revealed in an incident from *A Sword of the Old Frontier*. The hero, Raoul de Coubert, has been imprisoned by Indians

---

[4] Zane Grey, *The Last Trail*, 28.

with a British officer, who keeps his distance until de Coubert's rank is revealed. He says, " 'Oh, that is decidedly better', with new cordiality in his voice and manner. 'We can at least meet upon social equality, which has its value.' "[5] A similar admission of this status consciousness is seen in the appellation "Colonel" given to Eb Zane in the Grey novels.

The several heroines, as daughters of high-ranking officers, are part of this classification. Their fathers' superiority is transposed to them; they are accorded the singular treatment that befits prestige and power.

When he is not filling the role of officer, the hero acts as an independent scout. As such he is not subservient to anyone, gaining status therefrom and standing apart from the general population. In this role he is sought for advice and leadership, frequently by the military. When this happens, he associates and acts with the officers. John Lee, an ex-officer, serves in such capacity in *The Wilderness Road* during his self-imposed exile; he later regains his commission and position.

This pattern of having the man of the frontier act as a scout for the military is not uncommon in subsequent novels either. However, a distinction exists in the degree to which the scout associates with and becomes a part of the life and class of the officer. Generally in those later books we are told of scouting expeditions; the emphasis is on the ways and manners of the scout, who usually springs from, and identifies with, the frontier element and holds himself somewhat aloof from the military. In contrast, the novels of the first decade emphasize, in these encounters, the habits and concerns of the officers; the scout becomes a part of this picture with but one exception. Generally, the battles are shown from the vantage point of the authority figures from astride horses. The hero is often entertained in salons by the lovely daughters of the household; he is apart from the common frontiersmen.

Wealth, either past or present, is another indication of status.

[5] Randall Parrish, *A Sword of the Old Frontier*, 246.

Glimpses of John Lee's Philadelphia mansion in *The Wilderness Road*, which is somehow maintained during his long absence in the woods, of Alan Gordon and Rance Poole's plantations in *The Throwback* and *The City of Six*, are replete with ease and luxury. Beverley, too, has these necessary trappings, while Ramon Bell establishes his position with evidence of careful dress, horses and servants—including D'ri, the humble frontiersman, as a kind of family retainer-companion. Raoul de Coubert's lapsed fortunes are made much of in *A Sword of the Old Frontier*, as are those of the Randolphs in *The Heritage*.

Wealth is invariably associated with a prestige of family which is part of the "old family" tradition. There is an assumption of rank, an expectation of service and respect which permeates the behavior patterns of the hero and heroine. (This is with the exception of those maintaining a complete disguise.) The hero is spared the more menial activities. Rance Poole readily adopts an attitude of the leisure class—unsoiled, not needing to work, pursuing gaming interests. Ramon Bell quite naturally leaves his horse to the care of D'ri; while Ramon is entertained in style, D'ri sups with the servants.

In creating the distinction of rank and position, more subtle indicators are used with the exiled aristocrats living as pioneers. These cause them to be both distinctive and distinguishable. Similar distinctions are given the heroes with nonaristocratic heritage which place them above the common lot and in a position, so it seems, to have dealings with their superiors. These patterns further reinforce the idea expressed earlier that a plot requirement of this period insisted upon an upper-class hero and heroine. Their essential superiority and gentility are clear to the reader even though they masquerade on a lesser level.

In their self-imposed exile, the aristocratic heroes have thrown off the outer aspects of their former lives. Often declining to comment upon their past, they successfully identify with the frontier elements. However, in their appearance, their behavior, their expressed attitudes, they are set above their fellows. They do not fully fall into the ways of the common people. The presentation of the several heroes who lack aristocratic lineage is comparable. Unlike the exiles, they do not have their heritage to fall back upon. Nevertheless, their surface characteristics, their behavior and their acceptance by those labeled as aristocrats make them distinctive and separable from those of common mold.

The composite picture of each of the exiled aristocrats is of inherent nobility. First, he looks the part. Typically, Raoul de Coubert, the declassed French nobleman in *A Sword of the Old Frontier* has a "good face"; he is described as having fine features and the look of a gentleman. Tom Moonlight, alias Alan Gordon, in *The Throwback* is thus identified by the author:

> . . . his face was high and noble, and he carried an atmosphere of command.[6]

The inherently noble aspect of the hero, which belies his outward class status, is furthered by his manner, especially in relation to others. Bearing, stature, and a distinct personal dignity communicate to the hero's actions an aura of superiority; a sense of isolation, of independence, creates distance and separation from the multitude. In the presence of the upper classes he evinces a silent confidence—a coupling of pride and modesty, but without humbleness—that evokes esteem and belies his low station.

The outstanding hero of *The Virginian* is a case in point. In the early chapters, the immediate visual impression created is of the man's splendor and grandeur; the Virginian radiates strength and personal presence. He stands out in a crowd as someone special, even to the stranger. Upon first meeting the narrator, who is a guest of his employer, the Virginian's cool reaction to undue familiarity gives the guest pause and begins to establish his special status.

> I abstained from further questioning the "trustworthy man." My questions had not fared excessively well. . . . But neither did he

[6] Alfred H. Lewis, *The Throwback*, 43.

purpose to leave me familiar with him. Why was this? . . . If he
had tried familiarity with me the first two minutes of our acquaintance, I should have resented it; by what right, then, had I tried it
with him? It smacked of patronizing: on this occasion he had come
off the better gentleman of the two. Here in flesh and blood was a
truth which I had long believed in words, but never before met.
The creature we call a *gentleman* lies deep in the hearts of thou-
sands that are born without chance to master the outward graces
of the type.[7]

The author here starts his sometimes contradictory campaign to
recognize the essential nobility in man, or this man, at least. (It is
contradictory, for, although he creates the Virginian in this noble
guise and make him a better man, he also creates a situation
which implies his class inferiority.) The portrait of practicing
nobility is enhanced throughout the novel by his manners and
actions: his gentleness of speech and conduct, his desire for advancement and education, his strict code toward women, his
usual calm assurance with his superiors, and the like. The Virginian stands head and shoulders above the other cowpunchers
and even the elite of the novel.

A major part of this presentation in evolving the undercurrent
of rank is the recognition of the hero's distinction and acceptance
by others of the upper class. Particularly outstanding is the generally uniform reaction of the aristocratic heroine. She senses the
nobility of the hero, the essential quality and spirit of the declassed pioneer, even though it is masked. She permits herself to
have dealings and conversations with him; some permit themselves secret admiration. She comes to rely on him and eventually
to doubt his disguise. It is fairly clear that the initial encounters
are circumstantial and that these men are acceptable only in
these special circumstances. However, other pioneers are not
accepted even on this level. For them a greater distance prevails.

Other aspects of superiority grow out of comparisons with
others found on the frontier. There is, on one hand, correct speech

[7] Wister, *op. cit.*, 10.

and clear diction and, on the other, crude and slurred speech patterns. An illustration from *The Crossing* is rather pointed in this respect. David Ritchie, who hails from a Tidewater family, grows up in the home of Tom and Polly McChesney. While Tom speaks in a semiliterate fashion, David manages to retain refinements of the Tidewater speech in both idiom and dialect. In addition to this greater literacy, the aristocratic hero invariably appears as more astute and intelligent. Leadership and wisdom are his basic characteristics while other frontiersmen, though stout at heart, are relatively slow thinking and unimaginative. Only in woodcraft do the common frontiersmen sometimes excel. The hero is also set off by his consciousness and adherence to acceptable manners in his contacts with women. Others, though well intentioned, display crudities and roughness.

The clearest overt indication of recognized rank and position is made with regard to young Stewart in *The Heritage*. Having been captured and adopted by Indians, he attains a large degree of Indian culture. He loses both memory and habit of white ways. In his third year of captivity he even contemplates marriage with an Indian girl. At this crucial point an old crone, a white captive, with whom he has had negligible contact, remarks covertly,

> ". . . a fine young gentleman like yourself don't need t'stay here among th' Injuns!"[8]

Although he has become an Indian for all superficial appearances, the old crone manages to recognize his gentleman status. She implies that Indian life, though good enough for her, could not do for him. This starts the self-questioning process that recalls his heritage, which results in his resisting the urge to marry. Later Stewart escapes and joins General Wayne's forces. Upon introduction to Wayne he is immediately appointed as aide to the general. His worth, stature, and class identity are not only readily apparent but are also sufficient to overcome his total inexperi-

[8] Burton E. Stevenson, *The Heritage*, 198.

ence. This instant recognition of class status and the automatic elevation to prestige positions are symptoms of the aristocratic pattern.

A construct of the nonaristocratic hero in *When Wilderness Was King* displays similar factors of status recognition. John Wayland is frequently described as having a noble face, a face showing honor and manliness, which is quickly recognized by the heroine. The hero himself asserts a vague class elevation: "I believe I can prove descent from an old and honorable race."[9] These give him access, unlike other men of the border, to society with the high ranking characters—officers and their ladies—of the novel, whose acceptance of him gives him prestige by association. While not readily apparent at first, thus emphasizing the initial reaction to the outward characteristics, John's education, cultured speech, manners and social graces solidify his status as a gentleman in spite of his rough dress and not-quite-acceptable pedigree.

The assumption of rank and expectancy of service is particularly apparent in the heroines. The females' own assurance of their superiority and gentility and their expectation of homage and respect indicates their adherence to a caste system. In some situations the authors attempt to deny this, sometimes contradictorily, by causing their characters to take note of essential elements of democracy. A previously cited quotation from *The Last Trail* illustrates this but also shows a contradictory consciousness of superiority. Less awareness of class differences would have been more indicative of its nonexistence.

These women are shown as determinedly keeping proper distance, a distance not solely fostered by moral propriety. They are somewhat regal and unapproachable, haughty, and expect the obeisance and respect that is afforded to women of their station. Their contacts with common people, including early meetings with the declassed hero, show their feelings of self-superiority.

Insight into such class consciousness is given through a rare

[9] Randall Parrish, *When Wilderness Was King*, 67.

meeting of the cultured female with the "common" frontiers-woman. In *The Crossing*, Polly McChesney, not of aristocratic lineage, is presented as part of the working, ordinary populace. When she comes in contact with the aristocratic Mrs. Temple, she immediately recognizes her as "gentry" and sets about "doing for" her. She asserts that what is good enough for herself is not good enough for gentry. Mrs. Temple accepts the hospitality but, though grateful, nevertheless considers the McChesneys inferior—beneath her; she sees them as crude, innocent "children of the woods." She knows that she would not be forced to be with them except for unfortunate ill chance. Her condescending manner causes the modern reader to be sympathetic to Polly, but the basic awareness and acceptance of class difference is not erased by this tone.

The hesitant relationships of the declassed men with these women are steeped with every evidence of a consciousness of rank and status. The heroes recognize their own lesser station. Although they permit themselves the freedom of falling in love with the ladies in question, their sense of rank and ethic keeps their ardor in check. They recognize the great social gulf which separates them from the consummation of their love. Without the prerequisite of rank they are unacceptable to their beloved. The hero knows this, as does the heroine. A major conflict of values hinges on this knowledge.

The full revelation of these facets is realized in the general design of the plots of these novels. The various threads, which might otherwise seem circumstantial or accidental are inter-woven in a pattern that seems unmistakable. The individual constructions are similar; their highlights, however modified, accent the aristocratic tone and the consciousness of class.

The first book of this chronological series, Maurice Thompson's *Alice of Old Vincennes*, provides a strong opening.[10] Bas-

[10] *Alice of Old Vincennes* was not only a best seller of its day according to *Sixty Years of Best Sellers*, but also compares favorably with other top sellers of the first quartile of this century in the lists of Mott and Hart in *Golden Multitudes*.

ically, the plot revolves around Lieutenant Fitzhugh Beverley, scout-officer and aristocrat of Virginia, who, having come west to Vincennes with George Rogers Clark's forces, falls in love with Alice. She is the vivacious daughter in a local French household. Her beauty, her charm, her education and culture draw him; her frank, impetuous manner intrigues him. However, a significant drawback presents itself:

> While joining in Captain Helm's laugh at the expense of [the people of] Vincennes, Beverley look leave to indulge a mental reservation in favor of Alice. He could not bear to class her with the crowd of noisy, thoughtless, mercurial beings. . . . His heart was full of her. . . . His youth, his imagination, all that was fresh and spontaneously gentle and natural in him, was flooded with the majestic splendor of her beauty. And yet in his pride [and it was not a false pride, but rather a noble regard for his birthright], he vaguely realized how far she was from him, how impossible.[11]

He admits his love to himself, but he forces himself to withdraw because of class differences: she is practically a peasant girl even though unaccountably educated and charming.

Despite the author's protestations about Beverley's "gentle and natural" preferences, his usual frame of reference concentrates on family and birthright. Gradually Beverley does rebuild his image of Alice to meet his prerequisites; he excuses her heritage by compensation—her beauty, her charm and grace, her manners, her learning—and decides to marry her. Even with the ever-present consciousness of class, this might seem to be a defeat for the aristocratic impulse. However, this is not a victory for the democratic impulse. By disassociating Alice from her environment, Beverley merely extends his discrimination of the frontier; the class consciousness does not actually diminish. Besides, the author does not leave it there. We learn shortly that Alice is actually the orphaned daughter of an old, aristocratic Virginia family; her dying parents had left her stranded on the frontier

---

[11] Maurice Thompson, *Alice of Old Vincennes*, 120.

in the care of the Vincennes French. The mantle of aristocracy falls easily about Alice's shoulders; her fondest day dreams have been of such a life. The couple returns to Virginia where Alice succeeds in charming everyone, adapting easily to her new life, and causing quite a sympathetic stir over her unfortunate experience in the wilderness.

The thread of class consciousness is represented in a similar manner in several other novels. In these, the situations are reversed in that the male is de-classed or outcast whereas the female holds the position of rank.

The most direct of these—in its statements, not in its structure—is Parrish's *A Sword of the Old Frontier*. Raoul de Coubert is frequently identified as a "mere *coureur de bois*," both by the author and by various characters. As such, he is unwelcome in the society of officers and ladies; his ability and responsibility are questioned, first as the protector and leader of the stranded ladies, and second in a special military role:

> "Why should we place any confidence in a mere *coureur de bois*, a wandering hunter, without position or prestige?"[12]

Out of context this would appear perhaps to be a sensible question, but the frequent repetition and the emphasis upon the elements of prestige and position deny any interest of the questioner in common sense and reveal as well the author's concern with social status.

The key relationship between Raoul and Alene is thwarted by this same factor. Alene's determined aloofness is fostered by his being a "mere *coureur de bois*." Her manner appears haughty and almost uncivil. In a moment of frankness and pique he remarks bitterly,

> "I was a mere French *voyageur*, an outcast of the forest, nor did you for one moment permit me to forget the wide social gulf between us."[13]

12 Randall Parrish, *A Sword of the Old Frontier*, 162.
13 *Ibid.*, 155.

This situation continues until Raoul is fully reinstated and recognized with proper status and prospects. Only then does he gain Alene's hand.

In their self-imposed exile, John Lee and Alan Gordon, who masquerades as Old Tom Moonlight, respectively the heroes of *The Wilderness Road* and *The Throwback*, are unacceptable to the heroines. The significant element in the male-female relationship is the lost status of the heroes. Each feels that he has fallen beneath the level of the secretly-loved lady. In keeping with their severe ethic they are sure that they do not deserve the ladies, and they deny themselves any real association with them. For reasons of the plot they are silent about their real identity and status; reasons of pride and honor do not permit such outbursts as those of de Coubert. They accept their self-denial with apparent stoicism.

However, the reader is not left with these sorry states of affairs. Both men are reclaimed: the mystery of their identity is solved. As a result they are free to reveal their love and the ladies may now reciprocate. The sense of aristocracy is preserved by their return to their original lives and status in the East.

The case of the Virginian is generally similar, especially in its view of class consciousness, though the conclusion is somewhat different. The Virginian and Molly return to the West, but not to his previous status. He becomes a partner to his former employer, a landowner in his own right, and a leader in the community. In a sense the aristocratic impulse is overcome, for the nonaristocrat has won the field; at the same time, the conclusion (as well as the basic characterization) subtly reinforces aristocratic values.

In his novels of the period, Zane Grey always manages to deny the existence of any class levels on the frontier while actually building situations that enforce the opposite attitude. His heroines arrive upon the frontier from the East. As already noted they are apart from the crowd, being educated, cultured and genteel. They initially have some difficulty in adjusting to their new situation. They cannot quite accept the people, though they verbalize acceptance. Typically, Grey has a lesser character advise Betty Zane:

> "I have learned to get along very well by simply making the best of it. . . . And to tell the truth, I have learned to respect these rugged fellows. They are uncouth; they have no manners, but their hearts are honest and true, and that is of much greater importance in frontiersmen than the little attentions and courtesies upon which women are apt to lay too much stress."[14]

These are the values being promulgated. But, though they are voiced, they are not enforced by the tone and activities of the novel which cast a spell of superiority over the Zane clan. Supposedly, the refined Betty does learn to respect the people, but it is Alfred Clarke, the Southerner from the old Virginia family, who woos and wins Betty. The backdrop of the frontier democracy fades.

In the other novels of this period, the conflict in status of the hero and the heroine does not become a central issue because they are equal to start with. There is constant evidence, as has already been shown, that the characters are superior to those about them. The characters pair off generally at their assigned level.

The sense of democracy gains barely a foothold on the frontier in the pioneer novels from 1900 to 1910. The aristocratic impulse looms supreme. The attitudes, manners and mores detailed are those of the aristocrat. A fairly distinct division is developed between this privileged class and the common folk on the frontier. Contact between them is limited; at best, the hero has transient associations with them. Winston Churchill's atypically sympathetic portrayal of the strength and goodness of Tom and Polly McChesney in *The Crossing* is overshadowed by his apparent acceptance of the fact of Mrs. Temple's superiority. Polly certainly accepts it. He also goes out of his way to build an aristocratic background for the central character. Although the

[14] Zane Grey, *Betty Zane*, 23.

modern reader may be empathic and recognize the actual superiority, the more essential heroism, of the McChesneys, he is submerged by the onslaught of the upper-class values. Even in the unlikely chance that Churchill intended a greater identification with the lower class, his is but a minor crack in the aristocratic wall of the period.

Owen Wister, who at times appears out of step with himself, provides a rare instance of an opposing value. He has his narrator give evidence on the truer nobility in man,

> "It was through the Declaration of Independence that we Americans acknowledged the *eternal inequality* of man. For by it we abolished a cut-and-dried aristocracy. We had seen little men artificially held up in high places, and great men artificially held down in low places, and our own justice-loving hearts abhorred this violence to human nature. Therefore we decreed that every man should thenceforth have equal liberty to find his own level. By this very decree we acknowledged and gave freedom to true aristocracy, saying, 'Let the best man win, whoever he is.' Let the best man win! That is America's word. That is true democracy. And true democracy and true aristocracy are one and the same thing."[15]

This is carried out in some ways in the novel and belied in others.

The literary tide seems to have left this group of novels high and dry. The apparent demands upon the plot in terms of social expectation and romantic overtones create a group of novels which in these respects is out of the main course of realistic literature. Whether these concepts had much basis in actuality is doubtful as compared to latter-day novels, at least.

Significance lies not only in the basic aristocracy of the major characters but also in the failure of the frontier to exert any lasting influence upon them. As has been shown, many aristocratic frontiersmen return to their titles and estates, forsaking and denying the frontier and its merits; others gain symbolic or actual

[15] Wister, *op. cit.*, 125.

status on the frontier that sets them above the common lot, thus establishing a reasonable facsimile of a neoaristocracy on the frontier. These do not detail the rise of a vital democratic force as an outgrowth of the pioneering process.

The Aristocrat's Decline

Where all the central characters of the early pioneer literature were either specifically aristocratic or suggestively superior in their status, the years after 1910 saw a decline in the emphasis on the high birth and breeding. Generally, the hero was of humbler origin. Through the years, however, the main character is occasionally presented as having aristocratic ancestry. Even when he does appear as such, certain qualifying factors alter the image so that the basic representation is not completely upper class in tone.

These designations of the hero as "gentry" occur sporadically in the novels between 1910 and 1950. There are several novels in each decade which in one way or another so identify the central figures. Proportionately there are more in the second decade for there are fewer novels in total. Some authors are direct in designating the aristocrat; others establish this identity through the secondary techniques which are part of the stereotype of high class (discussed in the previous section).

Certain superficial patterns closely parallel those used in the first decade's novels. The heritage of the Old South is paramount among these. The hero of *Erskine Dale, Pioneer* (1920), after years of Indian captivity from early childhood, is reunited with his wealthy Virginia relatives. Another is Yarbrough Whetstone whose Carolina plantation background is detailed in *Foundation Stone* (1940). Even as unlikely a hero as mountain man Sam Lash reveals in *Wolf Song* (1927) that he comes from "gentlefolk, halfway at least. . . . A white in Virginia and niggers and tobacco fields—."[16] Wealth and its accompanying ease help to classify Mort Sturdevant of New York who is escaping from his father's millions to be on his own in *Oklahoma* (1926). Webster "Black"

[16] Harvey Fergusson, *Wolf Song*, 16.

Brond, the upper-class hero of *The Red Road* (1927) is this portrait in reverse, the collapse of his fortunes forces his westward trek. Other heroes in such diverse novels as *The Covered Wagon* (1922), *Wind Over Wisconsin* (1938), *Don't You Cry For Me* (1940), and *Unconquered* (1948) also present heroes who manifest combinations of these symbols of status. Through speech, education, background or associations with persons having upper-class labels, they take on the aura of the aristocrat.

The approach to the development of these heroes varies. In the course of the years, there is less and less emphasis on the aristocratic elements in representing the character. Qualifying changes are introduced with passing time so that in the later books the characterizations are influenced but slightly by the superficial labels. In fact, in some instances the aristocratic heritage is all but ignored after the initial identification. The attitudes and actions of the characters, as well as reactions to them, create the character's class status.

Being caught in a crosscurrent of changing pressures, the novels of the early twenties dealing with aristocrats are not clear cut in their designations. Will Banion, the hero of *The Covered Wagon* (1922), is typical. He is given the outer designations of class: an ex-officer, an independent adventurer, wealth. He is well groomed, fine mannered, clear spoken, conscious of social niceties—more so than others. He is noble and romantic; seated on his stallion, he is an imposing and masterful figure. He is somewhat removed from the mundane experiences and occupations of the train. Yet, he, at the same time, is in frequent association with the other members of the train. He is accepted by them and he accepts them. There is little suggestion of class difference in his social manners. Banion falls in love with Molly Wingate, the daughter of the train's respectable but nonaristocratic leader. This position, of course, lends prestige and a half-way type of status. In addition, Molly has certain genteel characteristics which compensate for her lack of birthright. To complete the mixed portrait, Banion also participates in some activities which modify any excess of class that might have been developed—including an undignified and brutal rough-and-tumble frontier fight, conducted, however, in the duel tradition. The novels *Magnificent Adventure* and *Erskine Dale, Pioneer* present similar composite portraits which develop a qualified aristocratic hero.

A second group of these novels is much farther removed from an aristocratic tone. Once the hero's origin is established, there is no further development of class symbols in the character or events of the novels—except perhaps in the consciousness of the reader. The emphasis on fine manners, personal dignity, rank, and the extra-careful treatment of women disappears. There is no perceptible distinction drawn between characters on the basis of class heritage; associations between them are unlimited. Sam Lash in *Wolf Song* (1927), after his initial identification as being of aristocratic background, develops without restraint. The pattern of his life is not at all like that of his predecessors in print, and he is far from limited by the manners and mores that dominate their actions. He is true to the mountain-man tradition rather than to his "gentlefolk" origins.

Eventually Sam Lash does marry an aristocratic Spanish girl, but the emphasis is on physical attraction rather than class. Indeed, he is deterred by her background and attempts to take her away from her old life. The pattern of the early novels can be seen in the conclusion to the extent of Lash's return to the arms of his original heritage. But this is a secret satisfaction for the reader—if at all, for the characters are left unaware of such common ground. Lash's reversed decision is dominated by passion. These qualifications greatly undermine any aristocratic tone.

In the several other novels, the aristocratic mores of the past linger in some form, either as in *Wolf Song* in the identification of the hero as gentry or in the semigentility of the heroine. These elements are in minor key. New mores and values exert influence on the development of the events and the characters. These are especially apparent in the novel *Foundation Stone* (1940) in which the hero Yarbrough Whetstone intends to build a new plantation, to carry the ways of the Old South to the New South. Yet the concept of class that is conveyed through this novel is minimal. Whetstone is a driving, powerful force whose behavior evinces knowledge of social graces but also ignores them to suit his needs and purposes. He is top man, but he does not stand on his dignity, nor does he mince through the events in a self-conscious display of his own hereditary status. Rather, there is an emphasis of status through power and action and personality.

In general, then, the novels of this period on occasion identify their heroes as aristocratic by one means or another. However, the activities, attitudes, and associations of these characters are modified in varying degrees so as to limit the aristocratic portrait.

THE PULSE OF DEMOCRACY

Paralleling the decline of the aristocratic emphasis in the novels after 1910 is the rise of the sense of personal equality. The social-literary motives that required the heroes and heroines to be stereotypes of certain criteria of gentility have faded, though not disappeared, as the previous section indicates. The realist forces active in the literary milieu of the day had begun to affect this type of popular historical novel, the effect being especially apparent in the identification and interaction of the major characters.

A literary concentration on the lives of ordinary people is the essential prime mover of the new emphasis on equality. The hero is cast in the mold of the common man; he does not, for the most part, profess a heredity superior to others about him. Nor is heredity and background particularly important to him. He is of the people and proud of it. Unwin Shaw in *The Far Country* introduces himself with this clarification:

> "I will not let on that Maria and myself can lay no claim to aristocratic forbears, but am proud to write, we come of plain stock."[17]

By making the ordinary man the hero as well as heroic in the

[17] Marthedith Furnas, *The Far Country*, 3.

majority of the novels, the shift away from the aristocratic influence is achieved.

The emphasis on equality is heightened as a result of the leveling force of the frontier. No matter what their previous hereditary or social background, once on the frontier the characters are accepted on terms of equality and are expected to act accordingly. The thought, "She knew that on the border there was no distinction of rank",[18] expressed in *The Last Trail* is echoed to an ever-increasing degree but without the unconscious awareness of rank that qualified the early statement. There is no question of acceptance or distinction of treatment based upon class. The pioneer is not subservient to anyone. In *Bridal Journey*, this concept is exemplified through a minor character's astonishment and disbelief when he beholds what appears to be the bowing to class by frontiersmen:

> Bethel was flabbergasted. They called her Marah as if she were one of them. But they treated her as if she were a young queen. These packers and movers and militiamen were not the kind of people likely to stand in awe of her because she was rich or because she was marrying a county lieutenant.[19]

It is accepted that the pioneer is not impressed by wealth or position and would not lower himself before such. The frontier society is built upon a solid foundation of equality.

This independent attitude is more exactly stated in *Genesee Fever* in response to a conflict situation between classes.

> "I regret," said Nathan ironically, "that in these Yankee woods we have not kept up the genteel practice of fawning servility in the presence of superior beings."[20]

Nathan Hart's sarcasm reveals not only the attitude of equality associated with the man but also suggests the evolution of that spirit on the frontier.

[18] Zane Grey, *The Last Trail*, 28.
[19] Dale Van Every, *Bridal Journey*, 12.
[20] Carl Carmer, *Genesee Fever*, 158.

Any inequality that may have existed before the pioneer's entrance upon the frontier stage is soon diminished in value and effect. The trials of the trail, the work of the early farm and settlement, the perils of the Indian raid do not distinguish because of rank. Indeed they are the catalysts in the leveling process. In general, the pioneer heroes neither affect a superior attitude nor take an inferior role in terms of rank. This is well illustrated in the novels of the mountain men. As a group they do not recognize any class differences nor do they exhibit any hierarchy among themselves—except in terms of ability. Significant in this respect is Sam Lash, the hero of *Wolf Song*, whose gentle birth is of no consequence in his development as a mountain man. A common denominator of rank on the frontier is also reached among the immigrant pioneers. As in *The Emigrants*, the varied class backgrounds of the central characters, which confined them to different social strata in Norway, are soon eradicated on the frontier. Such a process is also evident on the overland trail. Although they are migrating from a plantation, the Johnsons in *Don't You Cry for Me* pretend no superiority to their companions nor are they treated with any special deference by them. They take on their share of the train's work without question.

The gradual but marked change in the heroine of *Each Bright River* attests to the influence of the frontier. Kitty Gatewood is a wealthy, strong-minded Southern belle who is stranded in frontier Oregon. Her sense of superiority of person and culture is challenged by the people and the environment of the frontier. Once she recovers from the shock of her destitution and adjusts to her new life, she finds that she is neither above the people around her nor above work. She is accepted on a par with others.

The leveling process is also expounded in *Oh, Promised Land*. The early chapters of the book, which take place in the Tidewater South, make the class levels explicit. The hero, Sam Dabney, who has grown up in the backwoods, is definitely lower class. Yet, once on the frontier this distinction is unimportant and not invoked. On the frontier,

There were no social barriers between the Chadbournes and the Dabneys. The Chadbournes were Scots, the Dabneys were Irish, and they were equal in the newest section of a new land. Sam didn't know there was such a thing as social barriers, and neither Donna nor Pierce ever would have told him.[21]

The social barriers break down before the frontier's ignorance of them and its straightforward conduct of social relations.

On the frontier, a man was what he was and what he could do, not what he came from. He was superior who proved his leadership and courage, who excelled in skills. The free, open society permitted a man to develop on his own merits—without the sense of hereditary rank. In these books and others, the men and women of vision and strength make the greatest achievements.

Built into this sense of equality is a self-acceptance and self-assurance that act to deny any inferior status. As a result, though the pioneer may recognize certain qualities of culture—fine manners, greater education, or wealth in some of his associates or in nonpioneers—he does not feel basically inferior to them. When the frontiersmen in *Lamb in His Bosom* go on their yearly trading journey to the coast, they go without subservience; they do not lack assurance or self-possession. They do not feel beneath other farmers or the traders and, in fact, feel themselves better for doing their own work rather than depending on slaves. In *The Fields*, Sayward Wheeler recognizes the quality of the school teacher in comparison to her own "woodsy" unschooled background, but she does not diminish her own accomplishments. She sees the relative merit of the individual qualities and lacks neither self-respect nor pride. She sees that her children achieve the education that she lacks for the quality she does lack is attainable.

Aside from expressing his equality through his associations and activities, the pioneer on occasion distinctly spells it out: he claims his independence of action and represents it as a chief

21 James H. Street, *Oh, Promised Land,* 42.

code. A conversation recorded in *The Forest and the Fort* shows this consciousness of the frontiersmen.

> "Who's your master?"
> "No one," said Salathiel. "I'm neither a soldier nor a servant, my friend. The chest, however, belongs to . . . Captain Simeon Ecuyer . . . ."
> "No offence, no offence," cried Mr. Yates. "Ecuyer's one of the finest, even if he is a Swiss. You might well be proud to sarve him."
> "I am," replied Salathiel, "but just because I'm doing something useful, I'm not a slave." . . .
> "Damme, I like your spirit," replied Mr. Yates. "This is America and you can suit yourself."[22]

The frontier environment is specifically represented as the developer of this equality. The pioneers express a desire for equality of chance and life and an expectation of finding it on the frontier. The frontier symbolizes a new life and, as stated by Yancey Cravat in *Cimarron*, ". . . no class distinctions, no snobbery, no high-falutin' notion."[23] Unwin Shaw also predicts a defeat of classism that has limited the advance of his life and that of his sister, Maria Prettymans, who had married above her station and suffers constant humiliation as a result.

> So I said to Maria, there was no Prettymans in California. Her boy could grow up free and equal there. He would not be raised by snobs, but in constant communication with the natural grandeur of these regions, would develop into manhood uncontaminated by civilization, relying on his inner man rather than external distinctions of wealth or family.[24]

True to his predictions, class structures are left behind. Self-realization and self-confidence grow out of the fertile pioneer atmosphere. The results are the same in *Buckskin Breeches* and

---

[22] Hervey Allen, *The Forest and the Fort*, 241.
[23] Edna Ferber, *Cimarron*, 173.
[24] Furnas, *op. cit.*, 27.

the causes are similar, though the hero does not have an inferior status. But the frontier represents the chance for the individual to rise to his own level and not be held down by constricting attitudes and deteriorating elements of society.

However, the frontier is not presented in these novels as totally devoid of class feelings. Both characters and events are depicted which play up at least a minor consciousness of rank. Although the hero may represent equality in his thoughts and actions, not all of the characters follow suit. Hints of inequality either encourage respect or raise doubt about the total effect of the frontier process. Not all of the novels present this problem; in few is it a major theme. If shown at all, it usually forms part of the network of relationships and feelings that make up the background of the pioneers' lives.

A positive view of the frontier role in this respect is seen in the representation of the aristocrat and the outcome of conflicts between the several levels of society. The sense of equality is effectively portrayed in *Drums Along the Mohawk*. Clearly, the hero and a great proportion of the inhabitants have no pretensions about origins or rank. Indeed a part of the rationale of their revolutionary fight for independence is against such notions fostered by their English neighbors. Only an occasional frontier character, notably Mrs. Demooth, the wife of the local militia leader, talks of "gentry" and shows a consciousness of society and rank. Her pretenses and haughty concerns are made to seem petty as well as unpopular. The frontier society rejects Mrs. Demooth's concept of the right way of things; there is no place on the frontier for such old-world concerns, just as there is no place for the weak, the dependent, or the unable. Although he recognizes authority and education, the hero, Gil Martin, seems unconscious of class; his response to the Demooths is as honest, straightforward and self-respecting as to his other neighbors. The novel conveys the sense that it is men like Martin out of whom a nation is shaped. With the negative evocation of the English aristocrats and their consorts, the ordinary people gain the honors as well as the land.

The evocation of frontier equality in contrast to aristocratic codes forms a subtheme of *The Far Country*. The contrast is brought out through the hero, Unwin Shaw and his brother-in-law, Basil Prettymans. In the tradition of the aristocratic temperament, Basil holds himself aloof from the "common" people; he refuses to do some types of work or even to walk when it becomes necessary to. He is critical of Unwin and at first easily and arrogantly demolishes him. However, the rigors of the trail cause Basil to falter while Unwin rises above the hardships of the situation; Unwin's breed builds the country while Basil's dies out. This obvious symbolism is fostered by the one-dimensional, unsympathetic picture of the one and the favorably strong portrait of the other. Unwin's outspoken anticlassism, his independence and self-respect, his refusal to be bought by security or bribed by favors make him a very positive character.

The clash between aristocrat and common man becomes a major aspect of the plot in *Genesee Fever*. The issue develops out of the desire of a wealthy group to transplant a system of landed aristocracy to western New York. Nathan Hart, who gains tentative acceptance among the aristocrats because of his education, character, and leadership, is nonetheless passionately opposed to "big estates, with lords to own them and peasants to fill them. . . . I would have every man own his own land and work it . . . and no man touch his forelock to a master."[25] Hart argues and practices equality. Independence without servility is his watchword, and he does not permit himself to be bribed into compromising this credo by acceptance into the aristocrat's circle. He does not lose touch with those who have had fewer advantages and whom he considers his kind. The aristocratic establishment is finally defeated.

The negative image of the aristocratic type that emerges from

[25] Carl Carmer, *Genesee Fever*, 199.

these novels is enhanced by his occasional appearance in several other novels, and it becomes more emphatic as the decade of the forties is approached. The figure is depicted as incompetent and weak or as shrewd, materialistic, and calculating. He is self-interested and unprincipled, often enough to the disadvantage of others. He is obsessed with pride and social graces and is contemptuous of the lower classes. He seems somewhat effeminate in close proximity with the vigorous frontiersman. A contrast of these dual images with their representations in the novels of the first decade is revealing. In the earlier novels such a comparison favored the aristocratic type for the common frontiersman was frequently crude, uncouth, and unlearned. The current emphasis compares the strength and true nobility of the frontiersman with the false superiority of the aristocratic type.

Although the aristocrat as exemplar and hero has fallen by the wayside, there is still a consciousness of class that is somewhat antagonistic to the developing democratic image. The sense of equality is not entirely pure; even though all on the frontier are represented as equal, some are more so than others.

One delineation of this attitude represents the hero in a better light than his associates. In some instances, as has already been discussed in the previous section, the hero is given outright upper-class attributes; in other cases, though of non-upper-class origin, the hero is given associations or attributes that place him above the others of his class. These patterns are less frequently emphasized and even negated by a great proportion of the heroes so identified in terms of the frontier's effects. There is, however, a contradiction between what these heroes represent by their basic identification and what they are said to represent in the enactment of the frontier drama.

A second strong pattern creates a somewhat less acceptable group on the frontier. Several novels present a neoaristocracy based not upon heredity and wealth but upon a distinction in cultural attributes and way of life. Wealth becomes an associated factor when discrimination grows out of the degree of comforts that have been achieved. Another symbol of this attitude is the sense of respectability in terms of the standards of behavior of the dominant group.

A few of the overland trail novels create such an impression of class consciousness. In *The Way West* a typical situation of this type is presented: one family, nearly destitute and shiftless in character, is looked down upon by others in the train. It is considered inferior by other travelers, excluding the hero; he and his family are sympathetic and helpful. Some of the negative reaction seems reasonable in terms of the family's inadequate equipment, haphazard operation, slovenly habits and the parents' ineptness. However, the figurative sniffing of some of the pioneers is beyond what these faults merit; it is based more on righteousness than honest scorn. Their feeling assumes a class distinction, an inherent deficiency of status that precludes sympathy for their past misfortunes or understanding of their present plight.

Novels of the developing frontier show similar patterns. Two early ones, *Vandemark's Folly* and *Heroine of the Prairie*, show a more marked sense of class. The better-established pioneer looks askance at the less fortunate or the new comers, who are necessarily cruder in their way of life. The first comers are hardly surrounded with comforts but they hold themselves aloof. However, the central characters do not accept a menial position and prove themselves better than those who maintain a superior attitude. Vandemark particularly refuses to accept the permanence of his lesser economic position, and he is not bound by the social barriers that are raised. In overcoming the attitudes that prevailed on the frontier being described these characters give evidence of the pioneer's strength in overcoming class attitudes.

A variation of this theme presents, in *Oklahoma* and *Early Candlelight*, squatterlike groups whose members are quite poor. They are kept apart and not welcomed in association with their betters, a group which includes the heroes. Mort Sturdevant's excursion into "Pore Folks Haven" in Oklahoma is an uncommon event. His sympathetic reaction and his liberal associations there are not in keeping with the attitudes of the general population.

This level of class distinction is also brought home in the novel *In the Hands of the Senecas*. In the face of extreme conditions—capture by Indians and servitude—a number of women still maintain concepts of exclusiveness. They are indignant or outraged because a low class young man becomes friendly and protective of a girl of higher class. She should have nothing to do with him. Recognizing the prevailing social limitations on this romance, the boy at first urges the girl not to take advantage of a chance to return to the white settlements. Among the Indians they can be together; among the whites they may be separated. He particularly fears that such influences will cause his sweetheart to disassociate herself from him upon their return.

The significant factor is not in the existence of these modified class patterns but in their apparent general acceptance by the people of the novels, the hero's attitude notwithstanding. In reaction to overt conflict between an aristocratic element and the common man, Nathan Hart comments:

> "It isn't the political opinions of people like your [aristocratic] family I resent," said Nathan, "it's the acceptance of inferior station by people like me and Whirl here. . . . Why do they accept such contradictions as the use of the word aristocracy in a democratic Republic?"[26]

It is the leadership of strong men like Hart that prevents the resurgence of the upper class and servile domination of the freeholders.

Further evidence is provided in several novels through the tendency of one group of pioneers to hold themselves apart from another. Factors of snobbery and superiority are joined by a distaste or hesitancy for the unfamiliar; a separation line is drawn in terms of the standards of respectability or achievement of the

[26] *Ibid.*, 265.

group. The settlement-minded pioneer therefore withdraws from the free hunter, dealing with him only for his skills. This is noted in some of the incipient settlements as in *Long Hunt*, but is particularly strong in the overland trail novels. The people of the wagon trains accept the assistance of the mountain men guides but cannot accept their nonconforming behavior and strange habits. The mountain man, far from being awed, is himself contemptuous of them for he holds himself superior, a reaction similar to that of the free hunter regarding the settlers. The foreigner is also such an outsider who is subjected to negative attitudes in those novels where there is contact between them and pioneer Americans. This latter type of novel is rare, however.

Turnabout being fair play, it is curious counterpoint to note the anti-American aspects of the several novels dealing with the Southwest. The Spanish, who feel invaded by the Gringo, regard him as inferior in class. They scorn his ill-mannered, boorish behavior, his lack of culture and social graces, his forwardness, his aggression. They attempt to bar his entrance on their domain, but they do not succeed. Of course, the Mexican is also lowly. This society was highly structured even before the entrance of the Yankee.

A final superiority pattern is closely related to the exclusiveness of each group. The interplay of these attitudes creates for the pioneer a concept of himself as superior to the nonpioneer. This is a superiority not of rank but of ability. A man unable to fend for himself, unfamiliar with basic means of self-help and self-preservation, no matter the degree of education, is not worth his salt. Common sense, practical knowledge, independence, individualism: these are the measures of the man.

This last idea, though it is steeped in outright prejudice and blanket disapproval in some instances, brings the concept of the frontier around in full circle. In the recognition of quality based upon personal achievement and ability rather than heritage, it represents the frontier ideal. The undercurrents of class attitude and the residual stream of aristocracy would seem to question the democratic influences of the frontier environment. But these undercurrents are dominated by a spirit of equality represented in the actions and beliefs of the main characters and the final victory in the novels is of this democratic ideal.

7

Go West, Go East, Go West

A CURRENT of conflict between the frontier West and the civilized East runs through the pioneer novels. This conflict takes distinct shape in some of the novels as an element of the plot or in antagonisms between characters who represent the two areas. In other novels this stream of thought forms a muted background to the events, usually as general opinions or reactions of the characters, or as assumptions inherent in the presentation. There are references to the East—fond memory to some, despair and lost opportunity to others, escaped drudgery and servility to still others. Contrasting visions and emotions symbolize the West. In the minority is the novel which makes no reference, direct or indirect, to this theme.

Go West, Go East

In the novels of the first decade, 1900 to 1910, this theme develops as a pattern of contrasts and contradictions. A number of ideas and prejudices have been interwoven into the novels, both individually and as a group. If any pattern of thought is discernible, it is one of overlapping acceptance and denial of both cultures: a favorable impression of the healthy frontier against an unjust, stifling East; a favorable portrait of the civilized East contrasted with a crude, uncouth West. The authors seem to have been caught in the middle of conflict, not knowing which way to turn—turning first toward the frontier West and then back towards the civilized East.

Two distinct plot patterns evolve from this group of novels, these being the basis for the development of the concepts of the two cultures and the contradictions in values represented. The stronger of these patterns centers upon the aristocrat as the pioneer hero. He is a relative newcomer on the frontier. Presumably he adopts the frontier; he acquires the status and skills of the pioneer while maintaining essential elements of his initial character. He exhibits some of the crucial values of the frontiersman, at least for the time of his frontier interval. However, he returns, at the book's close, to the civilized culture of the East. The second pattern depicts an equally noble hero, although he is not necessarily an aristocrat by birth, in like situations but permits him to remain on the frontier. However, he, too, joins the forces of civilization and at the end of the novel resigns from his untrammelled life. These patterns quite clearly overlap. Certain central, developmental ideas and inner contradictions are uniform.

The contrast between the frontier and organized society—or the frontiersman and the Easterner—is instrumental in the development of the conflict. A key element is the positive presentation of the frontier and its people as opposed to a negative view of organized society and the Easterner. The virtues of the West are numerous and varied, ranging from physical and social attributes to character development.

There is a strong reaction of the main characters to the beauties and openness of the wilderness. There is rarely a direct comparison with the East, but there is fairly frequent marveling at the breadth and grandeur of the West in a manner implying superiority to the closed-in Eastern community or the prosaic farm.

The preference for the wilderness is built upon a series of interrelated attitudes. One view is expressed by Joe Downs in *The Spirit of the Border* when he attempts to explain his motivations. "I wanted to come West because I was tired of tame life. I love the forest; I want to fish and hunt; and I think I'd like to—to see Indians."[1] Thus the frontier is associated with adventure and vitality. It signifies a relatively free and open occupation, one unhindered by demands of time or season, and unlimited by space. It is a refuge from tameness and narrowness as well. When questioned about his reasons for traveling westward, the Virginian amplifies Joe Downs' vague desires.

> Oh, looking for chances. I reckon I must have been more ambitious than my brothers—or more restless. They stayed around on farms. But I got out. When I went back . . . they was talking about the same old things. . . .[2]

An aura of limitation, of stupefaction, of fearful sameness is attached to the life of the settled East. A man of vigor and spirit, a man seeking challenge and self-development could not be satisfied there. Presumably, such a man went west.

The West represents something more than wilderness and the glamor of blazing trails; it also meant freedom of movement and being on one's own. The frontiersmen want the frontier to remain unchanged; they guard their wild life jealously. They attempt to remain aloof from the settlements and resist settling down. These symbolized the eclipse of their unhampered lives. Typically Tom McChesney denounces the crowding of the woods and the resultant departure of the game. The Virginian and his friends sneer and poke fun at those of their members who have given up the free range for the fenced-in plot of land. The Virginian, though he professes ambition, scorns those who settle down with the thought of advancing themselves from a nomadic existence; he's initially motivated by a desire to preserve an open, free life.

A more explicit denunciation of organized society is presented in *The City of Six* in terms of its limitations on the spirit and its narrow view of life.

As for Dot, she was a bird let loose, an irresponsible creature

[1] Zane Grey, *The Spirit of the Border*, 23.
[2] Owen Wister, *The Virginian*, 225.

fascinated . . . free from the fetters and shackles that exacted rigid compliance with the narrow customs and the need for established properties, founded on generations of Puritanical limitations. She looked back on the social village life, where the least step outside beaten paths, the slightest departure from unwritten but well understood laws of conduct, called forth the scathing criticism of the village gossips. It was all so different here.[3]

Apart from the denunciation of the East is the corollary attitude enhancing the attributes of the frontier. These go hand in hand with the hero's love of the open life. His freedom is cherished as a consequence of these limitations.

The frontier is a more deliberate refuge from civilization for a number of pioneers. These express a stronger reaction of escape; memories of the East are bitter. Injustice, faithlessness, disloyalty; these drive the hero into exile. John Lee in *The Wilderness Road*, Alan Gordon in *The Throwback*, Raoul de Coubert in *A Sword of the Old Frontier*, among others, turn to the frontier to erase their experiences with organized society. Essentially their criticism centers upon its narrow prejudices and patterns which stifle or destroy the individual. When put to the test, society failed in its sense of fairness, in its recognition of duty and merit, in its preservation of honor. Western society judges men directly by what they are and what they can do. In their bitter retreat from the East, these heroes find solace and self-development and a true spirit on the frontier.

The frontier accounts for various advances: the wilderness cleanses and revitalizes; it gives purpose and identity; it develops manhood. Indeed, the fruits of the forest are great. Boys become men; men—on their own—gain strength and wisdom. Stewart Randolph in *The Heritage* returns to the East after three years captivity in the wilderness a self-assured, responsible, capable man where he had been a romantic, ineffectual boy. Alfred Clarke in *Betty Zane* comes to the frontier a soft, unskilled and somewhat useless individual. However, in the company of the

[3] Chauncey L. Canfield, *The City of Six*, 157.

honest, practical frontiersmen he develops physical as well as inner strengths. Other heroes develop in similar ways.

Associated with the manhood of the pioneer is a characterization which is closely related to his sense of justice, selflessness, and faith. This characterization is developed not only in the manners and principles of the hero, but also in comparison with a counterpart Easterner. In pitting the one man against the other, there is a symbolic representation and a sometimes obvious negative image of the Easterner. He becomes the evil symbol of all the hero left behind.

On a rather simple level in *The Virginian*, there is the juxtaposition of the hero and his stalwart associates with the tenderfoot from the East. The men of the West are self-sufficient; they have what it takes; common sense, skill and knowledge, perseverance. The tenderfoot is helpless and soft and dependent. More dramatically, in *The Wilderness Road*, John Lee is faced with his serpentine cousin Jasper while in *The Throwback* Tom Moonlight's nemesis is his cousin Robert. In each case the Eastern cousin is a sly, vicious plotter who attempts to ruin the life of the hero to foster his own selfish purposes. The hero's openness, honor and courage are matched by the villain's deviousness, deceit and weakness. Naturally, the man of the East lacks skills and knowledge of the woods, thus seeming, in addition, ineffectual. He is quite unsympathetic.

Another element is added to this image in *When Wilderness Was King* and *The Crossing*. In addition to weakness and selfishness, the characterization of the man from organized society includes foppery and falseness and idleness. John Wayland's manliness of manner, his simplicity and directness, and his sincerity are contrasted with the perfumed flirtatiousness, the trickery, the prideful conceit, the superficial concern for dress and manners of De Croix. John's admirable qualities in relation to his frontier background and in contrast to the artificiality of De Croix are no less obvious than the similar construction of David Ritchie and Nick Temple in *The Crossing*. These two were brought up together in early life. The frontier has made Davy a dependable, sober, effective citizen while Nick is an idle adventurer, emotional and intemperate. He has been brought up in a doll's house existence apart from reality. Though honorable and decent and charming, he leads a wasteful life devoid of meaning for himself or others.

In these several cases we see, at the culmination of the novel, the defeat or the deterioration of the Easterner. This defeat is achieved by the hero through skills and attributes that he has presumably developed on the frontier. Without these, the Easterner cannot succeed.

The presentation of the image of the Western hero is furthered by an occasional glimpse of the general populace. These glimpses favor the wilderness men as vigorous and healthy and reject the later comers and the Easterners. Compare the description of two military groups:

> The line of backwoodsmen, as fine a lot of men as I ever want to see, bronzed . . . strong and tireless . . . expectant . . .[4]

> It was certain that these were not men who knew the wilderness road; the ways of the forest were strange to them. I remembered the type. Their faces showed a lack of healthy colour; they were white in the cheeks and black under the eyes, and their muscles were loose and flabby.[5]

This sort of comparison is frequent. In battles the frontiersmen are fearless, undaunted and persevering; the motley collection of Easterners is easily cowed, routed and broken.

Glory lies with the original settlers. The West requires men and requires also that a man do everything well. He cannot succeed in the game unless he is able to prove himself. It is clear that the feats of the pioneer would not be possible to the Easterner. The West builds the man or breaks him. The weak are defeated or, in the face of danger, depart. The later comers, the "ill-

[4] Winston Churchill, *The Crossing*, 143.
[5] J. A. Altscheler, *The Wilderness Road*, 34.

assorted humanity" who came when the frontiersmen had made the land safe, are parasites who beat the frontiersmen with their land speculation, with their activities that are not very honest, forthright, or generous. The wholesome pioneer is overtaken by the selfish settler who manifests the attributes of Eastern society, or is forced to go farther afield, as was Tom McChesney in *The Crossing*. Such incidents and characterizations emphasize the honesty, the directness and manhood of the frontier West.

Other value elements of civilization are also negated. Certain characters, having been brought up in the East, need re-education for life in the West. The novels frown upon loose coquetry and falseness. Betty Zane, though basically a fine person, is tainted by civilization. She is flighty, egotistic, even discourteous in her town manners; her family, as well as the author, is critical; frontier manners are more sincere, less superficial. Similarly are Helen Sheppard in *The Last Trail* and Rose Carew in *The Wilderness Road* altered by life on the frontier. Rose Carew, depicted initially as spoiled, haughty, and self-centered, develops under its influence into a warm-hearted, thoughtful person who can see the merit in a man aside from title and status. Other characters: Mabel Wood, in *The Virginian*; 'Toinette, in *When Wilderness Was King*; and Alfred Clarke, in *Betty Zane* show a similar though less extreme personality rehabilitation.

Taken thus in total, this series of relationships would seem to lead to a generally positive view of the frontier, a view opposed to organized society. However, civilization is not completely negated nor is the frontier always in a favored light. In fact, all these attitudes notwithstanding the final denouement points to the supremacy and value of organized society.

A significant consideration in this regard is the particular position of the hero of these novels. As outlined in the preceding chapter, he is an aristocrat in pioneer trappings or is otherwise ennobled. As a transplanted Easterner enjoying the fertile soil of the West, or as a noble Westerner who has accumulated some Eastern culture, he is the fruit of two worlds. His superiority stems basically from this combination of the best of both environments. He outwits and overcomes with knowledge, skill and courage bred on the frontier those Easterners symbolic of all that he detests. Yet, he is able to at least match them their education, their social graces, their poise. And it is these which place him in a position superior to other pioneers. Though worthy people, courageous and warmhearted, they are unlearned and crude. He is not of the common lot, he is a leader of men by virtue of his dual background. He can meet the challenge of the wilderness in the pioneer's terms. By thus manifesting the special elements of both areas, the hero achieves his singular position of overall superiority. Perhaps this image is the expression of the ideal of the period—or indeed of the American ideal: the hero has all the solid endowments of manhood and advanced culture assimilated from his life on the frontier and his associations with the East and none of the negative aspects of either environment.

The hero's comparative stature in these terms is evidenced in many of the novels. In *D'ri and I*, the presentation of D'ri is decidedly less favorable than that of Ramon; D'ri is common, rough. Such heroes as Fitzhugh Beverley, the Virginian, John Lee, Raoul de Coubert, John Wayland are depicted as superior to the people about them. Tom McChesney, for all his heroism in *The Crossing*, does not measure up to David Ritchie. The characterization of McChesney is that of a steady, good and generous man, skilled in his own trade of the woods, whose dignity is personal—the outgrowth of his selfless, straightforward nature. But Ritchie is all of this and more; a leader among men, based, as is suggested, on his education and background as well as his frontier upbringing.

It is pertinent to recall at this point that in this decade, the novels show a stratification of classes. Such a stratification makes the divergent concepts possible. Although the description of the common frontier folk creates a more positive view than that of the Eastern populace, there is no particular carry-over to the total impression of the novel, for the hero is in a different class. The total impression of the background pioneer is of a hearty, whole-some, good people—but somewhat beneath the level of the hero. (It should not be inferred that he necessarily acts so or thinks so.)

It is this impression that first creates the sense of the final supremacy of civilization. On the one level, there is the conde-scending attitude of a few heroes, like Fitzhugh Beverley in *Alice of Old Vincennes*, toward the populace, or the conscious-ness of class on the part of Raoul de Coubert in *A Sword of the Old Frontier*. In *The Crossing*, excuses need to be made for Tom McChesney's limited social graces and poor speech. The impor-tance of such graces is made apparent in almost every novel; the hero's poise and command of these stands out as a positive factor, especially in comparison to the less fortunate frontiersmen.

Basically, then, the novels contain an underlying assumption of the merit of certain attributes of culture, attributes which are based, in these novels, on civilization; attributes which are not found in the pioneer class. This partly results from the fact that the main view of the frontier is through the eyes of the hero who is but a few steps away from aristocracy and culture. By this means a subtle prejudice is built up which, if not antipioneer, is quite favorable to organized society.

The full and final victory of civilization over the frontier takes shape as an element of the plot itself. The two patterns—one which returns the hero to the East, the other which has the hero embracing a settled life—both signify that the values associated with an organized society—progress, family, settling down—are accepted. The hero, seeing value in society, joins its ranks and is saved. This happy ending does not permit the hero to wander endlessly in the wilderness but returns him to the fold.

The hero's return to the East, a change of horses in midstream, is marked by contradiction. He returns despite the fact that he has with but one exception stated his abhorrence of civilization and so accepted the life, values, and habits of the pioneer as his own. The shift in values and objectives that the change repre-sents might be expected to have been preceded by some evidence of conflict in the hero. Having made a difficult decision, he might be expected to evince a shade of regret for the lost life. This is not generally the case. Only in a few novels is there even slight evidence of either feeling; for the most part the shift is easily—sometimes hastily—made.

Typically the hero decides he cannot deny his past, his upbringing, his race. He returns to the East—and love—and takes up where he left off. The decision for John Lee in *The Wilderness Road* lacks conflict. When he suddenly realizes that all is not lost for him in the East, that he might clear the blot from his honor and good name and renew his old life—and claim the hand of Rose Carew, he leaves the previously preferred frontier without further ado. Similarly does Tom Moonlight respond in *The Throwback*. A preliminary conclusion he comes to has the additional effect of negating the wilderness life:

> From this treasure [Ethel] . . . I might . . . fashion freedom for myself. I had thought I owned the wilderness. I now see that the wilderness owns me. This treasure would mean my liberation.[6]

For both men all semblance, habit, and memory of the pioneer life depart as swiftly as a dropped cloak; all fascination for and allegiance to the frontier fade away.

In a parallel pattern, the heroes in several of the novels renounce their wild, free life and adopt the life of the settlement. They, too, show little conflict in this turnabout, nor is there particular regret shown for the life they have championed. Zane Grey in *The Spirit of the Border* at least has the wilderness-styled brother die before giving the mantle over to his settlement-oriented twin.

Two characters are typical of the manner and cause of change. The Virginian, who opposed encroachments to the free life, not only forgets his antipathy when he meets Molly Wood but accepts the sense of progress and strives to make himself over to be able to meet her requirements. This happens after no previous

[6] Alfred H. Lewis, *The Throwback*, 75.

sign of ambition or desire to develop his life. Jonathan Zane, who has vowed a life as a free hunter and wandering protector of the border, seems to put aside his vow with little regret once he finds he is acceptable to Helen Sheppard. The contradiction between Zane's love of the wilderness and his protection of the settlements is unquestioned in the novel.

The wanderer is defeated or like Tom McChesney forced to wander farther afield. The solitary life with its associations of free movement and manliness succumbs to the presence of love, to a new vision of progress and settlement. Individual progress is related to the progress of civilization. The function of the pioneers in the novels is to break down the wilderness; their settlement is the symbol of advancing civilization.

The final solution of this group of novels depicts the primacy of organized society and culture as a way of life and as a goal of life. The novels are punctuated with notes approving the virtues of the frontier and decrying the ills of society. But the tenure in the forest of the hero is a brief taste of Eden; it is a temporary adventure. Having drunk the nectar, the foraging bee returns to the hive, to the organized life. He is perhaps the better off, for his experiences have taught him truer values. The frontier itself is temporary. The single adventurer served a purpose but progress lies in the advancement of civilization. The new communities in the wilderness, as the old ones, symbolic of institutional stability, law, order, authority, followed upon the taming of the wilderness.

It is difficult to impose a philosophic organization upon these novels, for their general tone does not permit it. However, a scattering of thoughts come together to suggest the inevitability of progress—defined as higher culture and civilization. Force—epitomized by the frontiersman—breaks down and subdues the savagery to give civilization a chance to root. But force dies: the heroes adapt to advancing civilization. The death of Joe Downs, the rough, free hunter, in *The Spirit of the Border* is symbolically the death of a type of man and a way of life; left to carry on is his milder, educated twin brother, identical in every other respect but representing a newer spirit of the border, that of progress and the community.

Go West, Stay West

The shift in attitudes in the conflict between wilderness and civilization after the first decade's novels is gradual and subtle. First it is a shift in direction. The pattern, so strong in the earliest novels, of the hero returning to the East to reclaim his heritage dies. The direction remains westward in the novels after 1910. Once the hero and heroine have turned their backs to the East, they do not look back.

Two novels of the second decade, 1911–20, which are written in the tradition of the earliest works, illustrate the permanent shift away from the East. The heroes of *The Magnificent Adventure* and *Erskine Dale, Pioneer*, the first raised among Tidewater aristocracy, the latter in the wilderness by Indians, go from wilderness to civilization and back again on several occasions. Equally acceptable in either society, their final choice lies in the West. At the conclusion of the second work, Erskine Dale heads into the wilderness with his Eastern, aristocratic bride to found their home and fortune. In the earlier novels the opposite direction would have been the choice. These mark the turning point.

Later novels are farther removed. Rare are the characters who even think of returning. Several do: the plainsman-trapper Lige Mounts, prairie farmer Abbie Deal, and mountain man Boone Caudill, central figures of novels of different character and periods, *Morning Light, A Lantern in Her Hand* and *The Big Sky* respectively. They return to satisfy some lingering cultural association, craving or curiosity. They are dissatisfied with what they find—small, hemmed-in, dull lives—and they do not stay.

While the direction of the pioneer—and the novels—shifts to the West, the point of view of the pioneer also changes in its purpose and overriding interests. This is inherent in the changes in literary tradition—romanticism waning before the growing strength of realism—and parallels developments analyzed in earlier chapters. Elements of certain attitudes found in the earlier novels that do remain are redeveloped and redirected to match the new literary patterns.

Two chief patterns emerge concurrently in the later novels. The greater proportion of those concern the pioneer who travels westward to reproduce an organized society, a society essentially similar to the one from which he came; the other pattern develops the image of the pioneer who strongly rejects society, deliberately searching out the wild lands. There is not a particular numerical emphasis in the distribution of the two groups of novels, though there is proportionately a slight increase of the wilderness hero type in the more recent works. There is some overlapping in the values expressed in the mass of novels; as shall be seen, analysis of individual works shows that the lines of demarcation are not always clearly drawn.

The underlying concept basic to the settlement group of novels is progress. This is particularized in some novels as the chronicle of an individual or family and in others as the settling of an area. The wilderness is but the place of opportunity—opportunity for advancement of the individual or the group or the nation. The subduing of the wilderness is in the natural course of events; the advance of civilization over barbarism or crudeness is inevitable and heralded. To progress, in the majority of the novels, is to create a solid, sufficient life; an orderly secure community. All efforts and activities, all will and energy of the pioneers bend to this purpose. The face of the land is changed: trees axed down, soil broken and plowed, homes raised. The specific activities vary according to the locale but whatever the task or the interruption—war or overland trail—the goal is apparent and generally achieved.

In some novels this advance is a simple re-creation of the old life; in others it symbolizes a chance to effect changes, to start a society with a fresh outlook. These variations of purpose and

185

minor shifts in emphasis over the forty-year period in the attitudes of the pioneer and the character of the novel exist, but the final goal is quite the same.

Those pioneers who share this significant goal are not completely of one mind in their valuation of wilderness or civilization. In some a heightened sense of partisanship toward one or the other exists; in others the conflict is neutralized.

There is a substantial number of novels—about thirty per cent of this group—which remain neutral. This is not a solid block of novels. They are spread over the four decades. However, there is proportionately a greater number in the 1911–30 years than in the two subsequent decades. In these novels, there is no comment in favor of or in opposition to either the wilderness or civilization. There is simply an acceptance of the situation and conditions of their lives. The behavior and activities of the characters show an unquestioning, automatic expectation of the establishment of an organized community life. Such a development is seen as inevitable.

This assumption, though the novels are not identical, is basic to the texts. Just as they recount various activities and events, so do they spell out a difference in tone and spirit. The propelling energy and driving force exhibited by the hero of *Giants in the Earth* (1927) make the efforts of the hero of *The Cabin at the Trail's End* (1928) seem mild in comparison; however, John Wainwright's determination and sense of purpose are not less than Per Hansa's. The sensitivity and concentration on character in *The Great Meadow* (1930) and *Lamb in His Bosom* (1933) only mask the day-by-day toil and struggle against the physical barriers to progress; beneath the surface, it is this struggle which is accented. Later novels, such as *Oh, Promised Land* (1940), *Foundation Stone* (1940), and *A High Wind Rising* (1942), superimpose a tone of action, adventure, and momentous events over the basic current of creating a new life out of the wilderness. This current of progress, however, underlies all of these novels.

This group is matched by another in which the proprogress

sentiments are clearly expressed, as in *A Lantern in Her Hand*. The strivings, the values, are evident not only in the day-by-day efforts to effect change but also in the stated yearnings and recollections.

> "We can fight to keep civilized . . . can fight to keep something before us besides the work."
> "We dreamed dreams into the country. We dreamed the towns and the cities, the homes and the factories, the churches and the schools. We dreamed the huge new capitol."[7]

In these terms, the disappearance of any aspect of the wilderness is considered a great advance. Particularly is this so in the eyes of the women, but the men strive also for progress. Signs of society are sought and welcomed: the nearness of neighbors, the coming of social birds, curtains on windows, churches, schools, wooden buildings on the prairies, board buildings in the forest, the railroad. Each of these is cited as a step forward even by heroes who otherwise question certain aspects of organized society and indeed, as in *Nebraska Coast* and *Oklahoma*, left the more settled areas to escape certain attitudes and attributes of civilization. The value of civilized life is also brought home in the novel *Beyond Law*, in which Lige Mounts, the prowilderness hero of *Morning Light*, does a second turnabout. In the earlier novel he had rejected the settlements as evil and small minded; in the sequel he rejects the wilderness for the good things the settlements have to offer: schooling for his young adopted son and a measure of stability and safety in which to rear him.

These factors of stability and safety are significant values in this group and other related novels in terms of both law and order and social developments with their accompanying restrictions. The establishment of law and order in the defeat of the Indians and other violent elements is a primary role of the pioneer. This is self-protection to be sure, and Lige Mounts acts on his own to safeguard his family. He returns to civilization,

[7] Bess Streeter Aldrich, *A Lantern in Her Hand*, 114, 280.

aware that where there is no law the unscrupulous take over.[8] The defeat of the terrorizing mob in *Mighty Mountain* is laid to the rise and strength of forces of civilization which force the decline of the power and prestige and the eventual defeat of the undisciplined marauders. These illustrations are extreme, but they identify an important value associated with the advance of society.

On the social level, advances run the gamut from neighborliness to the establishment of clubs, societies and other institutions of community life. As the communities develop, as in *Heroine of the Prairies* and *Cimarron*, these appear in greater profusion. They are the marks of advanced culture according to the heroines involved (the heroes are not often concerned). The foreigner-pioneers, although their memories of the Old World are not wholly pleasant, nevertheless hold on to former social customs, and they early manifest desire to redevelop them. The haunting remembrance of the past life in *My Antonia* is glowingly favorable toward society in contrast to the life of these immigrants on the prairie. Old times and distant places reflected with measures of longing and sadness and mixed with the urgency to rebuild a like life in both *The Emigrants* and *Giants in the Earth* help to convey a positive view of organized society. And the reminiscences of Sayward Luckett in *The Trees*, Martha Murray in *The Day Must Dawn*, Bethany Cameron in *Edge of Time*, and others are cut from the same cloth. Each hurries the achievement of these social aims as well as the restrictions associated with them, restrictions of manners and mores that are part of a highly organized community.

The attitudes represented in these proprogress novels are not one sided nor are they completely consistent. A few characters maintain a distinct prejudice against too much civilization or some aspects of it. Others promote progress while wishing to maintain vestiges of the wilderness *status quo*, something like

[8] The contrary presentation of this concept in *Morning Light*, the first book of this series, is discussed in the pro-wilderness segment of this chapter.

those who despair biting into a magnificent fruit because it looks so good, yet cannot put off eating it either. Fragments of conflict between characters or ambivalences within them reveal that no attitude toward the wilderness was without qualifying shades of opinion.

The wilderness itself is not completely negated. A few heroes seek out the wilderness in preference to the settled areas, while promoting, at the same time, self-advancement and progress. The motivations of these men are loosely connected in the desire to escape the press of people, the tameness of settlement life, and the restrictions of organized society. Typical of one wing of this group is Hugh Murray, young hero of *The Day Must Dawn*. The raw Ohio territory beckons him away from the barely tamed Pennsylvania country. He desires the open country partly for its own sake and to escape the already "crowded" conditions. On available free land he can develop and prove his self worth—he can be his own man. The heroes of *Oklahoma*, Mort Sturdevant, and *Green Centuries*, Orion Outlaw are similarly motivated. In addition he feels the imposition of restrictions: laws, taxes, social rules; he wants to be free of them. These men combine, then, a sense of independence and adventure with a desire for progress. Interwoven is the suggestion that to advance as well as to remain independent required the giving up of ease and security. To gain new lands and opportunity required men of spirit and strength to strike out on their own.

The juxtaposition of the characteristics is also evidenced in the overland trail novels. There is somewhat less emphasis on the desire to seek open country for its own sake, for as a group these pioneers are less adventurous in spirit. They do go west to seek free lands and greater opportunities, to escape crowded conditions and a closed-in life.

These men who favor the wilderness for its own sake strive mightily for their own degree of comfort and organized life but reject full community progress. Orion Outlaw resents activities that would recreate the social order he left behind; he discourages the coming of too many people. The hero of *Wind Over Wisconsin* feels similarly; he semiactively hinders the growth of settlement about him. He knows people will ruin the prairie and cut into his idyllic isolation. The sense of progress in these men is couched in individual terms and, in that regard, limited in nature. Nonetheless settlement and progress it is.

For a considerable number of heroes, the wilderness presents a different vision; their preference of the frontier is not merely the result of their hostility to oversettled regions. They define progress, as has been suggested above, in terms of their strong opposition to the prevailing structure and manners of society. The wilderness West, therefore, is not only a chance to realize individuality, to strike out on one's own, to find opportunity. It is also a chance to eradicate certain social ills and to build in a new mold. Clearly these heroes do not reject society completely. For the most part they do not particularly desire the retention of wilderness aspects of the frontier as do their companion heroes.

The most impassioned and continuous condemnations are issued by Yancey Cravat in *Cimarron*. He is antagonistic to the false social niceties which do not distinguish true from false feelings; the fancy, meaningless customs and mores; the "middle-class respectability" and provincialism; the people's superficial concerns for such things as clubs and dress styles. He also condemns society for destroying people and then scorning them; he defends Dixie Lee, the prostitute, as just such a victim of society. As a reformer he wants to create a world where such superficiality and social prejudices will not develop, where people can be themselves instead of being blinded and harnessed by narrow customs.

Closely allied to Yancey Cravat and his breed, but concerned on a more personal level, is the hero of *Buckskin Breeches*, Jesse Ellison. Disturbed by the slovenly, immoral life of the settled community and the lack of challenge in his own life, Ellison becomes increasingly alarmed by the society consciousness of his wife, who neglects her family interests and duties; the physical softness and the weak, parasitic values of his children; and the general deterioration of the social scene. He turns to the West to refashion their lives by forcing the family to be on its own. The force of his beliefs carries over into the community that is developed.

The critical attitudes toward society encompass a range of specific negations drawn from the group of novels. Fairly representative are these: the condemnation of the narrow-minded religious prejudices in *Nebraska Coast*, the hostility to the fancy, pale patterns of the Old South in *Foundation Stone*, the ready-made life of the East in *Oklahoma*, the class divisions of Norway in *The Emigrants*, the resentment toward class snobbishness in *The Far Country*, and religious-social narrowmindedness of New England in *'Forty-Nine*.

This subgroup of novels exemplifies the dissatisfaction with the Eastern settled areas and the search for a new, fresh life in the West. The new country is the place where a man can amount to something, where he can make something of himself and create a new world. And in this new world these particular social ills would be guarded against. The heroes, socially oriented, have chosen the vigorous life of the frontier rather than vegetation in the settlements. They are akin to their companion heroes but more determinedly reformist and less isolationist.

Taken in total, there seems to be only a scattering of hero-pioneers who clearly reject the advances of organized society. When these are augmented by a group of secondary but significant figures, a more numerous and stronger effect is created so that this presence is not so minor. These are joined by several other heroes who, although they seem to follow the paths of progress for a time, offer strong resistance to elements of civilization which confront them. As shall be seen, the members of this latter group enjoy or suffer the consequences of their partial compromise and then either break away or give way completely. However, for the most part they stand with this prowilderness group.

A distinct evolution or preponderance of this wilderness image of the pioneer is not clearly evident. In terms of numbers, there are more of such heroes in the novels of the later thirties and the forties. This compares with none prior to 1920 and only a few in the twenties. Certain attitudes and prejudices typify this figure, though to a lesser degree these are also in the make-up of his counterpart, the pioneer of progress. In some of these attitudes there appear certain modifications and emphases with the passing years. However, these variations are but barely evident for they are both subtle and overlapping.

The man stands out as an exponent of freedom and individualism. This is expressed in his choice of a way of life, his devotion to the wilderness, and his attitude towards settlements and settlers. His code of behavior is both a determiner and a result of his attitude.

In a single phrase this hero could be described as an independent spirit. Although he may travel with another or several companions, his alliance with them is based upon a kinship of soul and understanding. Between them there is a close loyalty and mutual responsibility, but there persists also a sense of separableness and self-isolation; there are bounds which even the closest companion cannot invade. Also, the hero is frequently alone in actuality, or remains within himself when with others.

The earlier books of this series represent the more modified view of this independence. In *Morning Light* (1922) the kinship and interdependence of Lige Mounts and Dad Lamkin are quite strong, having a father and son quality. Similarly in *The Long Rifle* (1930) is the relationship manifested, but in this case Andy Burnett does not follow Joe Crane exclusively. Once Andy has matured, his behavior and values are not automatically those of Crane. A much later novel, *The Big Sky* (1947), finds the basic ingredients of the relationship unchanged: a young man under the tutelage of an experienced older one. However, although there is certainly understanding and strong bonds between them, Boone Caudill gives up little of his identity and independence to Dick Summers; he remains basically a loner.

A comparable number of these pioneers retain a completely

individual status or favor such isolation after an initial period of training with a group. Such are Sam Lash of *Wolf Song* (1927) and the hero of *Johnny Christmas* (1948). In keeping with the general tendency indicated above, it is of note that Johnny Christmas is a more determined isolationist, more closely drawn to himself in his avoidance of people.

Other heroes permit themselves to have infrequent associations either in some frontier enclave or in a settlement removed from the frontier. These men, like Murfree Rinnard in *Long Hunt* (1930), Harley Boydley in *Free Forester* (1935), and Abner Gower in *Bridal Journey* (1950), take off for the woods whenever they wish to and actually spend more time there alone than with others. Their independence is primary. Of this group of men Andrew Benton, the hero of *This Land Is Ours*, and Michael Beam, in the novel so titled, stand apart in the frequency of their association with others. However, they insist on a freedom to roam the nearby woods: to hunt, to scout, to wander.

A heightened concept in this stress on independence is freedom from responsibility. This is associated with a refusal to settle down or an inability to be or stay married. Murfree Rinnard is the epitome of the former. When he says, "Married men don't fight so good, anyhow. They've not so much to lose,"[9] he expresses his basic tenet and an underlying current of thought in the novel. Close associations and family ties make a man less able to act on his own, to do what he wants to do. He is hampered by having to be aware of the dependence of others. In order to maintain his essential freedom, Murfree permits no close associations; he does not join even in principles with others of his race. He shuns major or lasting responsibilities and successfully resists marriage. He does aid the settlers in their resistance against Indians, but he reasons that he has more to lose than they.

To this hero the greatest value is placed on freedom of movement. Marriage is an encumbrance and a trap. In *Bitter Creek* (1939), Ray "Spur" Talcott expresses this in his despair over his

[9]James Boyd, *Long Hunt*, 369.

Indian friend's burden: a wailing wife and a dying son. In *Wolf Song* an older mountain man conveys scorn for the weakness of young, women-chasing men. To him this is indicative of deterioration, the weakening of manly values.

This intense need for and valuation of freedom of action is also represented in *The Gilded Rooster* (1947). In this novel the mountain man is pitted against the military system. The extreme variance between Jed Cooper's creed and the regimented army system particularizes the essence of the free man. Cooper's reaction to the hampered life of the soldier and the soldier's inability to think and act as a man—rather than as an extension of another's orders—is monumentally depreciating.

More acutely is this value seen in the several heroes who do marry and take a step toward settling down. In these instances, the hero makes an attempt to adjust to a nonnomadic and routine settled life. Enjoyment is short lived. Gradually, his spirit becomes hounded with a longing to break away; short trips into the woods do not suffice to alleviate his frustration and unhappiness at being chained. He sees his manhood warped by the petty details and tasks. Then, apparently unable to take any more of his bound life, he disappears, leaving his wife and family to fend for themselves or in the care of relatives. Gabriel Sash in *The Limestone Tree* (1931) goes away forever; Blaize Ormandy in *So Free We Seem* (1936) and Worth Luckett in *The Trees* (1940) reappear many years later, the latter in a sequel novel. Another type is exemplified by Harley Boydley in *Free Forester* (1935), who reappears from time to time but takes no responsibility for the protection or support of his family.

These characters' escape from responsibility is not entirely negative. There is sympathetic treatment in most of the works of the spirit of these men and their quest for freedom and manhood. The failure of their attempt to maintain the responsibility they had undertaken (with the exception of Boydley) is put in terms of their utter frustration and inner destruction. Blaize Ormandy, upon his return after almost twenty years, instructs his son to no avail as to the particular value that has driven him. (He makes his point in terms of an antislavery uprising.)

> Blaize shook his head. "It's not as simple as that," he said vehemently. "If you measure it all by property of course right and wrong are easy enough to see. But those blacks tonight had a chance to get away, to get into a free state where they could run themselves . . . and instead they turned traitor. . . . To my mind there's some things more important than property—freedom, for instance—."[10]

Ormandy defines the issue squarely. He suggests, too, that freedom could not be understood or valued by those who had never tasted it and that those who completely measure values in terms of property could not comprehend freedom either. Property-bound persons are indeed slaves of another variety, is his implication. His son shows the other side of the coin—as well as his lack of identification with his father's value, in a further comment:

> "He [Blaize] doesn't care for anybody, so long as he needn't be bound—. He isn't interested in building things, or seeing things grow, finishing jobs. All he wants is to be free—why to God didn't he stay free, and not come back?[11]

Other heroes maintain a compromise relationship between these values by marrying Indian women. These women do not demand homes and stability as do white women; they require a minimum of time and attention. Boone Caudill's devotion to Teal Eye and Lige Mount's love for Bluebird do not prevent either from long trips of several months' duration away from them. Apparently, this goes with their notion of manhood and freedom.

The factors of freedom and individualism are also expressed as a passion for the wilderness and an antipathy toward organized society. The relationship to independence is quite direct, for the wilderness allows a man to do as he and circumstances of

[10] Helen Todd, *So Free We Seem*, 342.
[11] *Ibid.*, 347.

terrain and climate permit, while organized society does not. It is natural, then, that a man with these cravings should keep to the open country.

At the core of his existence, then, is his desire to live close to nature. Although his reaction is based, consciously or otherwise, upon his desire to escape from the settlements, it is also founded upon his response to the natural grandeur of the untamed, unpeopled country. He has an overpowering need to travel, to see unknown places, to trod upon virgin ground, to be face to face with nature. He expresses disdain for the smallness and closed-in aspect of the East. He grows with the sights and expanses of the West. Inescapable in his thought is the desire not to be harnessed by daily routines or tied down to a farm. He seeks solitude and self and distant places. For occupation, trapping or hunting serves; for sustenance, game suffices. Life is untroubled and unbound by either natural or man-made fences.

Paralleling these emotions are those which expressed aversion for the life of the settlements, even the incipient variety. They see the fences and houses and the excess of people as the destroyers of their way of life: the game was driven away, the space was taken up, and the woods scarred and cut down. They do not want the natural surroundings destroyed. A rather mild rebuke is offered at one point by Andy Benton in *This Land Is Ours*. Before his conversion, he contemplates the pressures of the fast organizing settlement.

> "Town ways!" he brooded. "A wilderness of land for the taking and freedom to roam in it and his own son was for fencing it to keep neighbors out."[12]

This attitude toward fences and farming and settlements is standard for these men. They go as far afield as they can.

The settlement represents customs and regulations—a way of life—that dismay them. The wilderness hero is uncomfortable in settlement surroundings. The smell, the dirt, the smoke are

[12] Louis Zara, *This Land Is Ours*, 581.

dreaded. The small rooms and crowded conditions give him a smothered feeling. The seemingly unimportant interests, the routine tasks, irritate him. He frowns upon the concentration on comforts as unmanly; he sees illness, physical softness and ineptness as compared with the hardness and skills required by his own existence. In several novels, *Bitter Creek* for example, the settlement or community is the scene of evil and debauchery, quite in contrast to the clean life of the open country. In this respect, similarity with the reforming hero and the isolationist settler can be seen. The view of society is founded on the same base; the reaction to it is differently expressed.

Of Boone Caudill in *The Big Sky*, the author says, "It didn't suit him to be where people were so thick."[13] Very simply this suggests an antisocial pattern found in the works concerned with this hero. He is not, in general, comfortable with people, especially in large numbers; he does not always trust them. A relationship to the attitude of the isolationist settler is evident, but here it is more extreme.

The people of the settlements take on negative aspects in the eyes of this hero. The settlers seemed unable to think beyond their farms, their mundane tasks and ambitions. He sees them bound by their narrow lives and fettered by their customs. He sees them also as rather miserable people. "These greedy, smelly, loud-mouthed pushing men were trying to cut up the western wilderness into truck patches and hog lots."[14] This description is definitely prejudicial to the settlers. The wilderness hero distrusts their ambition and despises their smallness, their way of life; he determines not to be trapped.

The frontiersman's antipathy finds a source of complaint in the laws and the hobbling customs of the settlement. These do not permit free decision and action and often enough go against the grain of common sense and natural desire. Since his code stresses individual action and fulfillment, these binding laws are

[13] A. B. Guthrie, *The Big Sky*, 112.
[14] James Boyd, *op cit.*, 123.

197

unnatural handicaps and severe limitations. There are instances in several novels which tend to be sympathetic to this view and to justify the frontiersman's disapproval of organized society. The officials of the law protect the thief of Boone Caudill's rifle in *The Big Sky* and make Caudill the culprit. The law unjustly victimizes Lige Mounts in *Morning Light* for a murder he did not commit; this murdered man was killed by Dad Lamkin, a very sympathetic and honorable character, in vengeance for certain vicious deeds after there had been no satisfaction from the law—indeed the law had protected him. In a later instance, Mounts himself returns to civilization only to be robbed and beaten by ruffians; he determines, therefore, to return to the "lawlessness" of the plains. There where laws are not particularly needed, he can protect himself if he needs to. In the settlements, the laws are false protectors and a man is not permitted to take the law in his own hands, which makes him helpless as well as victimized.

Certain customs and attitudes are similarly shown to hinder the individual in his self-expression and development. These chiefly, as illustrated earlier, have to do with the emphasis upon certain decreed social patterns and interests. In *The Forest and the Fort*, Salathiel Albine cannot continue a friendship with an officer when he undertakes a particular job. In *This Land Is Ours* the Easterners exhibit class prejudices unknown to the frontier, and it is similarly implied in *Bridal Journey*, *Westward the River*, and others that such prejudices are developed in society. These are amply illustrated in the novels which emphasize the settlement scenes, especially those which deal with the reform impulse.

The wilderness permits a man to develop above the level of shallowness expressed in the lives of others. "I couldn't never see how any men could be small or ornery and live on the plains. It seemed to me that men ought to measure up to their country, someway, and be like it was."[15] In the unspoiled purity and strength of the wilderness, the true nobility of spirit develops; honor, loyalty and brotherhood are manifested in daily activities.

[15] Frank Linderman, *Morning Light*, 148.

Personal dignity and respect for the individual are in the forefront of man's relationships. The code of the frontiersman is high: honesty and fair dealings prevail. Binding these together is an independence of man, fostered and developed by the unlimited frontier, that was, in effect, the driving force and result of their strivings.

A final composite analysis of the patterns of conflict between the forces and ideals of wilderness and organized society reveals the interrelation of the several elements of the design. The several strong strains of progress become merged into a general pattern that reflects the purposes of the pioneer settlers and their eventual domination of the scene. The pattern also conveys the values of the frontier codes and the strengths of the pioneers—strengths developed by the very wilderness they were subduing—especially as compared with later comers or those who came not at all. Within this pattern there is the presence—distinct yet nearly overcome, as a vivid thread caught in a conservative weave—of the extreme wilderness ideal. He represents the optimum individualism and independence, the greatest distance from society. The sense of progress of the dominant attitude modifies the essence of his character; contact with the frontier keeps the dominant attitude in a related pattern.

The entire group of novels generally presents a portrait of the Westerner as superior to the Easterner and the frontier as superior to the settled regions of the East. This image is constructed out of comments by both groups critical of organized society and its residents in relation to the implied and stated virtues of the frontier and the pioneer. In turn, by citing values inherent to the frontier, comparative weaknesses of its settled regions are displayed. This is so despite the intended mirroring in some novels of those same settlements; the whole value structure of the pioneer comes into play. Thus, in pitting the two cultures against each other, the frontier assumes a more advantageous position.

A crucial aspect of frontier life is its verve, its solid strength and vibrant health. Life demands much and leaves no room for softness or falseness. It is hard and rough and fearful; the people are forced to meet each challenge. They are typified by their vitality and purposefulness. Their initial decision to head westward rather than remain safe, secure and comfortable at home identifies a basic pattern and points to key characteristics: resourcefulness, courage, determination to outstay the hardships. By comparison, life in the settlements to the east is superficial and protected. It is a soft life dominated by the mercenary and the false and emphasizing the selfishness of its people.

When these are compared in the novels, there is no room for doubt as to which is favored. It is a continuation of the prejudice conveyed in the novels of the first decade but without the ennobling man-of-two-worlds overtones, although some of this remains in the 1910–25 novels, as noted in the discussion of class patterns. Such a comparison is made in *Foundation Stone* and *Buckskin Breeches* between the vitality and strength of the west-moving heroes and the soft degeneracy of those left behind. In *This Land Is Ours*, the plain, wholesome, and warm frontier folk are sharply contrasted with the haughty and self-centered Easterner. The hero of *Westward the River* expresses strong disapproval of the lack of knowledge about life and inability of the supposedly typical Easterner to cope with ordinary needs and affairs on the frontier. Certainly the characters representing the East in this novel suggest the useless, powdered, conceited dandy, while the rough, willful and somewhat unprivileged pioneer comes up as a progressive individual. The pioneer does not always have all these values, but he is usually superior in his attitudes, skills and his way of life.

In addition to his general superiority to the Easterner, the pioneer himself may be placed on a continuum. A pattern is revealed in the novels which is particularly pronounced in those depicting the wilderness-oriented hero. This hero is in the extremest position on this continuum partly because his comparative description constructs him in more startling diversity and thus he is more emphatically and individualistically superior; he is generally unequaled. Also the attitudes of these heroes, so disdainful of those who don't enjoy their particular brand of independence and singular skill, as previously noted, and the admiration he receives from others solidify his favored position. The first arrivals of the settlement-oriented pioneer take the second position. Indeed, the more aggressively individualistic he is shown to be, the more pronounced his separateness from the mass, the more is he respected and admired. The large bulk of pioneers outshines the later arrivals, particularly those who come after the real dangers are past, who take advantage of the opening created by others. (This is reminiscent of the feelings expressed by the hero against the later arrivals in the 1905 novel, *The Crossing.*)

The relationship on the continuum changes in one basic way. The individualistic mountain man when he is seen as a wagon train guide is given a mixed portrayal and a mixed reception. He is at once the object of contempt of the industrious, purposeful pioneer and that of respect, sometimes grudging, for his knowledge and skills. He, in turn, is contemptuous of their ways and petty concerns. The portrayal is usually sympathetic to the sturdy wagon train group, presenting the mountain man's creed harshly and not clearly. The major exception to this is *The Way West* which represents both figures equitably and, apparently, honestly.

This continuum is significant in its representation of the attitudes toward the peopling of the frontier, that is, toward the conflict between the code of the wilderness hero and the purpose of the pioneer of progress. The relative strength of the several attitudes is discernable; the overlapping values and concepts reflect particular significance. Certain attitudes and concepts exemplified by the wilderness hero are favored in this delineation, but the image is modified by the persistence, purpose, and the numbers of the hero of progress.

The tone and episodic reactions which conclude these novels give some data and final understanding to the conflict's outcome.

The drama of the wilderness hero is more fraught with decision and tragedy. Although for the most part the main group of pioneers meet with success, there is a qualification suggested in the development of some of these novels.

A few of the wilderness heroes maintain their pattern of life, but with a disillusioning note expressed at the end. Andy Burnett in *The Long Rifle* flees westward when the actions and misunderstandings between his Indian friends and trapper associates cause his ideal world to crumble about him. In *The Big Sky* Boone Caudill returns to the mountains after an unhappy visit to the family farm. There is little sense of victory conveyed in this action, for he foresees the end of his way of life.

Several heroes return to the wilderness with full conviction. Some of these, the brother-heroes in *The Brothers in the West*, the father and son in *The Trees*, the husband in *The Limestone Tree*, had tried marriage and settling down. Blaize Ormandy in *So Free We Seem* is in this category, except that he returns to his family some fifteen years later; he indicates that he had wanted to return earlier. Love and some sense of responsibility call him back but shame kept him away.

Two extremely strong characters are killed at the close of the novels in deaths which seem symbolic. Neither Murfree Rinnard nor Jed Cooper, heroes of *The Long Hunt* and *Gilded Rooster* respectively, can adjust to the changing scene, both being too completely committed to their own way of life. Cooper is clearly vanquished by the society he abhors. Refusing to compromise, unable to see the need for escape, he comes into head-on collision. The strong intuitive animal is outmaneuvered by the man of thought.

Almost half of the heroes of these works, when faced with the inevitable displacement of their way of life by organized society, make a change. Typically, Sam Lash in *Wolf Song*, a complete wilderness man, after much conflict and self-torture gives up his free life for marriage and a ranch. He rationalizes that his life will still be in the open country. There is less conflict in *The Red*

Road; "Black" Brond, somewhat like the first decade's heroes, simply reverts to the predominant life force about him—and a loved woman. The situations vary in *Shadow of the Long Knives, Westward the River, Wind Over Wisconsin,* and others, but the sense is the same: settling of the frontier has caught up to the holdouts.

A number of novels stop just short of the conversion of their heroes, but there is a strong suggestion of their accepting the life they had previously declined. Harley Boydley seems about to end his wandering days to return to his family in *Free Forester.* Ray "Spur" Talcott, recognizing the end of his old life in an open West, seems ready to come to terms in his bitter feud with society. Even the unwavering Johnny Christmas vaguely mentions the possibility of a ranch, and Abner Gower's departure with Marah in *Bridal Journey* gives a clue to a less nomadic future. These heroes seem to be facing up to the reality of change.

This evolutionary design is also apparent in those works which initially evoke allegiance to the wilderness credo and a denial of specific aspects of settlement life, usually the congestion or the value structure. However, the movement toward eventual progress and settlement is proclaimed by the activities and proposals of the heroes. Hugh Murray in *The Day Must Dawn* chooses the further frontier of Ohio over the safety of settled Pennsylvania, but he proposes to build there. Mort Sturdevant is motivated by the challenge of the wilderness, the call of action and adventure in comparison to his New York associates who take "their adventures in an armchair. . . . Do you think . . . that I could spend my life grubbing in some dusty office?"[16] He goes to Oklahoma to escape this life, but after a relatively brief period his outlook alters: he comes to envision a glorious expansion, a future of settlements and people—the very thing he had attempted to avoid. Other novels representing different periods, *The Covered Wagon, Michael Beam,* and *Thunder on the River,* present sim-

[16] C. R. Cooper, *Oklahoma,* 8.

ilar situations of men drawn to the wilderness who eventually
accept a modified settlement life.

Nowhere is this evolution from wilderness orientation to organized society more emphatically expressed than in *This Land Is
Ours*. Although his life became a limited compromise, the hero
resisted the trappings of civilization to go his own way. However,
a distinct change is seen toward the close of the novel:

> "I reckon I understand what they mean by 'pioneer-folk'. When
> I was a youngster bringin' in my first furs I knew some of it, the
> pride of livin' free. . . . Now I have a different feeling, a pride in
> this growing town."[17]

The final effect, then, is of the inevitability of progress. Those
characters who tried to maintain a life that was insupportable in
a changing world are swallowed up or vanquished or forced to
retreat. The strength of this point grows out of the pressure of
numbers of novels as well as the characterizations and conclu-
sions. The hunters in such novels as *The Trees* become secondary
figures; the hunters in such novels as *So Free We Seem* become
outcasts while those whom they left behind harnessed to the
farm are the formulators of the future; the hunters in such novels
as *This Land Is Ours* adjust to new purposes; the mountain men,
in such novels as *The Land Is Bright*, become guides, disenchanted and outliving their original glory and purpose.

The wilderness hero is a passing hero; his passing is fitting and
justified. His immediate values and objectives are not sufficient
to the progressive movement, to the wave of the future.

> ". . . you've known only to go farther and farther into the West.
> Rivers, mountains, valleys—to you they've only been new pastures
> to cross, new places to see. They've meant new land but not to be
> taken . . . you've been so much a part of the wilderness . . . that
> you've wandered from one section to another. . . . I know your
> blood's gone into this land, and your sweat, too. I know you've
> won the land. But you haven't settled it."

[17] Zara, *op. cit.*, 772.

". . . but there's a time for all things and the time for wandering here is nearly over. I love the land, too. . . . But I want to get down to it, maybe feel a handful of clods, maybe fence in a piece and put it to farming."[18]

Although an eventual or assumed affinity for settling down and progress is displayed, the wilderness tradition is also promoted. The attempt to maintain vestiges and values of the simple, uncrowded frontier life remains in force. A decision to move further westward, as in *The Day Must Dawn* and numerous others, including the overland trail novels, identifies the opportunity and the challenge of the frontier. A specific comment in another novel which promotes progress is revealing:

"Here in Salt Lake City, everything's made too easy. I want my children to know what it is to start from nothing, the way we did. I guess I'm a born pioneer, for when things get settled and finished I want to push on somewhere's else."[19]

Such a decision also points to the values that are critical of organized society, as has been discussed.

The wilderness tradition is also maintained, unexpectedly, by a few novels which show the complete development of communities. Besides portraying the achievements of the pioneers and the progress of life, they profess dismay over the dilution of frontier values. The novels *A Lantern in Her Hand* and *Spring Came on Forever* particularly urge the return to the simple, wholesome realities exemplified in the early frontier day. These have become lost in the deification of luxury, social position, and indolent living. Life has become dishonest; the people prideful, superficial and false. Progress—the advance of culture and the elimination of crudeness—had been a glowing objective in these novels.

This turnabout is dramatically displayed, symbolically as well as literally, in the Richter trilogy: *The Trees, The Fields*, and *The Town*. Sayward's lust for the destruction of trees in the first novel

18 Zara, *op. cit.*, 612.
19 Susan Ertz, *The Proselyte*, 304.

is finally replaced by a realization that the trees "wasn't something fierce but tame and beneficient to man." She complains that ". . . houses and mills shut in all my land now. I can't see the country anymore," and she goes about planting trees. Her original urgency for people and settlement is also replaced by a concern about the pride and greed of the people who push out and destroy everything in their way in the name of progress.[20]

And the wilderness hero himself is not totally repudiated. He comes to take second place but he is not completely a loser. He was necessary to the development of the land. His strength and manhood is undoubted; his quest for independence and freedom forms the core of his successors' values. His spirit and vision shine through his deficiencies. Especially when the weaknesses of the developing society of the settler become apparent are his values shown to full advantage. His passing through enriched the country, and his seed, appearing happily in later generations, is the seed of strength, character and manliness. It is this which assists later generations to rise above the failings of society and the people who have made it.

In the final conception of these cross purposes, the dream of progress is foremost, but it is a dream founded on the frontier and a progress which recognizes the values taught by the frontier. The wild and the tame are mixed in the formulated dream. This idea is symbolically represented in *Each Bright River* in the nature of the hero and heroine, their goals, and the conflict between them. He, representing the untamed, free West, comes to admire and desire her culture, her respectability, the aura of the future which she represents; he also despises her pampered, careless self-indulgence. The clash between the forces of their wills and the life they represent is resolved in the modification of their natures and principles. So, too, does the view of the West represent such a modification with both progress and the frontier values in the driver's seat.

This simplification of the tone and sense of this group of novels

[20] Conrad Richter, *The Town*, 272–75.

derives from the accumulated factors that have been detailed: the impetus toward adventure and independence; the escape from the evils or narrowness of the settled areas; the opportunities in the new lands; the urge to prosper, to build a home, a community, a land. This image is complemented by the simple prosaic portrait of the pioneer who had no particular ax to grind other than the honing of his own future in a land where the future beckoned. He saw the future emanating from the hopes and struggles of the present in a more secure, comfortable life.

Part and parcel of the presentation is the effect of the frontier upon these people and, by implication, the effect of the individual people thus formed upon the character of the nation. Sundry comments like those which follow proclaim and describe this effect:

> "Such a country would breed a race of heroes, men built and knitted together to endure. . . . A new race for the earth."[21]

> . . . these robust people he had found inhabiting the lower South. He liked their crassness, their joviality, their pigheaded self-interest that begot bravery. . . . Gracey (Old South) was ineffectual on this soil fertilized for the Gerdas of the time.[22]

> "The prairies took me, an ignorant, orphaned canal hand, and made me something much better."[23]

The independence, the spirit, the confidence and leadership of this Western breed, their determination and dreams, made the West the land of the future. These people, who opened and built the West, were also builders of the nation.

[21] Elizabeth M. Roberts, *The Great Meadow*, 13.
[22] Lella Warren, *Foundation Stone*, 214.
[23] Herbert Quick, *Vandemark's Folly*, 420.

8

Some Minor Themes

Cᴇʀᴛᴀɪɴ relatively minor attitudes and values are represented in these novels. These are labeled as minor not because they lack significance but because they are less emphasized in the presentations, though a particular idea may recur fairly consistently, or because the attitude may occur only in a special group of novels distinguished either by locale or time. The more significant of these will be discussed in this chapter.

Tʜᴇ Pɪᴏɴᴇᴇʀ's Vɪᴇᴡ ᴏf ᴛʜᴇ Iɴᴅɪᴀɴ

Since the Indian was usually an integral element of the frontier, his occurrence in these novels is regular. On a frontier that ranges from the western slopes of the Appalachians to the waters of the Pacific, he was, of course, of various tribes and not the same Indian. Therefore, some difference in his portrayal might be expected in the various novels. The view of the pioneer on the successive frontiers should, theoretically, be amended to take in these differences but with modification. It is probable that the pioneer's assumptions and expectations would be influenced not by an awareness of the variances of the Indians to the west but by knowledge of those already contacted. In these terms, if any uniformity of attitude did exist, it might still be expected to appear on a particular frontier. Although there is evidence in the novels of such patterns, another variant alters the picture. This variant apparently has little to do with the frontier itself but is a manifestation of changing attitudes toward the Indian in the half century in which the novels under consideration were published.

In assessing the attitudes toward the Indian in the novels, primarily the views of the hero are used. These often coincide with those of other characters but not always. The contrary views are used at times to emphasize those of the hero—which may be those of the author—and will be clarified when they seem significant. Certain conflicts point to the general frontier attitude in the novels against which the hero (and the author) reacts. Indeed, the hero sometimes represents dual views or manifests a change in feelings towards the Indian.

Chiefly, the attitudes fall into three categories. The first of these builds on a negative stereotype but includes an acknowledgment of strength and individual nobility; the second displays the Indian as a simple creature of an inferior culture; the third represents a sympathetic response to the mistreated Indian and recognizes his unique culture. Somewhere between these latter two is a neutrality of response to the Indian. In the novels in which this is manifested, either no attitude is expressed or certain defensive activities are carried out with but limited expressed emotion. The implications are more positive than negative and will be discussed in detail in due order.

The first of these attitudes is displayed most prominently and with fewer qualifications in the earlier novels. These organize a two-dimensional portrait which seems to highlight contradictory views. However, these views are corollary and have root in a like romantic deficiency: a stereotype of sweeping qualities without depth or comprehensiveness. The coexistence of contradictory views is typified in this descriptive quotation:

> . . . a type of inhumanity raised to the last power; but under the hideous atrocity of nature lay the indestructible sense of gratitude so fixed and perfect that it did its work almost automatically.[1]

On the one hand, the Indian is known to be a cruel savage, intent on the destruction of the pioneers. On the other, he is given

[1] Maurice Thompson, *Alice of Old Vincennes*, 276.

certain positive attributes that do not necessarily redeem him but function in the further stereotyping of his character: inexpressive manner, immobility of feature, automatic loyalty and gratitude, and childlike simplicity.[2]

This is the pioneer's vision of the barbarian Indian, evil and malignant, silent and strong. He is termed a savage and shown in various cruel poses and activities: ". . . every wind brought the sound of the savages sharpening the scalping knife."[3] As such he is the enemy to be killed without mercy; the pioneers must stand against the Indians—against torture and scalping and murder. The pioneer hero usually accepts this view and is depicted as active in relieving the frontier from this menace. This killing is at times conducted with malice and aforethought but sometimes is simply an automatic act of defense against the murdering savages. A strong example of the venomous, vengeful anti-Indian attitude is the dominating figure of Louis Wetzel, who figures prominently in the three Zane Grey novels of the first decade; his sole, driving purpose is to take the lives of the Indians in payment for their massacre of his family. To him, the only good Indian is a dead one. This outstanding negativeness is modified in other heroes who do not display such an excess of hate. Jonathan Zane in *The Last Trail* and Tom McChesney in *The Crossing* see their roles as protectors of the frontier to include killing Indians and they do so but with less show of emotion. John Lee's activities in *The Wilderness Road* are further qualified by his strong friendship with an Indian companion (who stands out as apart from and quite different from the average of his race—he is given a "broad brow" and "great width between the eyes," aside from his barbaric nature). In some of the works, too, the hero expresses a sense of admiration for the Indian's skills and bravery despite his savagery, but the latter concept is still present and most impresses the pioneers.

[2] There is a relationship between this aspect of the stereotype and the second attitude toward the Indian.

[3] J. A. Altscheler, *The Wilderness Road*, 64.

Paralleling this view of his inhumanity in these novels—sometimes in unison—is the acceptance of the Indian as a simple creature with his own code of behavior, which inexplicably shows itself in isolated moments. The code is only slightly and shallowly depicted, the generalizations being both flat and sweeping. The sense of the pioneer's notion of the Indian's simpleness is conveyed in the following: "They are like children. I swear, I almost believe their lot in life is happier than our own!"[4] In *When Wilderness Was King* and *The Crossing*, pioneers use this attitude to excuse or show understanding of the Indians' savagery: the "misled children" are forgiven for not knowing right from wrong. (This, of course, skirts the real issues, the problems and the basic needs of the Indian.)

An incident in *The Heritage*, following the capture of the hero, suggests this attitude through both its statement and tone.

> So I looked at my captors for instructions, and when they motioned me forward, away I went between the lines as fast as my feet would carry me, reasoning that the quicker I got through the fewer blows I should receive. I got enough as it was, for they banged me over the head and across the shoulders, with little grunts of satisfaction, in a way that left me sore for a week. They ran me down to the river, and would have begun all over again, but that one of my captors intervened, . . . and permitted me to wash off the blood from a little scalp wound. . . . I could not help laughing . . . for the event had been so much less dreadful than I had feared, and they all stood around regarding me so solemnly. He stared at me for a moment, and then strode up and linked his arm through mine. "Man," he said, "No squaw! Come."[5]

Aside from the unreality of this torture scene, particularly as compared with those depicted in later novels, the Indians come over as wooden—doll-like, animated but without intellectual or social consequence. The hero's reaction to them as well as their portrayal as ineffectual, wild creatures conveys the stereotype of

[4] Emerson Hough, *The Magnificent Adventure*, 182.
[5] Burton E. Stevenson, *The Heritage*, 213.

their simplicity. This same feeling is developed in other works which show the hero easily outmaneuvering the Indians who, though strong and savage, lack depth of perception. They are creatures close to nature, wild and simple.

The concept of the noble redman is slightly revealed in this point of view. Direct statement of this view is not made, but it is inherent in the attitude that creates a simple but strong Indian—notwithstanding his savagery—and implies or reveals certain attributes associated with the noble nature. Individual Indian characters—the hero's companion in *The Wilderness Road*, a worthy chief in *The Spirit of the Border*—and, in isolated instances, the race, display such a presence: dignity of person and manner, loyalty, honesty, inscrutability; they are majestic and magnificent physical specimens. The heroes respect these individuals. Generally, however, these noble strokes are colored and offset by the basic simpleness of the Indian's nature.

A minor attempt is made in several early works to show the pioneer's awareness of the Indian issue and character. In each of the Grey novels, for example, there is mention made of the pressures of the land-seeking pioneers who pushed the Indians to acts of desperation and of the rum-selling French traders who brought him degradation. This harassment ruined their honest, simple and enviable life.

> . . . the real nature of the redman. The Indian's love of freedom and honor, his hatred of subjugation and deceit . . . the Indians had reason for their hatred of the pioneers. Truly they were a blighted race.[6]

However, this generous attitude and a further recognition of skills and ways of life does not prevent this spokesman from applauding the heroics of the Indian-killers or from pursuing the settling of the land. Such luke-warm, superficial consciousness of the Indian as a human being without giving any degree of culture or character delineation tends to support the noble-

[6] Zane Grey, *The Spirit of the Border*, 95.

simple image: default by omission. It also permits it to be structured with the savage aspects of his nature.

In the novels of the subsequent years, after 1920, some of these attitudes are carried forward; others—the image of the Indian as a barbarian and the accompanying vengeful reaction—change in quality. Often enough the Indian is savage and cruel, and the pioneer acts against him in defense and also in revenge. The difference in tone is created by the addition of a quality of knowledge and of understanding of the Indian drives and ways—though this is not always on the part of all of the members of the pioneer society. This tone will be discussed in relation to these changed views of the Indian.

These later novels do depict a view of the Indian which is closely related to the image of him as a simple child of nature and perhaps emanates from this early picture. This view represents an attitude that categorized the Indian as beneath the class and cultural level of the pioneer. It is not difficult to imagine this as an apt rationalization of fear of the savage or as a justification of pioneer aggression. However, the novels that point up such a comparison of cultures do not accent Indian savagery or the social issues involved in the westward advance.[7]

Statements of several heroes in novels of various locales illustrate the point of view that the white man—the pioneer—was inherently superior to the Indian. When he says, "I was a white man and she was only an Injin woman,"[8] in alluding to the Indian girl he has come to love and whom he wants to marry, Lige Mounts reveals the prevailing attitude among his companions that placed the Indian in a lower class. His friend and mentor, Dad Lamkin, speaks for society when he argues against Lige's interest in the Indian girl, pointing out her unacceptability. Indeed in the early works the hero is not permitted an alliance with an Indian woman. Similarly does Orion Outlaw in a later work

---

[7] A number of novels which portray such social issues are discussed in subsequent paragraphs.

[8] Frank Linderman, *Morning Light*, 227.

declare the pioneers' view of the Indians in his remarks when first viewing the Indian village: "It looks like a town, with real folks in it!"; "I don't know. Sometimes they act just like real folks, don't they?"[9] These comments reveal a concept of sub-standard culture which considered the Indian way of life as perhaps savage or animallike and somehow below the human level. A majority of the mountain men show a decided negative reaction to the Indian, particularly in the novels of the 1920's. The strong, early attitude is exemplified by Sam Lash: "He knew always that brown skin was to shoot at and Indian hair to lift."[10] This is part of the mountain man's cult of superiority, but in seeming to react to the Indian as to an animal, this response distinguishes him from other men. Lash and his associates act out their attitude by freely killing Indians without particular concern or reason—other than to prove their manhood.

Several novels with but a very limited degree of Indian-pioneer conflict—and thus a limited sense of fear or hate—present a slant that fits into this negative point of view. Aldrich—who is other-wise rather noncommittal—conveys the belief in Indian inferior-ity and cultural lag in scenes in which the pioneer heroine is faced with unexpected Indian visitors, scenes which appear almost identically in two of her novels of the prairie:

> They spoke among themselves in their low, guttural tongue, seem-ing amused at her fright. . . .
>
> From that time they began a systematic search of the cabin, handling . . . uncovering . . . drinking from the jug of precious mo-lasses. . . . For a long time they entertained themselves childishly . . . they appropriated the jug of molasses and without a backward glance departed.[11]

Thus, in the guise of thieving, moth-eaten gypsies, the Indian is made to seem both foolish and simple and low class. Aldrich

[9] Caroline Gordon, *Green Centuries*, 271, 307.
[10] Harvey Fergusson, *Wolf Song*, 16.
[11] *Spring Came on Forever*, 96

creates this image with direct description, with language that creates a negative impression, and with the reaction of her characters. These, after getting over their surprised fright, are either incensed, indignant, or determined to remove all stains of the visitors. Hargreaves' main characters, while reacting with more humanity toward the outclassed Oregon Indians, voice one set of values but act according to another. They evoke kindness and sympathy; however their humanity does not recognize the essence and value of the Indian culture but is based on an initial assumption of his inferior status. The comment, "white man hold nothing sacred that belongs to an inferior race, not even the dead,"[12] shows criticism of white men's behavior but also a consciousness of the Indian's lower cultural-social level.

In a few novels where the usual frontier conflict between the Indians and the pioneers exists, there is some inclination to belittle the Indian's cultural background as well as his capacity to fight. Of these, the former is the more discussed, taking the form illustrated by the comments of Orion Outlaw in *Green Centuries*. When these feelings are combined with a general war antagonism and sense of fighting superiority, the comments sound like those of Berk Jarvis and his friend in *The Great Meadow*. Responding to a remark that Kentucky is Indian property, Jarvis says,

> "If the Indian is not man enough to hold it let him give it over then. It's a land that calls for brave men, a brave race. It's only a strong race can hold a good country. Let the brave have and hold there." . . .

> "They're a poor sort, under their paint and war noises. If you guard yourself against surprise he got a mightly little advantage. I never . . . saw one Indian keep his courage up when he begins to lose a fight. Run, he will then."[13]

In view of these attitudes, the hero and his friends act to protect

---

[12] Sheba Hargreaves, *The Cabin at the Trail's End*, 195.
[13] Elizabeth M. Roberts, *The Great Meadow*, 105, 107.

themselves as against any scourge. There is little attempt at first to recognize the Indian point of view, his rights to the land, or his way of life. It is force against force. Though Jarvis' reaction to the Indian changes after several years of captivity, representing the shifting view of the Indians in the later books, the bulk of the pioneers maintain this attitude.

Another aspect of this shifting view is the position of relative neutrality apparently adopted by a group of characters. These appear in novels written during the three decades after 1920 and form a kind of second chorus to the rising hum of sympathetic feeling for the Indian. Indeed some additional main characters, like a few already mentioned, evince a generally neutral attitude for the most part with only occasional show of feelings in trying situations or before experiences render changes in their concepts.

The usual pattern in representing this attitude is the general lack of reaction—negative or positive—to the Indian as an individual or as a race. Such heroes as Dan McMasters in *North of 36* and Tom Kirby in *The Last Frontier* fight and kill Indians only when it is necessary to do so. There is no evidence of hate or contempt. McMasters shows, in addition, some awareness of civilized ethic by vehemently objecting to the ruthless killing of Indian women. In a later novel, *Free Forester*, the hero seems indifferent to Indians. He does not care about them even when they interfere in his life, and he seeks revenge only when goaded by others who are more vehement than he; there is in his action neither hate nor pleasure. This kind of indifference shows up in *Plume Rouge*, in which the sense of business enterprise dominates, and in several novels featuring pioneer women. In two of these, *Lamb in His Bosom* and *The Trees*, the heroines lean toward acceptance and curiosity rather than animosity.

An element of fear among some pioneers alters this neutral reaction; however, the extent of this alteration and the general presentation are such that the tone of these works fits this category. The mildest of these is a group of prairie novels, particularly those dealing with immigrant settlers. The people in *Giants in the Earth* and *The Emigrants* dread the unknown Indian, the unknown in this case having been fortified with tales of savagery. There is little hatred, however. When the test comes, Per Hansa, in the former novel, reacts with compassion and humanity and no fear. In the latter, there is a reaction of numbness but there are no incidents. The general feeling of the prairie settlers is one of distant concern, at the worst. Even the pioneer-Indian encounters in the Aldrich novels which convey a negative quality seem to have little consequence for no further mention is made. The mild tone toward the Indian in this series of novels may be due to the lessened menace in this period and locale, as well as to the period of publication. It is interesting that the non-American authors are less involved in any emotional response.

Fear and animosity cannot be separated from the pioneers' reactions in numerous forest frontier novels, but there is a noticeable absence of racial hate and emotional vehemence of the quality noted in the earlier novels. Typical of this development are the novels *Unconquered* and *Drums Along the Mohawk*. The emphasis is on the Indian as the enemy; in the latter novel, the Tories are feared and hated on a par with the Indians. The Indians' unceremonious activities are not whitewashed to be sure, but they are delineated with less venom. The Indians themselves are characterized with more dimension and are not treated as identical red blurs creeping through the forest. The hero in the latter novel exhibits respect for some Indians and affection of a sort for one old brave, Blue Back, who is both welcomed and trusted. This is not to say, of course, that the main characters do not become involved in the terrible struggle with the Indians for survival or that they are free of emotions. Some lesser characters exhibit extreme passions and ferocity, but the heroes and key characters are generally removed from this. (As will be discussed subsequently, heroes of other works take a more definite stand, often positive, despite contrary feelings of the populace.)

Several of the overland trail novels, which, like those of prairie locale, have fewer Indian tensions, create an impartial tone by expressing individual reactions to individual Indians. They are seen alternately as powerfully built, supple and handsome or pitifully poor, miserable creatures; they are thieves or drunkards or examples of kindness or determination to withstand invasion: all these characterizations in the same works. By thus being neither hateful nor sympathetic in attitude, impartiality is expressed in such novels as *The Far Country* and *Don't You Cry for Me*. These responses are generally those of the hero figures as well as the general wagon train population.

The strongest trend in these novels of the second quarter century is a sympathetic response to the Indian and his problem, a sympathy apparently imbued with a growing understanding of his culture. This trend starts earlier with sporadic examples of these attitudes and gradually gains momentum in both quantity and depth so that it becomes the dominant expression of attitude toward the Indian. Included herein are those novels which display conflicting impressions, the hero usually being on the sympathetic side of the Indians or developing to that point of view in opposition to other pioneers. Such a conflict pattern was also rare in the first two decades, there being then a near uniformity of attitude. Rather than being a contradiction, as might be supposed, this conflict pattern enhances the trend toward sympathy and understanding, for it points up the human issues involved.

The earliest clear-cut sympathetic response to the Indian is in Eleanor Atkinson's *Johnny Appleseed* (1915). The hero, a romanticized version of the fabled traveling orchardist, is portrayed as unconscious of any differences between men and practices his creed of brotherhood with red men as well as white. He preaches peace and helpfulness between races and neighbors as well as respect for Indian rights. Appleseed believes the Indians can be taught white men's ways, thereby bringing peace and amity. These beliefs are not completely divergent from the ideas expressed in later novels; but the emphasis on brotherhood, helpfulness and humility and the romantic tone distinguish this novel from those to come.

Through the mid-nineteen twenties the thread of sympathy is slight, found chiefly in vague, occasional allusions to Indian strengths and culture. The earlier Zane Grey novels show, as has already been noted, the contradictory sentiments about Indian rights and the pioneer's purposes. A later one, *The Thundering Herd* (1925), further illustrates this ambivalence. His hero vacillates between indifference and sympathy: he had shown unconcern for the Indian's plight in the destruction of the buffalo, and then, suddenly, he is troubled by their loss of food supply. Later still, he kills them freely and vengefully when he thinks they have captured his beloved. Such are the patterns of several other works with the main characters mildly advocating a sympathetic reappraisal of the Indian or peaceful coexistence, that is to say, the Indian adopting white men's ways. Individual Indians in several works are portrayed in positive terms as friends or companions. However, the attitudes in these works are muted.

Attitudes of greater strength and consistency mark the turn of the quarter century. These show the other side of the coin of Indian life and character. The Indians display favorable qualities and the other characters recognize and appreciate their merits. Some outspoken characters denounce or decry the methods and purposes of the pioneers as impinging on Indian rights.

One series of heroes particularly identifies with the Indian's way. These usually prefer to live with the Indians (with varying degrees of association with whites) and often show contempt or disapproval of the pioneer settlers. Their regard for Indian life is closely related to a strong sense of independence, a love for the wilderness and anticivilization tendencies. Disenchanted with their own race, they're critical of their greed and self-interest, their softness, their fussing talk and complaints, their destruction of the wilderness. When a final choice must be made they often side with the whites, however. Even so, Murfree Rinnard is able to favor his newly avowed enemy: "Yes, sir, if I was a slave, I would have small craving for an Indian fuss. What makes an Indian fighter is that he's free."[14]

Such preference is also tied to an understanding and appreciation of the Indian's life and character, which, brought into the foreground, are favorably and carefully depicted.

Angus McDermott, a character less involved than Rinnard in the need for freedom and isolation, finds Indian life inviting.

> He was conscious . . . of an urge to try to find a place for himself among the Indians. He had an understanding of them, a sense that they were not so far removed from his own forbears, even though of these he knew actually nothing. They all carried themselves as free men, fought for each other's rights, and their sachems and chiefs claimed no superiority over the rank and file as persons. The family ruled, and each member in it had an equal right. He liked them for this personal dignity, which was an attribute of their simple government. He liked the chieftains, not one and all, but Blue Jacket, who had courage and yet no fanatical temper; Little Turtle, a man of McDermott's own age, but brighter and more inquiring, a full hearted, swiftly flying warrior.[15]

McDermott's respect for Indians is based upon their faith, dignity, honesty, and justice. He sees them as victimized by the whites and sides with them and the British in the wars against the Americans; the latter are viewed as trespassers upon treaty rights. Similarly do Andy Burnett and Boone Caudill, respectively heroes of *The Long Rifle* and *The Big Sky*, react to Indian life: their fineness of spirit, their faithfulness and humanity, their freedom and self-determination. Milder reactions like those of the heroes of *The Way West* are no less positive. Lige Evans objects to the view that Indians are varmints; he, along with Dick Summers, shows recognition of human qualities and is generally sympathetic. This attitude of the hero pioneer comes close to the image of a noble native except that it is more precise in

[14] James Boyd, *Long Hunt*, 356.
[15] Thomas A. Boyd, *Shadow of the Long Knives*, 216.

identification and description of Indian character on a real life level, particularly in the more recent novels.

These attitudes are particularly emphasized through those heroes who markedly change their opinion: as captives of Indians they view and gain understanding and humanity. Jim Dalrymple in *Perilous Journey* awakes to the reality of Indian character and life and questions his prejudices:

> Jim . . . found it hard to reconcile the nobility of the Choctaw's dark face and the dignity of his bearing with what he knew about the Indians. . . . there must be some richness to Indian life that lay within and accounted for the dignity and magnificent bearing of the race.[16]

Not all of the reactions of the heroes are based on so superficial an analysis, but this is illustrative of the learning process that others go through.

The other heroes' experiences are longer and fuller. Berk Jarvis in *The Great Meadow*, embittered by the massacre of his mother and the assault of his wife, sets out to wreak vengeance. He is captured and forced to live with the Indians for some years. Upon his return he recounts his experiences, detailing the lives of the people: their customs, feelings and fears. He has come to see them as warm, full-hearted human beings. Archy Outlaw in *Green Centuries*, to his brother's amazement, refuses to leave his Indian home and Indian sweetheart. Portrayed in this regard are some sensitive scenes which show the measure of wholesomeness, love, and loyalty that the Indians' lives hold.

The later novels also convey interactions between the men and women of the two races. Beyond the sexual encounters, several of the male heroes love, marry, and live happily with Indian women, who are portrayed in positive, understanding terms. Several white women, usually captives, marry Indian men who are similarly portrayed. Through these relationships the Indian is seen in a favorable light. The shamed inability of the heroine to

---

[16] Clifford N. Sublette, *Perilous Journey*, 218.

return "home" with a half-blood child and, when one does, the horrified rejection of her white husband do not diminish this effect.

Needless to say, not all of the heroes reject their own culture or face the trials of captivity to come to this point of view. And they maintain their attitudes despite existing conditions of war or peace. These men do not pretend to judge the Indian; they understand him. The Indians are credited with ability, courage, and strength; their own culture and values are recognized; their cruelties are defined as part of their custom; their fight against the whites is honorable and necessary for them. For example, even during the height of battle and racial friction, in the midst of hatred and passion, Yarbrough Whetstone in *Foundation Stone* voices respect for his enemies, for their inherent dignity and the justice of their cause. (This does not keep him from fulfilling his own, of course.) Others—the heroes of *This Land Is Ours, Oh, Promised Land, Bridal Journey, Mighty Mountain, A High Wind Rising*—follow suit. Their many associations with Indians bring them to affirm the values inherent in Indian culture. They learn to judge Indians on individual merit, just as they would judge white men. In response to a negative comment about an old friend, the following comment is made: "He was a man if an Indian," said Anna Sabilla wrathfully, "God made him. Don't talk ugly."[17] Although the others might not adhere to the religious sentiment, most would no doubt echo the sense of the comment.

The flow of sympathetic response to the Indian is not limited to a show of recognition and understanding of his life and ways. There is also a strong sense of dishonesty, greed, and dishonor among the white men and the grave injustice done the land's original inhabitant.

In these many novels, a constantly repeated refrain is: The land belonged to the Indian before it was usurped. Though the

[17] Elsie Singmaster, *A High Wind Rising*, 178.

tone and direction of such comments vary in the novels the sense is quite the same, as the following sample quotations display:

> . . . the Saints, troubled though they were, agreed that the Indians could not be greatly blamed for their behaviour. They were being driven from their lands, their game preserves were now in the hands of their enemies and destroyers.[18]

> "White men are so smart in some things . . . and so dumb where red men are concerned. This was their country first; it was their land, their forest; the game was their game. By what right did we come and claim it?"[19]

> But it was the Indian's land they were taking. The Indians have never been given a chance by the settlers . . . but the settlers think it queer that they aren't glad to give up their land on which they hunt and fish.[20]

The heroes in these novels see that the Indians are being driven from their lands by the never-ending incursions of land-hungry pioneers. In their initial sincerity and innocence, the Indians believe and trust. At last, after continual encroachment, they are forced to the extremity of defense and war. And in defeat they are shown as noble, valiant, and righteous. Particularly so are the Sacs of Wisconsin, led by Black Sparrow Hawk, and the Oregon tribes. These are a tried people who are vainly seeking peace, justice, and a place in the sun. The fury and hostility of the pioneers is undeserved. A number of heroes, looking on or participating in actions against them, are most sympathetic and wonder if they would not do the same if in the Indians' situation.

The righteousness of the Indian is seen from two sides of the coin: the unscrupulousness and meanness of the whites as compared to the honor and honesty of the Indians.

> "It's only that, having known them and dealt with them, I understand . . . and often there's more honor among them than among

[18] Susan Ertz, *The Proselyte*, 304.
[19] Ethel Hueston, *The Man of the Storm*, 245.
[20] Mary Schumann, *Strife Before Dawn*, 10.

my own fellow men, so many of whom don't know what honesty is unless it can be turned and bent to suit their own ends."[21]

Injustice is charged to the pioneers. They knife the Indians in the back, literally as well as figuratively, with false promises and broken treaties. These treaties are not only flagrantly disadvantageous to the Indians and easily disavowed, but all too frequently the methods used to achieve them are based upon trickery, deception, and force. Treachery, murder of innocent, peaceful Indians, greed and lust are depicted as the method of the pioneer. In several novels, notably *Cimarron*, the accusing finger is also pointed at the government:

> . . . a government that has cheated them and driven them like cattle from place to place and broken its treaties with them and robbed them of their land.[22]

Thus is compassion built up for the Indians, both the hunted, unfortunate tribes like the Sacs and the more warlike ones. Both are given rationalization and cause for their actions, the distinction between them being the nature of their strength and character.

Where does the later pioneer hero stand? Generally, in sympathy with the Indian and in opposition to the horde of avaricious pioneers. At one extreme he is the frontiersman who is not interested in land and who opposes the settlers directly. In another he is the rather more complex frontiersman who, while settlement oriented, finds it necessary to act with or help the Indians. Typically, the heroes in the Derleth novels, *Wind Over Wisconsin* and *Bright Journey*, and the hero of *Mighty Mountain* work to avert war, to bring about justice in Indian dealings, to prevent vengeful killings by pioneers, to practice and lead to peaceful coexistence.

At times the sympathetic hero seems to contradict his own

[21] August Derleth, *Wind Over Wisconsin*, 98.
[22] Edna Ferber, *Cimarron*, 32.

purposes, for he, too, is often striving for land; he also accepts the pioneer's cause. Thus he maintains dual allegiance. His compromise calls for a degree and method which are above reproach. Andrew Benton clarifies this special attitude that distinguishes the pioneer hero from others:

> Most of the settlers . . . Andrew reflected, held that the life of an Indian was worth no more than the life of any animal of the wilds. Other bordermen were, like himself, hungry for the land and wanting it dearly, but not so much as to bleed the Indians to death for it. Perhaps what Simon had reported about Tecumseh's talk of a buffer land between the white men and the red men was not impractical at all. Then the game would not be driven away, trade would not cease for lack of peltry, the redskins might be chastened and still be educated to better ways, and there would be days of peace.[23]

Such characters manage the feat of leading two lives. They successfully thread their way between the two forces, maintaining their convictions sincerely and honestly.

It would be amiss to imply that these later novels are one sided in the pioneers' view of the Indian. Although the majority of the novels present a hero who shows understanding and sympathy, often he stands outside the pale of local opinion. As has been stated, he himself is not necessarily stable in his reactions. And there is a sufficient number of major characters, including a few heroes, who represent the contrary view.

In the novels of the mountain men, from *The Long Rifle* to *The Big Sky,* when the hero stands in sympathy with Indian friends, he is not joined by his associates. The majority of the mountain men in both novels hate the Indians or want to undo them; they look out for their own interests. The Indian is beneath them.

This attitude is not isolated to the mountain man novel. In *Cimarron,* while the hero lustily exclaims against government deception and group treachery, while he shoulders the burden of

---

[23] Louis Zara, *This Land Is Mine,* 620.

the Oklahoma Indians and expresses their virtues, his wife equally energetically preaches and practices the opposite. She teaches
her son:

> Indians are bad people. They take little boys from their mammas
> and never bring them back. They burn down people's houses and
> hurt them. They're dirty and lazy, and they steal.[24]

She means it, and the majority admit to her point of view. In such
novels as *The Great Meadow* and *A High Wind Rising*, the
populace in general is fearful and withdrawn at best; few achieve
the friendliness or compassion of the heroes; in the former the
hero's change of heart comes late in the novel.

Several other characters display mixed reactions: the favorable
attitudes to the Indian are subject to reservations; the convictions
are less completely held. *Michael Beam* presents a vacillating
hero who repudiates the prevalent white man's conception of the
inferior Indian yet cannot give up his white man's heritage.
Angus Drumlin's thoughts signify his spirit of fairness and general acceptance but also show a degree of disenchantment.

> . . . he did not mind the Indians. Murdering, scalping brutes when
> they chose; heathen to be destroyed, if you listened to your min-
> ister; never trust most of them as far as you could spit, certainly;
> but it was stupid to keep plaguing them . . . [he] kept his word
> with them.[25]

This quotation also indicates this character's general separation
from the multitude. Such is also apparent in the comment of
Mark Elderidge, who manages to show his weak principles as
well.

> "Of course they're savages. They're also human beings. But the
> government tries to make them Christians and treats them like
> dogs!" . . .
> "I don't know as I like most of them either. They're too bar-

[24] Ferber, *op. cit.*, 60.
[25] Meade Minnigerode, *Black Forest*, 7.

barous for my taste. But you don't have to like a man to treat him decently."[26]

Thus does this character present a measure of humanity, necessary perhaps for the time of publication, while preserving his superiority, and remnants of attitudes of the past.

It still remains to explain the defeat of the Indians in view of these sympathetic sentiments. Various reactions of characters make this possible. Some, as has been shown, come to an awakening sympathy after assorted experiences—after the cause is won. Others are relatively isolated in their feelings and either cannot or do not affect their neighbors; the tide moves forward despite them and their kind. A few of these manage relatively minor successes, but history is against them. In several novels, from Grey's *The Thundering Herd* to McNeilly's *Each Bright River*, the hero is forced into responding with defensive or even offensive measures. This happens to characters who had not shown much feeling (Berk Jervis in *The Great Meadow*, who becomes re-educated subsequently), to those who had shown ambivalence (Tom Dean in *The Thundering Herd*), to those who had advocated a practical approach (Curt Fletcher in *Each Bright River*), and to those who profess general sympathy (Murfree Rinnard in *Long Hunt*). The cruelty of the Indians on the warpath offers excuse as well as reason for defense and reprisal. Such a change of heart is clearly evoked in *Long Meadows*. The chief characters had been raised on this philosophy of the father:

"We've brought it on ourselves. . . . Fire water and unfair tactics! An Indian is a good fellow, if you trouble yourself to pay him proper respect."

But the developments on the frontier bring about this change in the son:

"The reds would have *loved* to scalp us, one or both, after they'd taken a shot in the dirtiest, meanest way on earth—not giving us

[26] Charlton Laird, *Thunder on the River*, 247.

even a scrap of a chance to defend ourselves. There was a time once when I was sorry for them and looked on the whole business the way Father does. But not anymore. If they shoot on sight, so will I."[27]

A final group displays the undercurrent that carried the pioneers to fulfill their purpose. The novel *The Day Must Dawn* typifies this in the extreme. Both attitudes toward the Indian are presented. The hero, Hugh Murray, who is very much convinced of their evil nature and who bears a revengeful hatred of the redskins, eventually recognizes the good side. He begrudgingly accepts this but limits it to certain Indians. This attitude does not prevent his seeking out the land to the west. In final development of this work, the tone of Murray's attitude becomes one of self-protection rather than intolerance; the sympathy of the novel is with the pioneer and his cause—his fight for self-preservation—but a measure of sympathy has also been given to the Indian. This attitude is very close to the almost clinical approach found in the novel *Drums Along the Mohawk*, which has been previously described. It is this current of feeling that permits the pioneer to fight the Indians, to guide armies against them, yet to remain basically loyal to his own creed.

THE QUEST FOR WORK AND PROFIT

The role of work in the lives of the pioneers was of no small consequence. Life for these people was one task after another with but occasional respites; there was not for them a forty-hour work week and two-week vacations. The novels display the work of the pioneers with varying degrees of intensity, dependent upon the nature of the novel—the locale and the adventure—and the time of publication. Beyond this depiction of the work load and more significant in terms of this study are the frequent allusions in a group of novels to the merits of work and to certain associated values. These representations are particularly strong

[27] Minnie H. Moody, *Long Meadows*, 362.

in the novels of the 1930's; there are manifestations in other years as well, but they are less pronounced.

Exceptional for the total lack of emphasis on work are the novels of the first decade, 1900–10. The characters are not shown in the situations of labor nor is there particular reference made to this aspect of daily life. The concerns of these novels are adventurous and romantic and are not keyed to day-by-day routine existence. In short, these novels are typical romances of the turn of the century period. In decreasing frequency such novels are also found in the subsequent decades, with the realistic approach becoming more prominent as the years pass.

There are several exceptions in the romantic fiction of this period. The first is in *The Virginian*. Within the usual romantic structure and without really soiling the hero's hands, this novel through its hero expresses a doctrine of hard, honest work and rejects both the easy and illegal way of gain. A man has to earn his advances and has to show his worth before he achieves. This concept seems less foreign to the period when it is put in the context of the Rooseveltian philosophy—an active, working, strenuous life—that dominates the novel and the characterization of the hero. However, in these respects it sets a tone different from the other works of the period.

The second variation is found in the novels of gold mining in California which are introduced at the end of this decade. These novels present an idea about the efficacy of work which is repeated in such novels of the overland trail in which the characters must choose between the lures of California gold or Oregon land. And the lure—gold—defines a course of easy money which becomes repugnant to the characters.

The most direct pronouncements are found in the earliest novel of this type, *The City of Six* (1910). The main characters in search of adventure and gold are permitted to make a strike, to become wealthy—and to stay that way. They are able to do this because of the drive, efficiency, and business acumen of one of their members who organizes their efforts and manages their stake into prosperity. The mining-camp vices do not succeed in undermining the solid, no-foolishness virtue of this character. There are frequent sermons about the evils of shiftlessness, gambling, and spendthrift, carousing habits. Honest work and careful investment of time and income create wealth; good hard work also effects sound attitudes and habits, stability and acclaim. There is some contradiction in the idleness of the hero but he finds himself and his role in life eventually.

The characters in *Gold* are less astute and lose their sudden wealth; they realize, however, what they have found, as is shown in this conversation:

"... fresh gold is easy to get but almighty hard to keep."

"Do you know," he said suddenly, "I believe we're on the right track. It isn't the gold. That is a bait ... that attracts the world to these shores. It's the country. The gold brings them ... some, like us, will stick. And after the gold is dug and scattered and all but forgotten, we will find that we have fallen heirs to an empire."[28]

All the characters in these novels turn to the land, realizing that in it is true value, not as property but in terms of the merits of individual effort and accomplishment and the natural role of man. Those who have gained some fortune manage to make use of it to this end.

The Covered Wagon typifies the overland trail novels in which this conflict of gold and land is presented. In addition to the rejection of easy gains in terms of building and stability of character, the issue of country and man's destiny are thrown into the argument. The solid citizens go to Oregon; Banion, the adventurer hero, takes a short leave from his real destiny in Oregon to try his luck and skill in the gold streams. After achieving some fortune, he goes the way of other heroes—back to the land—symbolized in this novel by Oregon.

The novels of the fifteen- or twenty-year period starting at 1911 which are not strictly adventure stories begin to show the

[28] Stewart E. White, *Gold*, 437.

work and trials of the pioneer not through comments about work but through evidence of work itself. Cather's works, *O Pioneers* and *My Antonia*, Rolvaag's *Giants in the Earth*, and Quick's *Vandemark's Folly* illustrate the toil as well as the energy and enthusiasm of the pioneers. Other novels move in the same direction. In these there may be an occasional allusion to the value of and need for work to achieve both success and happiness, but for the most part such "messages" are indirect. (The less effective the novel in literary quality the greater is the frequency of the direct comments.)

In this respect do these works differ markedly from a group published primarily in the nineteen thirties. Going beyond a display of travail and hardihood, these novels offer a point of view about the nature and value of work. This view sometimes takes the form of simple sermons and sometimes ranges into superficial economic analyses.

One relatively uncomplicated expression of this idea can be seen in *Heroine of the Prairies*. These homely people striving for their degree of security against hunger and disaster are constantly at work. Everyone in the family is occupied at all times: the youngsters even knit socks while walking to school. Wasting time is sinful and there is none of it. The neighbors on the frontier are shown to be similar in their attitude and diligence. They are not afraid to add to their own tasks the helping of a distressed neighbor, with no thought of return.

A contrast to these plain people is suggested in several novels in the form of city people or the unemployed. A life of ease and wealth, of a do-nothing routine, is allied to personal and moral disintegration. The easy life leads to purposelessness and falseness, while hard, honest work is the essence of a complete and wholesome life. In *Spring Came on Forever*, for example, we are shown the growth of superficiality and false display along with personal weakness in the post-frontier generations. These characters have it too easy; they disintegrate with the lessened work. Only the return to the realities of work and land can save their

future. Similarly, in *The Limestone Tree,* the frivolous useless-
ness of several New Orleans–bred characters who expect to be
waited on is contrasted with those who work and do for themselves. It is clear that the latter represent the more positive value.

Another aspect of the value of work is illustrated in the Conrad
Richter trilogy. Basically, his heroine Sayward Luckett Wheeler
represents the concept that hard work is both honest and necessary for the proper training and development of people. She lives
and breathes this point of view. Her life is made up of work
performed naturally, without question or desire for anything
different. In later years, she argues against her youngest son's
feeling that working was disgraceful because they were rich,
that he should not have to work in the field like a hired hand. He
feels that release from work would lead to happiness and human
virtue. Sayward contends the opposite view: emotional disenchantment—unhappiness, dissatisfaction with life, inability to
deal with life—are brought on by lack of work.

> What gave folks "narve strings" today and made them soft so
> they couldn't stand what folks could when she was young? . . . It
> had taken a wild and rough land to raise the big butts she saw
> when first she came here, and she reckoned it took a rough and
> hard life to breed the kind of folks she knew as a young woman.
> If you made it easy for folks, it seemed like their hardihood had
> to pay for it. . . . which one of her young ones was it she had
> raised the softest, done the most for? . . . Wasn't it the same
> one that could take life and his country the least and wanted to
> change God's world . . . ? It was the same with sick folks . . . they
> got to feeling the world ought to be changed and softened, cen-
> tered toward themselves.[29]

A powerful figure, Sayward—competent, assured, stable, steadfast—symbolizes in herself the measured success and value of
this creed.

The relative value of money is denied particularly when seen
as a primary objective and when it blocks personal, develop-

[29] Conrad Richter, *The Town,* 409–10.

mental goals. In the cases already cited there are some indirect negative allusions to money and wealth as contrasted to the merits of land and work. In other novels, more direct reference is made. The hero of *Song of Years,* in a moment of self-revelation, is conscience stricken and sees himself defiled when he finds himself putting money and personal gain before duty, helpfulness to others, and honor. Other characters question mercenary values and show an approved disinclination for money. This attitude is expressed in the refusal to accept money for helpful services and in return for creative work. Happiness is gained from the pursuit of a simple, undemanding life based on the fulfillment of basic needs; happiness is derived from simple satisfactions for which you do not need much money or which money cannot buy. In *The Proselyte* the heroine points up this attitude. "How folks can imagine that riches bring happiness is beyond me. All history and all religion teach differently."[30]

The profit motive as well as the significance of money is discussed in *Long Hunt.* Rinnard, the hero, scoffs at the need for money. When a friend wants to increase his monetary return in a business deal, Rinnard exclaims that a man needs only enough to live on. Indeed, at a later time, he takes a job knowing that he is unfairly paid by current standards but knowing also that what he gets paid is sufficient for him. Only this matters. He seems to suggest that man should ask for less and be content with simple needs and satisfactions, not only to avoid greed but also in terms of economics. This concept is furthered by his reaction to profit made by a middleman who has not "worked" for it. The middleman's fifty-per-cent cut is not only a dishonest division of profit in view of his limited labor but also unnecessary for what he needs to live on. Of course, these ideas are not overplayed in this novel, but when they are read in conjunction with his strong disapproval of the greedy and the money-mad rich, his creed of independent activity and working to maintain oneself, and his tendency to ignore the money value of an enterprise—the highest

[30] Susan Ertz, *The Proselyte,* 322.

bidder gets ignored in favor of the neediest or of sharing alike—a definite economic attitude is suggested which seems related to the economic issues of the day.

The reactions of authors to the national economic situation can be seen in certain comments and motivational activity in some of the novels. (The authors are not always so subtle as in *Long Hunt.*) The hero of *The Invasion* enters the fur trade but resists joining a large fur organization to show greater profits or enlarging his own enterprise beyond his means or control. For him it is a matter of personal and economic independence. He wants to pay his own way, to stand his own losses if they arise, to keep his own credit—these all being noteworthy values in the novel. In his energetic work, financial stability, and pursuit of a steady life unaffected by the urgency of much money, power, or prestige, he stands symbolically above the problems of the twenties and thirties. Not everyone is so wise. The post-frontier generation in *Spring Came on Forever* loses sight of the values and principles of the pioneers and falls on bad days.

> ... if they had not bought so lavishly, had not gone so deeply into debt, had stayed on the first good old half-section without purchasing any more acres—above all, had *worked* it themselves, earning their living there, content with what it would bring, as his father and grandfather had been before him for their daily bread, this great indebtedness would not be looming always before him like some fearsome giant.[31]

Here again the idea of work and simple desires is posed in opposition to the accumulation of wealth and luxury, both of which are not essential to either well-being or happiness. These are persistent elements in the depiction of this value.

This aspect of the discussion would not be complete without mention of the comments relative to government intervention in a few of these novels. In *All Ye People*, the hero witnesses a scene in which an old, poorhouse woman is being auctioned for

[31] Bess Streeter Aldrich, *Spring Came on Forever*, 264.

her keep, apparently an early form of relief. When the price gets low enough, the old woman bids to care for herself and gets the privilege, to the acclaim of the hero for her spirit of independence and self-esteem. Less subtle is the response in *Song of Years* to a proposal to exempt debtors from their just debts.

> "America's based on honesty and fairness. That's what America *is*. . . . Our liberties we prize. And our rights we will maintain. They'll never in this world be humans with *equal* brains or *equal ability to get ahead*. Consequently they'll never be equal amounts of property owned . . . so the results of man's labor will never be equal.
>
> ". . . some of 'em has more ability, foresight, ingenuity, and gumption than I have, and others not as much. But gettin' out of my debts because I didn't do so well as some, or seein' my neighbors shuffle off *their* debts because they didn't do as well as me— *no, sir.* . . . That ain't America. Our rights we will maintain.
>
> "It might be nice and benevolent to try and fix over the laws to help out some poor cuss. But even if it looks benevolent on the surface it ain't good horse sense. . . . I hope our *benevolent* friends won't tinker up the law to prevent a honest feller from payin' his debts if he wants to."[32]

The attitudes of these authors and several others who speak out against government bureaucracy and government intervention are not far removed from the ideas presented in the earlier portion of this section. A line of relationship can be drawn to the concepts of self-help and honest work. In fact, these authors find glory in work as well as the positive personal development of the pioneer. In thus speaking out against government intervention, in thus contrasting the independent, fierce pioneer spirit to the poor unfortunate who cannot stand on his own feet and making it seem as if that same governmental sympathy is cutting the legs out from under his strength and pride, the value of work—in association with simplicity of life and a dogged individual effort to succeed—is enhanced.

[32] Bess Streeter Aldrich, *Song of Years*, 226–27.

The novels of the forties are similar to those of the preceding decade in the general impression of pioneer life and work routine, there being an equivalent emphasis on presenting a realistic view of frontier life. The greater proportion of the novels are generally ungilded tales of pioneer life and progress. The adventures are proportunately equal in number, but they, too, show the characters performing the tasks of their trade or those necessary for life in the particular locale.

In these terms, the attitudes toward work are somewhat automatic in response. Generally, the characters throw themselves into the job at hand, making it an accepted part of their lives. Indeed, there was no lack of this type of portrayal in the novels of the previous decade. The chief difference between the novels of these two decades is in the extent of discussion about work and its merits: fewer characters comment about it in the forties; fewer situations point directly—with seeming author's aforethought—to this value.

The specific values presented are cut of the same cloth as those already discussed. Idleness is frowned upon; it is important to work one's way. Making money—particularly easy money—is not important; profit should come from one's own labor and not at the expense of others. One hero expresses his credo of enterprise and work through a sarcastic note: "Strike rich, go crazy, peter out, die pauper."[33] This and other illustrations in the novels also suggest the role of work in the strengthening and building of a man.

As one would expect from the softer line in these works, there are few of the allusions to the broader economic or government issues that are evident in the novels of the thirties. The general pattern reflects the concept of free enterprise which develops parallel to the image of the strong independent man. These concepts permit certain characters to act in their own interest, not only in pursuit of "amounting to something" but also with his sights on his profits. In several novels, a profit and business-is-

[33] W. D. Steele, *Diamond Wedding*, 232.

business attitude prevails, a stress contradictory to that of the preceding decade, sometimes in juxtaposition with a helpful, friends-and-country-first ethic. In this regard these heroes act in achieving of personal goals despite the law or in knowing disregard of the law. Part of the rationale for this lies in the independent nature of the frontiersman: he makes his own way; he objects to being ordered; his interests are more vital to him than those of the government. A less frequently cited reason refers to the American way:

> Our fur traders did not have government subsidies. . . . That is because we are a democracy and we give special privileges to none, equal privileges to all. . . . But ours is a system of private enterprise—not government aid and protection for one group of stockholders in one favored company.[34]

In another novel, *Perilous Journey*, there is conjecture over a communistic community as opposed to the American idea, but it meets with revulsion. As the several novels develop there is a tendency for the self-interestedness to be tempered by a realization of broader human and national interests, but it is never entirely discredited.

The total presentation of the concept of work shows the influence of both the literary and social environment. The gradual demise of the romantic influences on literature permitted the development of a down-to-earth portrait of the pioneer and allowed for a view of life that encompassed mundane activities. These are more or less emphasized according to the locale and stress of the work but become accepted factors in the presentation. The national economic disaster of 1929 and the subsequent political-economic activities are apparent influences in the 1930's and somewhat residually in the following decade. These events are manifested in veiled and not-so-veiled comments and reactions of the characters. The independent pioneer seems to have symbolized to these authors a way of life at variance to that being

[34] M. M. McNeilly, *Each Bright River*, 57.

created by a deteriorating society and an active government. The frontier novel became, in part, an evocation of the spirit of that past in terms of the nature and value of work in the development of man and country as well as an attempt—feeble though it appears—to speak out against the direction of the nation.

FRONTIER LAW AND JUSTICE

The frontier was not quite lawless. Without the fixed written laws of an organized government, the pioneer, who may have come with certain fixed ideas and habits, was forced by the very nature of the area to create law and to define justice—to take the law into his own hands. In displaying the several interrelated codes of law and justice, the novels reveal and further strengthen the patterns of character and values already established in earlier discussions. Also, the variance of emphasis in these representations offers further insight into the nuances of literary change over the course of fifty years.

In taking the law into their own hands—this phrase is used advisedly for it conveys the sense and the tone of their activity— the pioneers were not simply undertaking a task that no one else would do, at least not in all of the novels. This activity is shown through their manner and attitude to represent an essence of character and belief. These are men of independence and strength; they look to themselves for the most part. In this respect, making their own codes is a natural development of one of their chief characteristics, of one of their special, guarded drives.

One aspect of this code, particularly in the novels of the first two decades, concerns vengeance and man's need, justification, and authority to seek satisfaction for a wrong done him. In the early works—1900–10—seeking revenge is not only an accepted form of behavior, but, it is honorable and a factor of manly pride and self-respect to seek retribution for a slight or injury. Acts of vengeance, found in many of these novels include killing the enemy, usually with an appropriate comment regarding the hero's honor and justification. In *The Heritage*, Frederic's seeking of revenge is seen in this favorable light; one can perceptibly see the author patting him on the back for his courage and manly values, his maintenance of personal honor. The right for vengeance is certainly given the hero in *The Throwback*, whose life and fortune are threatened by his unscrupulous cousin. Negating law, he puts the conflict on a personal level maintaining an eye-for-an-eye code which is consistent in all of this man's activities; any slight or injury is repaid in kind. The three Zane Grey novels of the Ohio frontier present Louis Wetzel, whose life is dedicated to the avenging of his family's murder at the hands of Indians as an admirable figure. Heroes who act in keeping with this value when the situation presents itself are similarly admired.

Inherent in this code is the attitude that a man has a right and duty to fight for his honor, his loved ones, his fortune. This is his very manhood. This attitude is repeated in other novels, in which the feeling of revenge is not specified and in which, generally, killing is not as acceptable. *The Virginian* presents such a hero who is essentially opposed to killing except as a last resort in a question of courage and manliness; but he will not back down from a fight. This sense of honor is also evident in *The Covered Wagon*, in which Banion, the hero, righteously fights Woodhull after some insult but refuses to take frontier spoils—gouging his eyes—or to kill his enemy after repeated treachery. An underlying conflict of values seems to exist in such situations between the code of honor and the image of a hero who cannot have blood on his hands.

This conflict represents a real issue in the early works, though it is not overtly discussed. While being honor bound to defend himself and his name—indeed circumstances give him no choice (and provide excuse for his actions)—the hero is often made to seem less brutal. Strict personal codes or extended rationale are provided; or the hero is rescued from direct killing through the intervention of a comrade who fires the fatal bullet or by resorting to hand-to-hand battle.

Despite the manner of battle, these activities and attitudes emphasize two attitudes in relation to law. One of these clearly regards it imperative for a man to act in his own behalf in both determining law and acting on it; this is a point of honor. The second aspect underscores the independent, free nature of the man's spirit and creed. The breaking of custom and even of existent law—though this is infrequently pronounced in these works—to preserve his individuality and special life is basic to his way.

Another development that parallels these concepts, though less frequently illustrated, is the resorting to mob action or lynching by organized groups as a method of resolving difficulties. In the novels dealing with the mining frontier, this takes the form of the vigilante committee which works outside the law to create order. Since the law of the land is ridden with corruption and poorly enforced anyway, these "unlawful" activities are made to seem appropriate and justified in subduing the rabble. The miner's courts are nevertheless not always thorough or fair in their actions and are shown to be subject to various prejudices and momentary whims. In *The Virginian*, the values of law and friendship come into conflict with honor and personal courage. He carries out the lynching of his best friend, for he has given his word and has agreed to the principles of self-determined law in this case and the method of retribution. These heroes are seen as honorable as their motivations are honorable and their purpose designed to create order rather than destroy it. They see in their acts not opposition to law but more speedy and direct enforcement.

Attitudes towards law representing extremes illustrate the variance and shift. In the 1906 novel *The Throwback*, Tom Moonlight believes:

> To one who, like himself, made an aggressive specialty of force, the situation was simple enough. Robert . . . his enemy . . . had the law on his side. . . . The sentiment sustained only the strong hand. The law was a trap—a gin—a snare, resorted to only by weak, scheming, criminal men, who possessed a vicious willingness to filch the goods of their neighbors, while wanting the

stark hardihood to go personally about the villainy. . . . He should not hesitate to confront the situation as became a man. He would shoot down Robert. . . .[35]

On the other extreme, Per Hansa in *Giants in the Earth* (1927), a law-abider, feels guilt and shame when he breaks a frontier land-claim law to save his friend from great loss. He and others like him represent responsibility and will not disavow their association with the community.

In these novels preceding the quarter century, the trend of development of this concept is generally related to the gradual eclipse of the romantic novel. Later works which shifted their point of view away from romance *per se* emphasized less the values of personal honor and self-made law (with the exception of the mountain man novels) so that the sense of justice became less personally oriented. Not the least of these changes are the decline of the revenge motif in terms of honor and the rise of disapproval of killing: the hero of *The Able McLaughlins* (1923), for example, seeks to avenge the rape of his sweetheart but finally decides another killing would not help the situation nor ease his conscience. The privileges of "frontier law"—the spoils to the victor in hand-to-hand battle—are also questioned, diminished by a sense of decency and nonbrutality consistent with a more developed community and social consciousness. In the novels detailing the world of commonplace events and progress, there is little space for such concerns. Indeed a large number of novels offer no incidents involving personal justice for discussion, particularly those of the prairie-farming frontiers.

The novels of the final two decades of this study do offer occasional evidence of attitudes similar to those already represented. The dissimilarity of the material may be taken as evidence of a varied outlook. Examples of the vengeance motif are limited; two of these are *The Great Meadow* and *The Day Must Dawn*. In the first, Berk Jarvis swears to kill his mother's slayer, an Indian. While a captive he comes to see the nonpersonal nature of the

[35] Alfred H. Lewis, *The Throwback*, 194-5.

killing as well as the human side of Indian life; he escapes without taking action. The second novel has the hero, Hugh Murray, agree to support his best friend, who has sworn to avenge a rape. In their plotting to have their act appear as an accident, it is clear they recognize it as unlawful, but they are unwilling to wait for law, and they take the law into their own hands. These characters do not speak in terms of honor but seem to act out of intense emotion. There are several other examples of revenge-seeking, particularly in novels depicting strong individualists as the mountain man in *The Big Sky* and the plantation settler in *Oh, Promised Land*. On the whole, there is an underplaying in these works of both the code of personal vengeance and the satisfaction of personal honor.

This is not to say that direct action on the part of the pioneer is eliminated. In some respects this is as strong as ever. This feeling is emphasized by the development of a strong, dominant figure in modern adventure fiction as well as the realistic approach to the problems of frontier survival. These men can and do take affairs into their own hands, but they do not all react in the same manner.

The use of force, though not necessarily out of direct impulse for revenge, is an expected reaction. Self-defense and offense in preserving their lands and hard-earned improvements are the sole recourse in many frontier situations. The pioneers act accordingly. Killing cannot be avoided; there is little hesitation—certainly not much from a sense of gentility—on the part of these men to kill when necessary. A man had to do what was required to sustain life.

A key concept is involved here. The pioneers could not wait for the militia all of the time. A man had to stand for himself. In matters outside war, the pioneers could not always wait for laws. Justice had to be meted out. Again, a man had to stand for himself, and for his principles. This is the code of independence and direct expression: a man takes action himself.

The interpretation of such direct action offers significant qualifications. A large number of heroes impose limitations and a sense of humanity on their behavior. Thus, although they engage in battles in fulfilling their pioneer roles, they avoid the cruel and the brutal; they oppose thoughtless slaughter and mass destruction. A particular reaction is in terms of Indians. The killing of Indian women and children, or other innocent victims is not condoned. Andrew Benton in *This Land Is Ours*, who leads forays against the Indians as a scout, opposes the treachery at Tippecanoe, both because it is underhanded and because these Indians are faithful to their contract. In *Strife Before Dawn*, Keith Maitland, who has suffered personally at the hands of the Indians, nonetheless is able to be compassionate toward them and to oppose their unwarranted slaughter. These characters manifest broad humanitarian feelings and understanding of the plight of these people.

There are, in addition, a number of novels which speak out through their heroes against violence, not only in terms of personal retribution but in general. This attitude is intertwined with developed feelings of humanity and justice. They oppose brutality and force; they act to avert Indian wars or to bring about assimilation of the races and cultures. In this light they argue against the eye-for-an-eye frontier law, seeking solutions through compromise and peaceful measures—substituting compassion and helpfulness for violence. Examples of such heroes can be found in a variety of novels, including the two already mentioned. Such opposite men as the strong and determined Hercules Dousman in *Bright Journey* and the relatively mild Unwin Shaw in *The Far Country* avoid through principle and temperament anything approaching physical violence. Dousman goes out of his way to remove peaceably a vicious trader who has been undermining his attempts to help the Indians rather than see him come to harm. Killing is equally repugnant to the staid New Englander, Martin Collins, in *Jornada,* and the lusty woodsman hero of *Michael Beam*. Beam suffers great remorse when he is forced to kill in order to avert war; life is a primary value and he opposes those who put their furs before Indian lives. A trend of such thought is suggested in several community-oriented novels, such as those of the overland trail—like *Don't You Cry for Me*—and the incipient settlement—like *The Trees* and *Genesee Fever*—in which a more organized society is evident. In these instances, the influence of women and the education of the hero often play roles in determining the stress on more humane or civilized values.

Taken as a group, the novels of the second quarter century present a theme of justice which is practically nonexistent in the first and second decades and only fleetingly introduced in the first half of the third. A consciousness of fair dealings, of honesty and high moral standards in human relations, is more and more apparent. This has been partially demonstrated in the foregoing discussion.

Many illustrations are seen of this concern for justice in the reactions of the many heroes to the Indian-pioneer relationships in such diverse books as *Cimarron, Wind Over Wisconsin,* and *Mighty Mountain.*[36] The injustice of the white man's acts, his deceit and the ignoring of the Indians' rights and claims are portrayed. The heroes oppose these activities, acting out a code of honesty and fair play that does not waver. Understanding and compassion keynote their reaction to the Indian; helpfulness and friendship their actions. The hero thus symbolizes humanity and justice.

Further examples, evident in these novels, replace the racial-political overtones with social-economic ones. Depending upon the nature of the novel, the point of view becomes one of vigorous defense of the downtrodden and the helpless—made so by a selfish society and a thoughtless government in *Cimarron*—or one of milder rebuke of smallness and stratification of society resulting from narrow, superficial attitudes toward people in *Heroine of the Prairies.* Other novels speak out generally against injustice

[36] This concern is related to the changing view of the Indian in a historical and social sense.

in human dealings in which understanding and compassion are replaced by inhumanity and selfishness in the names of safety, security, profit, or false honor. All of these stress faith and the duty of one human to another in the achievement of justice.

Several novels make a strong case against the government in terms of its handling of human and social affairs. The most outspoken of these are *Cimarron, Nebraska Coast,* and the Mormon novel *Children of God.* Politicians, corrupt officials, and lobbies of businessmen come in for their share of negative comments. Most of these are in terms of the common man, helpless before the machine and the powerful influence of nonfrontiersmen in government circles. The issues usually involve personal greed leading to the unjust division of land and resources. The Indian question is also involved, particularly in *Cimarron,* with the government's repeated deceit coming under direct attack. A host of other novels of this period add fuel to this attack by showing government officials in deceitful roles, although few are as outspoken as is the Ferber work. *Children of God,* which recounts the trials of the Mormons, emphasizes the loss of religious freedom and the lack of government intervention to prevent the mob actions and to protect the rights and safety of these citizens. In detailing the events and passions of this problem, the whole body of people as well as government faces the finger of guilt.

The attitudes towards law are mixed in these later novels. There is a recognition in several works that laws are not always equal to justice. The heroes in these works act according to their independent character and sense of right by opposing these laws. A few leave the law behind them in hopes of either permanent escape or of building something new. They do not bow to injustice merely to keep out of trouble. Yet, basically there is no opposition among the majority of these men to the idea of law. Value is seen in orderly procedures. It is the structure of the law process and the activity of the people which make it successful in preventing both lawlessness and injustice. If the people do not act to safeguard their rights, then the mob takes over, as in

Mighty Mountain, or petty corruption manifests itself, as in *Nebraska Coast,* or human indignity and suffering appear, as in *Cimarron.*

The totally independent man who disavows law and organized society and maintains this vow is somewhat the solitary figure. He exists unto himself without regard for any existing society. As has been pointed out in a previous chapter, escape from organized society is short lived as many of these fade into compromise or disaster. Their heightened code of individuality stands, however, as a beacon pointing out this element which underlies the nature of the other heroes. In effect, though it takes on a human-social consciousness, their stand in opposition to those about them is part of the same spirit exhibited by the individualists.

The concepts of justice and reactions to law developed in these more recent works show a social orientation not found in the earlier novels. This is so despite the continuing—though somewhat altered—presentation of the pioneer as an independent, direct individual. Activities and beliefs of characters are tinged with humanitarianism and social consciousness, as well as the more recent attitudes toward the Indian. In this regard, the role of law and the development of law is less a vague, nebulous question to quarrel with or to escape from; where there is escape, though it is a personal reaction, it has social overtones.

The development of realism has repercussions in the presentation of the idea of personal law in relation to social orientation. On the one hand there is much less of the personal vengeance code with its romantic aspects; nor is there the hesitancy towards the hero's involvement in direct killing. Realistically, killing in terms of self-protection forms a general backdrop; this is done rather matter-of-factly in some novels, while in others the frequency of notation represents an affinity with a trend toward violence in other contemporary adventure fiction. However, the social-humanitarian attitudes manage to temper the majority of these, as has been shown, so that the resultant image is somewhat a composite figure of the strict humanitarian and the ultra-free individual: a large group adopts some attitudes of both types. This hero acts according to the requirements of the frontier but remains cognizant of social-civilized mores of justice and human dignity. He becomes personally involved but less so from a self-centered code than from a social one.

THE SPIRIT OF THE FRONTIER

Such a country would breed a race of heroes, men built and knitted together to endure.[37]

A study of the novels of the frontier would be remiss if it did not mention the spirit of the pioneers that is woven into the fabric of these works. This, appearing in the novels throughout the fifty-year period, is like a glowing thread illuminating the pattern of the pioneers' lives and characters and attempting to show the glory and heroism of their trials and successes. Of course, there are novels throughout the period which make no apparent attempt to convey such feelings and which concentrate on telling their individual story.

Basically, the spirit of the frontier is portrayed in two ways. One of these is overt in that the author takes time out to call the reader's attention to some heroic purpose or attitude; the author may be somewhat less direct by putting such comments into the mouths of the characters. The other method is interpretive. Being indirect in approach, the work conveys the attributes and progress of the pioneer so that a sense of the spirit is developed. Clearly, the latter lacks the propagandistic, waving-the-flag quality of the direct approach and often defines glory and heroism in more solid terms as a result. Each of these, however, deals with similar concepts.

Many of the works eulogize the pioneers. Events dramatize their courage, fearlessness and dynamic strength; comparisons with nonpioneers point up their vitality and drive. Their fierce quest for independence, for an untrammelled life, is exalted as a holy goal. Their ambition and progress, their perseverance, their

[37] Elizabeth M. Roberts, *The Great Meadow*, 13.

willingness to face privation and danger are built into a tradition of Americanism, for though they may have been selfish as often as self-sacrificing, they drove the nation forward.

> Maybe this is the way it is. There's some that must go before and some that must come after. There's some that must cut down the wilderness and break the rough ground and maybe wet it with their blood. And then there's some that will come after and live on the fat of the land. God must sort out which is which.[38]

This selection for the forward position, this giving of life, defines the heroism that strode with the pioneers.

Novels approach this presentation from different avenues, sometimes depicting the single individual, sometimes the group. Though there may be a hero figure in the group canvas, the activities and character of the settlement as in *The Day Must Dawn* or the train personnel as in *The Way West* carry the elements of the pioneer spirit. The ennobling of an individual, be it female as in *The Trees* or male as in *Giants in the Earth,* is equally effective. Variations in literary technique can be shown in several extremes. Zane Grey's *The Spirit of the Border* in its very title and the explanations of a character-spokesman points to the heroic elements; indeed this spokesman figuratively pats the hero on the back. In John Weld's *Don't You Cry for Me,* one character rather obviously remarks, ". . . think of it as an adventure! We're pioneers—people of courage and fortitude!"[39] His fellow travelers need to be reminded as does, perhaps, the reader. This is quite an opposite effect from that in Willa Cather's *O Pioneers,* whose heroine needs no such words to express her remarkable qualities. The reader knows from her behavior what she is made of.

It does not take much in many works to scratch a pioneer and come up with an American personified. His qualities are somehow representative of the nation—the new breed of men. These define American superiority and indestructibility which

[38] Agnes S. Turnbull, *The Day Must Dawn,* 224.
[39] John Weld, *Don't You Cry for Me,* 53.

are either directly alluded to or evoked by the inevitable progress and success of the pioneer. The frontier is credited with begetting the man, with developing and enhancing these desirable qualities. For, the frontier notwithstanding, it is also suggested that certain characteristics precede the coming to the frontier, these being inherent in the national character (as the result of facing a frontier) or growing out of the American system and concepts of human nature. The freedom of the individual to express his individuality, and the opportunity given by the frontier for that expression are the roots of the matter.

> . . . Americans are a remarkable breed. By trusting human nature and putting folks on their own responsibility, we have released all kinds of energies and curiosities and talents.[40]

It is these elements fused and forged by the frontier—its demands and hardships—that make the American so remarkable and unbeatable. The more difficult the trial, the greater the outcome: "Hammer the American hard enough and you forge the best weapon in the world."[41] Place obstacles in his path and the greater the obstacle the surer his surmounting of it—no matter who or what stood in his way.

> "I don't say that the Americans have the right to come here and take your country away from you. But once they have set out to do it they will do it. You may kill a great many of them in your canyon, but the others will go over or around your army. We Americans are an obstinate race. If we want anything we don't stop to ask what right we have to it. We take it." . . .
>
> ". . . but there is something in their blood that makes it impossible to stay in one place. They cannot stop. . . . I think now they will go on until they reach the Pacific. Justice may be on your side, though I am told that you have not always been just to your own people. But they have a justice of their own. . . . It is called . . . manifest destiny."[42]

[40] Marthedith Furnas, *The Far Country*, 205.
[41] Hervey Allen, *The Forest and the Fort*, 157.
[42] Robert L. Duffus, *Jornada*, 219–20.

The attributes referred to in this quotation are not necessarily admirable in the long view, but this speaker and others propose them with pride and some righteousness. They are part and parcel of America's greatness and her successful progress toward the prophetic "manifest destiny."

The sense of purpose and destiny is a part of this pattern: the spread of the United States and its culture, the taming of the wildernesss, the broadening of the base of humanity, the promise of civilization.

> Men were going out to suffer— . . . to die—that others might live— and by living, build. That others might come in safety . . . to make plans with never an obstacle save . . . nature; that a generation might arise where they had fallen. . . . this was not a thing of today—it was a matter of Tomorrow![43]

Recognition of belonging to one's country, that it is worth striving and spilling blood for, grows out of these feelings. Such an attitude is illustrated in the many novels dealing with wars or the Oregon trail, and other areas wrested from other peoples. The destiny and good of the nation, its power and glory are prime considerations.

In this view of things, personal destiny is insignificant as compared with the nation and the future. Another aspect emphasizes the soaring of the individual spirit in expanding, in seeing the new and wild, in being free and alive. Here is associated the glory and passion of the individual pioneer and it forms the basic material for the sense of destiny. The preceding discussion of the American character shows the interrelationship of the individual to the concept of manifest destiny.

It must be pointed out in passing that this is not a persistent idea. A number of novels, particularly those featuring isolationist heroes, show no interest whatsoever in any destiny; their only purpose is to live and to live apart. Other works so emphasize

[43] C. R. Cooper, *The Last Frontier*, 198.

details of life and events that there is little direct concern for anything else.

With the inevitability of progress in the novels being the proof of the tasted pudding, the discussion comes around full circle. A series of novels, nostalgic in tone and sermons in quality, harken to the past in terms of the present. The work and character of the forefathers—the pioneers—is thus extolled and raised upon the pedestal for the unfortunate future generations who did not have the good fortune to be a part of those vital, grand times to look upon in awe and admiration.

The Image of the Pioneer

THE IMAGE of the pioneer in the American novel, 1900–50, is a changing one. Although the basic outlines of the image are similar—physical attributes, characteristics, attitudes—throughout the period, there are numerous variations in the details of the portrayal. In addition, the mechanics and underlying principles of literature have undergone marked alteration in the course of these fifty years, with a direct relationship between the changes in literary presentation and the changing image.

The pioneer also emerges from the novels as a regional figure. Each of the frontiers—the forest, the prairie, the mountain and range, the mines, the overland trail—has its type or types. Although there are certain overlapping qualities among all of these types, or at least among two or three, each frontier by its very nature calls for a variation of purpose or character and, indeed, of value system. Simply stated, it cannot be said that there is even one pioneer image of a changing nature. More accurately, there are several related regional images, each developing in more or less the same direction, in keeping with literary trends.

One notable aspect of change is the choice of locale of the novels and the frontier type being depicted. In the first two decades an almost exclusive attention is given the forest frontier; all of these novels portray the free forester type—the hunter and scout. Novels depicting this figure continue throughout the fifty-year period, but the exclusiveness ceases. After 1930, the farmer on the forest frontier, who had made a late entry as a focus of attention, matches in strength of numbers his wandering contemporary. Putting these together, the forest frontier locale is featured in the bulk of the novels in each decade except the twenties. However, the shift of emphasis—or the de-emphasis of the free forester—brought about by the introduction of the forest farmer, is strengthened by the novels of the prairie and the overland trail, both of which present the farmer pioneer. Although represented by occasional earlier works, these works appear in quantity after 1925 and 1930 respectively. Thus, together with the forest farmer novels, a concentration on the farm-oriented pioneer emerges in the novels of the last two decades. This trend is only partly modified by the novels of the mountain man, which are few in number, and all of which appear after 1926. The few works of the mining frontier, which are somewhat outside the general pattern, all appear prior to 1926. This general distribution is significant in the creation of the pioneer image.

A relationship exists between the eras of the different settings and the literary trends of the first half of the century. The romantic-idealistic tradition that overlapped from the Victorian period into the first decade of this century is evident in the choice of locale and the pioneer's motivation. The focus on the forest frontier permitted an evocation of this tradition by virtue of the elements of mystery, danger, and adventure associated with this frontier; the mining frontier is similarly endowed. The prairie frontier and the overland trail, less imbued with glamour and romance and more associated with arduous travail, were put aside. The plain world of working people could not meet the standards and impressions of the romantic tradition. Therefore, this world forms only a vague backdrop to the adventurous, romantic exercises of the early novels. The growing force of realism in literature reaches the novel of the frontier after World War I and affects the basic plot so that plain people and common affairs are depicted. The shift of emphasis to the farmer on both the forest and other frontiers illustrates this. Realism in literature affects other aspects as well, the character and values of the pioneer and the events and details of the frontier drama, which will be discussed in a later section of this chapter.

THE IMAGE

Marked uniformity of certain physical traits characterize the pioneer heroes throughout the entire period. These may be generalized with such terms as strength, endurance, vitality. The pioneer hero is usually foremost among his fellows in his ability to withstand the rigors and to meet the demands of the frontier. He frequently performs Herculean feats which are generally beyond the abilities of the others. In terms of size and stature, he is usually built upon grand proportions, being tall, solid, and broadly muscular. In this respect, too, he generally surpasses the other pioneers.

Two types of variations occur in the development of the physical image, one being relative to the frontier scene, the other to the literary fashion. Somewhat subtle changes can be seen from one frontier region to the others in terms of stature and breadth of the heroes. Compared with the foresters, the mountain men and the men of the range tend towards a rangier build, which perhaps fits with their occupational necessity of riding horses. (The rangy look is certainly in keeping with the more developed image of the cowboy of western fiction, the cowboy being a postfrontier relative of the pioneer of the range.) Many of the farmers, particularly those on the prairie and on the overland trail, seem less agile and bulkier, this impression being carried both by the nature of their lives and work and by their somewhat more heavy-set physiques. There is an age factor difference in the overland trail group, the hero frequently being older than the pioneer hero of the other regions. The more ordinary nature of this group becomes apparent in the wider range of description; it is not so easy to stereotype this particular hero as in some of the other groups of works.

The second variation in the physical description of the pioneer hero is in the manner of presentation. On the one hand there is a more detailed depiction of the hero's physical structure with the passing years. In some works there would almost seem to be a photographic muscle-by-muscle accounting of his attributes. On the other hand there is a tendency in the recent works toward a more rugged quality in the hero. He is less Godlike in his perfection of face and physique; the emphasis is on the strength and character of these. Presumably, these alterations are influenced by the realistic impetus in literature. By portraying the frontiersman as less nearly perfect, there may have been a conscious or unconscious attempt on the part of the authors to construct a more likely, a more real figure, thus being truer to life. Such a portrait may, however, be a manifestation of a societal inclination for more rugged qualities in its heroes. The greater physical display which grows out of the descriptive detail can also be related to broader acceptance in society of both discussion and display of the human body. Such detail as appears in the mid-century novel would have been horrifying to the average reader at the turn of the century; while the reader of today does not necessarily expect this as part of his diet, he is not overly sensitive to it. He would react probably with some distaste to the vaguely panegyrized descriptions found in the early works. This evidence relates in addition to the development of the modern, neoromantic adventure story which builds upon elements of physical display, sexual suggestion, shock and violence (also evident in other aspects of some of the recent pioneer novels) in keeping with a broader social acceptability and the demand of a segment of the public. The tendency toward rugged manliness of the heroes, the details and the occasional excess of display point to a sense of reality joined with a new literary-social tradition that organizes its own standards and mores.

Occupational skills vary in a more pronounced way from region to region. The association of skills with environmental needs is direct. The frontiersman of the forest is a specialist in woodlore and scouting, and he is a superb, phenomenal marksman; he is often adept with other weapons such as the tomahawk, the bow and the knife. His knowledge of animal habits and his handling of them enhance his scouting ability and marksmanship. In these respects he usually figures as the supreme exponent of ability in the novel with only an occasional legendary, historical frontiersman bettering him. Closely related to the free forester is the mountain man whose skills are basically identical, though there is less emphasis on marksmanship. The man of the range, in line with his forebears of the mountain, displays like skills. However, the environmental refinements of the range alter the emphases slightly. The stress on marksmanship is increased, but the greatest refinement is his horsemanship along with various accompanying skills of his trade. Like their forester counterpart, each of these heroes is rarely matched in ability by other pioneers. This semblance of uniformity in frontier skills is broken by the distinctly different emphasis in the novels featuring the farmer pioneer. A few of the farmers on the forest frontier have the skills of their nomadic contemporaries for the environment required such abilities, but the greater proportion lack both the extraordinary adeptness in the woods and the marksmanship; primarily this pioneer is a husbandman. So, too, are the pioneers on the overland trail and those of the prairie who exhibit even less skill with the rifle and practically none of the scouting lore. The one who does is a rare hero indeed, but every now and then the apparently traditional nature of these skills is adhered to and the hero manifests some of them. The novels of the mines illustrate the diversity of skills found in these regional works when they bring these several types—the hunter, the farmer, the cowboy—together into one novel. Each is distinct in his abilities and skills. Significantly, it takes several characters to promote the action, each offering his specialty in the plot's developments, for none is equal to all requirements.

On the whole, the novels of the frontier convey the extraordinary qualities of the pioneer. The sense of the unbelievable degree of skill appears more muted with the progress of the century, but this is not entirely because the extreme examples have been tempered with reality. At least, not directly. The modifying effect of the novels of the farmer pioneer, introduced primarily after 1925, does much to lessen the impact of the phenomenal skills, for, as has been noted, the farmers rarely perform prodigious feats. In comparing the depiction of skills of the forest pioneer in the early novels with the recent ones, there can be seen a like number of extravagant claims, though there is a decrease in the proportionate quantity. In the later works, however, there is usually given a background of education and training which help to make the skills more probable. The hero does not come from an aristocratic background and emerge suddenly as an accomplished scout as in some early works. Also, there are no obvious inconsistencies in the display of skills in the later works as there are in several of those of the first decade. A further example can perhaps be made of the mountain-man hero, even though it is not possible to make an internal comparison with early works. The figure, in many ways the most extravagant of the frontier types, does not manifest the excesses of proficiency that are identifiable in the heroes of the earlier decades. He is certainly very skilled, sometimes incomparable, but he is not infallible and he has followed the long, hard route.

The effort of establishing the probable degree of skill in order to gauge the extent of romantic-realistic influences upon this aspect of the image is made doubly difficult by my basic unfamiliarity with what was specifically required in the learning and performance of these skills, as well as the distance in time from the frontier. A sceptical outlook and an awareness of the crudeness of weapons of that day and of the raw, untrained quality of many of the pioneers is balanced to some extent by a consciousness that the very sustenance of life in such an environment must have forced the learning of skills. In the final analysis, the reading tells the story partly in terms of the overall context of the works and partly in terms of consistency and acceptability of details. The less extreme portrayal seems the more likely; the modifications already noted indicate that the novels of the more current decades generally can be accepted as plausible.

The character and values of the pioneer developed in the novels establish a similar pattern of uniformity and variance. The variances are generally regional in origin, the environment determining the occupation which in turn designates the purpose of the pioneer who came there. This further defines certain specific values that create other distinctions. Certain characteristics, however, deriving from basic drives that cause the individual to head west in the first place, establish a unity in the images.

One way or another the pioneers all want a new country. Although their specific reasons vary, they wish to leave the settled East behind them; there is a general distaste for the organized world they left behind for various reasons—crowded conditions, limited opportunities, the meanness of men and governments, hurt pride. However, there is not a like agreement of objectives among the pioneers. Two cores of purposes exist between which there are several modifications and around which cluster key variations in value structures. These two cores may be simply stated as being wilderness oriented and settlement oriented. The mountain men, many of the foresters, and the rangers thrive on the wilderness; the farmers basically are interested in building and settlement. Between are those who partake of both, who gradually shift from wilderness ways to settling down or who, having tasted of settlement life, abruptly return to the freedom of the wilderness. Any contradiction that may exist between the purposes of the builders and the pioneer's basic desire to "escape" from civilization is explained in terms of rebuilding a better society, finding new fields of opportunity, or simply seeking out life's challenges and adventures in the process of building individual character and the nation.

A basic search for independence unites the pioneers of each frontier despite the variations of purpose. They seek a freedom of action based upon either the removal of all shackles of law and custom of society so as to build an unstructured way of life or the opportunity to develop in their own way to the fullest extent of ability without the restraints of a preordained social and economic organization found in the settled areas. Each of these signifies a desire for individual identity, a need to be separate from the crowd and to feel one's own power. The ideas of standing up to hazards and trials, of utilizing and developing individual strengths and skills in the processes of survival and creation are paramount. These are emphasized by the pioneers themselves and by the negative representation of the nonpioneers.

The concept of independence is defined differently by the several pioneer types, however, the difference being in the character and strength of their desires. This coincides with their variance of purpose. The forest hunter-scout wants a minimum of association and maximum of freedom from restraint. He values his solitude and does not easily accept the kind of responsibility associated with home and family. Whereas close proximity to the settlements sometimes permits some break in the pattern for these men, the mountain men are less likely to be adaptive, are more fiercely independent of organized life. The ranger, in keeping with his transitionary position in the continuum from wilderness to settlement, shows some modification of this extreme position. He is, however, still basically a loner, holding out for as little hobbling by social organization as possible. In this respect he is reminiscent of the forest farmer, whose sense of independence, notwithstanding his desire to settle and build, is clearly based upon a concept of freedom of action and individual identity. He is his own man but, being rooted in the land and directed toward progress, he accepts responsibility for his family and in the incipient community. The pioneers traveling westward by caravan are imbued with some of this same spirit of freedom of action and building for oneself, but the escape-from-society motif is not so strong; the accent here is on opportunity and personal growth in a new, open land. Also, the nature of their enterprise—and the nature of the people—lessens the stress on individual identity. These novels project a group feeling unlike the individualism found in most of the other works. The pioneers of the prairie are somewhere between the forest and the caravan: the faster build-up of the settlements and the lessened isolation of the prairie engendered by the open space cause the essential spirit of independence to be quickly modified. It is there, nevertheless, and despite this tendency toward modification there is still strong feeling expressed against social organization. (Of course, it must also be kept in mind that this stage of the frontier was chronologically more advanced so that some tendency toward faster assimilation would be expected.)

The development of two cores of purpose and the distinctions in the character of the independence of the pioneer is related to the changes in choice of locale and pioneer type of the novels of the fifty-year period. It is also related to the shift in literary technique and principle from romanticism to realism that took place during this period. These brought about a shift in the relative emphasis of these aspects of the pioneer image. The romantic novels of the first two decades depict the independent scout who is oriented toward the wilderness and independence of spirit. This portrait is modified in keeping with the requirements of the genteel tradition which did not permit the antisocial or independent attitude to go too far or last too long. The antisettlement orientation of the heroes is sharply about-faced before the close of these works. The introduction of the farmer pioneer at the quarter century first focused direct attention on the settlement-oriented hero; this attention was emphasized by the interest in plain, middle-class people and by the realism of technique of these works. However, just as these literary techniques brought the farmer into the spotlight, thus defining his purpose and sense of independence, they in addition characterized the other pioneer types more distinctly. The wilderness ideal and the code of independence of the free forester and the mountain man are highlighted. The post-1926 introduction of the mountain-man hero, a particularly extreme type of individualist, illustrates this trend. By thus bringing out these distinctions, these novels organize the dual patterns of purpose. The settlement orientation is stressed by virtue of greater number of these works; the wilderness orientation is built up by the greater flamboyance of this hero and the development of the neoromance adventure story which gives him stature. Whatever the stress on purpose, the individualism and independence being portrayed are carefully enunciated both in terms of that purpose and as values in themselves.

The distinction of the purposes and the patterns of values that are part of the purposes is a matter of degree, a degree which is lessened by those heroes whose pattern of life changes as a result of a changing environment or as they accept elements of the opposite orientation. In the realistic novels this appears as a natural consequence of a developing frontier, thus converging the two purposes in these individuals. The central unity of the search for independence of all the pioneers and the emphasis upon this among the heroes—hunter, mountain man and farmer alike—also closes the breach between the two purposes. The divergence is, however, emphasized when the two points of view come in conflict, which happens frequently enough to be a significant element in this discussion.

Several other characteristics act as unifying forces in developing a single image of the pioneer hero. Generally typical of the hero of all times and places are such attributes as courage, determination, and resourcefulness. These attributes are closely allied to the pioneer's physical condition and strength as well as to his occupational skills. Together they make up the foundation elements in the building of the man and in establishing his success in the face of the varying frontier hazards. Equally prominent in his general make-up are his dependability, his trustworthiness, and his sense of loyalty. Once he has set out to do something or to fulfill an obligation, he can be expected to do so.

Loyalty is defined variously by the several types, particularly as it relates to their sense of responsibility and their intensity of independence. The free forester, the mountain man, and the ranger are likely to limit their loyalty to a few close companions;

such relationships are less frequent in the more recent novels as the strongly individualistic hero is developed. The settlement-oriented pioneer often extends his loyalty to include his neighbors near and far—or all of his race. To whomever it is given, however, the response is selfless, intense, and complete. The extreme isolationists among the more independent types express an attitude of self-interest to the exclusion of concern for others, but these are few and they sometimes modify their position at a crucial time by lending heroic, unstinting service to a group. This ties in with the trend of some pioneers who have previously denied the responsibility of a home and family, to adjust to the requirements of the more constricted life.

Personal pride and honor figure in the character of the pioneer though the interpretation of these varies with the chronological and regional range of the novels. In the early works, honor is bound up with the concepts of good name and reputation. The changing tempo of the later novels alters this to an emphasis on pride of accomplishment. Pride is an especially outspoken factor in the personalities of the more individualistic heroes; the greater his group consciousness the less the hero is likely to betray his sense of pride through overt behavior or self-acclaim.

The tone in the characterization of the pioneers is enhanced by their environmental-occupational situation. The widely different activities of each locale produce varying impressions, thus affecting the image of the man being created. In addition, the differences within the man which determine his choice of way of life and his reactions to the environmental situations also influence the image.

The stronger, vibrant tones are associated with the mountain man and the free forester. Their wilderness life and activities —hunting and trapping, scouting, roaming—accent their raw strength and manhood; their fierce independence exaggerates their hardness and forcefulness. This spirit is at times translated into ruthlessness and impetuosity. There is little room in their demanding and perilous lives for warmth and sentiment; their very isolation enforces silence and prohibits socialization. The more extreme members of this group—usually among the mountain men—emerge as rather abrupt, sometimes coarse types who exhibit wild, outspoken and swaggering natures when they are in groups or on public display. Closely allied in characterization in terms of isolation and hardness of exterior are the rangers, who very often are graduated mountain men. However, their demeanor, though tough, is more modest and betokens a warmer quality.

Not any less strong but certainly milder in total impression is the farmer pioneer, particularly the one found on the overland trail and on the prairie. The business of clearing the land of trees and breaking the prairie sod was not a task for a spineless man, but lacking the excitement and bravura associated with the wilder frontier, the life and the man take on slightly tamer—or less savage—hues. Although he is equally courageous, this pioneer's degree of caution—created by his concern for others besides himself—alters the nature of the courage. He is steadfast, unswerving in his duties, and deliberately aggressive if need be; rare is the impetuosity found among the more independent pioneers. The typical member of this group emerges as a simple, direct, and humble man. His manner is quiet, though not from direct isolation. He does not avoid his neighbors and often seeks them out. He is generous, frequently is warm and sensitive to people. However, he maintains a real degree of self-possession and determination in the pursuit of his goals which mark his independence and solid strength.

In thus describing these two character types in order to understand the diversity of personal structure, an implication of distinct types is created. It is necessary to point out that this is not completely accurate. There are heroes in each class who manifest characteristics that are more frequently associated with the other group. This cross-identification is especially apparent in those frontiersmen of the forest who are—by requirement of the locale as well as personality—both farmer and hunter-scout.

Another modification is found in the make-up of the hero of the earlier works. As compared with the later representations, he is aristocratic, significantly nobler in aspect and finer in his sensibilities. He is unblemished by crudeness and acts in keeping with high standards of propriety. This is true of the forest frontiersman, the ranger, and the traveler on the trail in those novels which appear in the first two decades. The later shift to a brasher, lustier hero with earthy qualities marks the shift in literary principles and techniques which will be discussed later in this chapter.

This modification in the presentation of the hero is readily apparent in the image of the heroine presented in the fifty-year period. The trend follows the developmental pattern indicated above: the heroine of the first decade is an aristocratic lady; the heroine of the later decades takes on down-to-earth qualities, strengths and abilities. As is implied in the phrasing of the first identification in comparison to the second, the early heroine is depicted as a nonworker, a fragile, feminine creature who is delicate and helpless. She exhibits civilized sensibilities, the highest gentility and purity. At the same time, and in this respect similar to the later heroine, she is influential in directing the progress of the frontier and in effecting changes in the hero's purposes. She stands for culture and civilization, progress; she values humanity and the manifestations of culture. The later presentation starts from a different premise: that the heroine's background is the farm and that she goes west to be part of the working frontier. And she does this, displaying her own brand of strength and reliance, a dignity developed from steadiness and assurance, a core of love and compassion. She, too, stands for progress and advancing civilization, and she projects these values in opposition to crudeness and lawlessness; she is influential in imposing these changes on the frontier and, at times, upon the frontiersman.

Certain values recur frequently in the novels over the fifty-year period; the pioneer's beliefs and behavior patterns in respect to these values make up a basic aspect of his characterization. At times the hero is seen as the exponent of the structure of values of the frontier; in some instances he is in opposition to what the frontier seems to stand for or to other pioneers on the frontier. However, these beliefs and the behavior of the pioneer hero are not static; they alter significantly in themselves and in relationship to other attitudes expressed on the frontier. These alterations, together with the chronological variations already noted, signify the overall change in the presentation of the pioneer. The pattern of change relates to the shift in literary principles and techniques, for the standards of the prevalent literary tradition helped to define the pioneer image.

The representations of class consciousness and gentility in the characterization and the values of the pioneer hero and heroine in the early novels are basic to the portrayal and point to key elements of the literary tradition of the period. There is a recurring emphasis in the novels of the first decade on the aristocratic background of the hero and heroine as compared with other "common" pioneers. This is expressed in several ways: their origin is specifically wealthy upper class or they are endowed with rank superior to the general populace. They have a nobility of face and manner. The hero is often an officer while the heroine is the daughter of one; their rank usually spares them from menial work; their behavior, in terms of social graces and manners, speech, and other activities, are distinctly cultured; they are educated. Their superiority is generally recognized by other characters—equal and lesser alike; the "common" pioneers are not only cruder in their representation but also accept the role of service to these people. The heroes and heroines reveal their response to this value through their consciousness of rank and their unwillingness, particularly the women, to develop relationships with those who lack the necessary status. Certain of the heroes who have been declassed by circumstances aspire to regain recognition and status. The relationship between the aristocratic heroines and the temporarily declassed males further emphasizes this consciousness of rank and status. While they are in the lesser station, the men cannot hope to develop a social relationship with the women and the women hold themselves aloof; a conscious distance is maintained between them until the hero's real identity and class status is established.[1]

The decline of this emphasis on class structure is apparent in the years following 1910 and a full rout of aristocratic forces is evident after 1920. Many heroes caught in a cross fire of transition are given some elements of the aristocratic characterization while they also maintain allegiance with the new, growing force, a force which might be termed democratic. This emanates from a change in the basic characterization of the hero: his roots are of humble origins. Such a switch to a concentration upon ordinary people emphasizes equality in the hero's identity. His sense of independence and his nonsubservience to anyone emerge as significant elements of his self-concept and his relations to others. As far as he sees it, there is no class rank. A man could prove himself on the frontier through his courage and skills; these gave him superiority and leadership. His self-acceptance, his self-assurance and confidence are as much a result of this as of his superiority of skills and strength.

The hero's sense of equality is accentuated in some novels by his antagonism to occasional manifestations of class consciousness. Aristocratic types, rare as their obvious appearance is in the later works, are granted no special recognition or privilege, either by the hero or by the majority of the pioneers. The hero also reacts against subtler class consciousness which establishes two

[1] Henry Nash Smith in *Virgin Land* (60–70, 96–101) points to elements of class consciousness in the development of the nineteenth-century novel. He notes Cooper's consciousness of social status in his lower-class representation of Leatherstocking in terms of background, speech, manners and dress as compared with other characters who are given the status symbols of rank. Later authors, particularly in the dime novels, altered this characterization by creating young, genteel heroes who had the skills of the frontiersman as well as the gentility and sensibility of the upper-class types. The Leatherstocking type reverts to a secondary role. In the later dime novels, the hero sometimes has a humble origin while manifesting all the cultural attributes.

levels of frontier society, one more acceptable than the other although neither is aristocratic in background. This stratification of society is at times acceptable to the mass of the populace; the stronger their acceptance, the greater the hero's reaction against it. In some works the author does not directly involve the hero in the subtle relationships that indicate class consciousness; the hero is rarely party to any feelings that would reveal any acceptance of distinctions of rank. The author often builds a negative reaction to such attitudes both through his delineation of it and through the hero's nonparticipation.

However, there is generally created a sense of superiority of the pioneer over the nonpioneer and in some respects of the wilderness man over the settlement-oriented one. This feeling is not only a matter of opinions and attitudes within the frontier group, but it is also found in the descriptive and discursive comments attributable to the author. However, it is stressed that this superiority is based upon ability rather than rank; this concept ties in with another frontier precept, one which compares the wilderness with civilization and defines the frontier's role in fostering the superiority of the pioneer.

Whether his point of view is specifically or indirectly stated, whether it is impassioned or moderate in degree, the pioneer generally favors the West over the East. This favoritism is based upon a number of interrelated factors, although each of these is not pertinent to every novel. The pioneer sees the openness and vitality of the West which gives rise to new opportunities for self-development; in comparison, the East is stifling and tame and closed in. The West symbolizes independence, that is, freedom from the legal or social restraints of organized society and freedom of action to pursue his own course. In this regard he sees the frontier as developing his manhood—his skills, strengths, and identity—while the East tends to soften and subordinate the individual. In the later works primarily, he also credits the frontier with a force that at once levels distinctions of class and permits each man to rise on his own merits. In addition, partly as the result of his experiences in the East and partly as an out-growth of this conception of the West, he associates the frontier with justice, selflessness, loyalty, faith, and other wholesome person-to-person relationships. These evolve from the frontier atmosphere, whereas organized society tends to subvert them. The frontier also gives an opportunity to build a new society, to eradicate the ills of the old—the falseness, the meaningless customs and mores, the provincialism.

A scrutiny of these factors shows the relationship to the pioneer's character structure and personal values. It also outlines the foundation of the pioneer's superiority to his Eastern counterpart. By comparing individuals and spotlighting the verve and purposefulness, the matchless skill of the frontiersmen, by citing the strengths of the frontier and the weaknesses of organized society, a positive aura of the frontier is conveyed.

The pioneers, however, part company at this juncture; their agreement does not go beyond this initial acceptance. In fact, as has been suggested, the character of their frontier orientation varies their outlook even on this issue. Their chief point of departure is in their basic objective; this alters the definition of this crucial value for it fosters acceptance either of an unchanging frontier or one which progresses toward organization.

The novels of 1900–10 present a particular variation. The heroes, after having stoutly subscribed to the strictest frontier wilderness principles, renounce them and the frontier in the end. They cease belittling the East and organized society; the majority return to the East while the others adopt the codes and objectives of organized society. This can be seen as an outgrowth of the aristocratic overtones found in these novels, for the major characters maintain allegiance to the world of culture as well as to the wilderness. By such a rather abrupt turnabout, these works finally depict culture and civilization as the ideal.

In the later works the chief variant is the degree of organized society or of wilderness acceptable to the pioneer. The greater proportion of the heroes are out to establish a settled life, a life basically similar to that left behind. The goal is progress: to transform the wilderness. Some of the pioneers project reforms or advances in the structure of the new society under the beneficent influence of the frontier. Others, particularly in the novels of the 1911–30 period, are indifferent to any conflict between the wilderness and civilization; these pioneers accept the situation and condition of their lives, but their behavior shows an unquestioning, automatic assumption of the establishment of an organized community life. However, a vigorous minority of frontiersmen wants nothing to do with the trappings of society but sees life's values only in wilderness terms. These heroes—the free forester, the mountain man and the ranger—look down on the tame and tied-down life of the farmer. Safety, stability, law and order—couched in terms of independence, individuality and search for challenge—are thus pitted against complete freedom of action, nonaffiliation and constant challenge. In a sense these diverse purposes represent the same antagonism to the social organization and restrictions of the older settlements; the various frontiersmen choose a different direction in which to expend their energies. Nevertheless their orientation is still toward the frontier.

The argument for progress represented by the majority of the novels is not undisputed. In comparative studies, the wilderness heroes are seen as more dramatic, more admirable, and, at times, more persuasive and heroic. They are looked to for guidance and support and are generally held in high esteem by the less adventuresome, except in certain overland trail novels in which the mountain men, though respected for their skills, are derogated for their crudeness and lack of purpose. It is significant to note that many of the wilderness heroes are forced to give way before the inevitable advances about them, but they do not do so willingly, as did the frontiersmen of the first decade. In their hesitation toward full-blown settlement of life, they are joined by those who have promoted progress but wish to pull in the reins and slow it down: they do not approve the complete effects of such

269

organization and wish to maintain some semblance of the frontier structure so as to preserve the values associated with it. This feeling is enhanced by the half-dozen heroes, sympathetically treated in the novels, who completely reject the neosettlement life and revert to the wilderness and freedom. However, despite factors which suggest the superiority of the wilderness and despite the nostalgia and regret associated with the passing of the wilderness hero, the trend toward progress dominates and is seen as inevitable.

The nostalgia goes beyond the "good old days" concept by depicting the strengths and undoubted manhood of the pioneer, which show up to full advantage when compared with the weaknesses in organized society. His existence enriched the country; his fine attributes show up in later generations as a source of strength and character.

Marked changes in the pioneers' moral codes and social behavior are evidenced throughout the period of this study. Prominent among these—and illustrative of the changes wrought—are the codes of acceptable behavior of love, the role of marriage, the concepts of law and justice, and the meaningfulness of work in the pioneers' lives. These changes are reflected in the activities of the major characters as well as in their attitudes, both stated and implied.

The change in the codes of love and in the behavior of the men towards the women is a gradual shift from standards of prudery to those of permissiveness. The heroes of the early works represent purity of thought and action in their behavior towards women. Overt expression of love is rarely resorted to; often love blossoms secretly accompanied by pangs and yearnings while a strictly formal relationship is observed. The heroes idealize the heroines and act to protect them. In their reactions they are gallant, courteous, respectful and deferential. Although they do not express their love, they nevertheless seek its fulfillment in marriage, a step which generally concludes their frontier experience by causing them to renounce their independence and frontier

270

allegiance. Marriage, which is somehow sentimentalized and given ethereal qualities, is seen as the pioneers' salvation and reform.

As the years pass, the impetus coming mainly after 1930, this idealization and purity fade. The pioneer's reaction to love takes on a dual coloration. Love and marriage are given a more practical foundation in personal relationships and day-by-day living; sex is introduced as a natural drive and, in some more recent works, comes to be a dominating force. While the home-loving, respectable, virtuous pioneer is still portrayed, a break-down in moral codes in the novels limits the extent to which virtue is adhered to or believed in: love is expressed in sexual relations; sex as natural to life is not limited to love or marriage. This attitude, plus the practical aspect of life, dilutes the romantic overtones of the relationship though, like virtue, this still persists. Marriage, despite the emphasis on sexual freedom, is accepted as a basic feature of life, and is not seen as a contradiction to the pioneer's principles of independence—which no longer implies complete isolation except for a minority of heroes. (This pattern is emphasized by the greater proportion of farmer frontiersmen in the works since 1925.) Marriage, being directly related to daily working life, has lost its ethereal qualities; it is built upon direct, deep human relations, with a frank consciousness of sex. In keeping with the lapse in the moral structure, instances of fidelity in marriage are matched by cases of infidelity: belief in double standards, yielding to temptation, and the like. Evidence of these changes in attitude is not limited to the activities of the heroes but is also apparent in the other pioneers in the degree of accept-ability of such behavior to the frontier society.

There is a similar though less extensively documented pattern of change in the pioneers' attitudes toward law and justice. In keeping with their independence and their isolation, their basic creed evolves from the concept of making and enforcing their own laws. The greater their isolation, the stronger is this dictum. In the early works in which the heroes initially take an extreme stand, a particular phase of this code is emphasized: the heroes' right and need for vengeance to maintain their honor. They react with an eye-for-an-eye creed which reflects this right and recognizes their role in determining law and justice. This emphasis on vengeance diminishes in the later works. However, direct action does not. The use of force on the frontier is viewed as necessary; the pioneers accept this as a matter of course. Killing, which was occasionally not permitted to the early hero, is fairly freely practiced in defensive and offensive measures. There is some ruthlessness. However, there is also a qualification, which is of increasing occurrence in the later novels, against brutality and thoughtless slaughter—against injustice. This definition of justice diminishes the freedom of action implied by "frontier law" and sets up a standard of decency and humanity, a consciousness of civilization to be followed. This definition relates closely to a greater acceptance of law in the later novels, particularly those of the settlement-oriented pioneer.

Paralleling these attitudes toward justice is the change in the pioneers' view of the Indian: the savage or simple Indian of the early novels eventually becomes a human being with a unique culture. A sympathetic response, sympathy imbued with understanding, and a consciousness of the Indian's victimization at the hands of white men are factors of this attitude which relate closely to the sense of justice and humanity, especially since these are often applied to the Indian. Significantly the heroes often are the most conscious of the Indian as a human being, sometimes in stark opposition to the ruthlessness or thoughtlessness of the general frontier populace.

The representation of work in the novels reveals the literary and social influence of the times on the values of the pioneer. The absence of any menial activities in the lives of the pioneers in the first two decades is related to the romantic tradition then prevalent. In a few novels the impact of the "strenuous age" is seen in the presentation of the concept of hard, honest work as part of an active life, but this is muted by the emphasis on gentility.

Later works, in keeping with the realistic techniques and the emphasis on the common man, heretofore barred from heroic stature, illustrate the full toil and struggle that made up the pioneers' lives. Generally this representation continues throughout the last decades, except where it gets somewhat overcome by the revival of the adventure story.

A special attiude is conveyed in the 1930's in response to the economic-social collapse of the nation. Comments suggest the negation of the frivolous, fancy life, the false display and superficiality, the deification of comfort, luxury and money; activities call for a return to a life of work and simplicity of desires and living standards, independent activity and personal responsibility, removal of middlemen and profits without work. Some novels preach against government intervention through their heroes by promoting self-help and honest labor. These harken back to the frontier spirit—what it meant and did for those who lived it. The novels that contain these comments diminish as this decade comes to an end, the war and a new national emergency drawing attention away from these issues.

The frontier novels of the first half of this century create a portrait of the pioneer that is not uniform; the presentation is not conducive to the development of a singular image. Rather, it is apparent that around a core of basic characteristics and values there are variations according to region and occupation of the pioneer. Where the demands of these are similar there tends to be a similarity in the expression of the specific characteristics and traits. Therefore, the forest scout, the mountain man, and the ranger have a unity of purpose and design beyond the basic core; so, too, do the farmers in the forest, on the trail, and on the prairie have characteristics in common. Much as there are parallel traits found in all, there are the distinctions of time and place. In this respect the forest pioneer, both scout and farmer, have some common points of unity which separate them from the later pioneers. The mountain man likewise has his distinctive qualities brought on by the nature of his life and environment. This might be said, in turn, of each group. There are also chronological variations in the image of the pioneer, this being most apparent in his values structure. The years show changes in his attitudes and beliefs that make the pioneer of a 1900 novel quite a different man from the one of 1950.

The Creation of the Image

Throughout the discussion and analysis of the novels, suggestions have been made as to the relationships of certain trends to literary and social influences. The changing patterns in the image of the pioneer, particularly the chronological variations which have some uniformity despite shifts in the locale of the novels, suggest the effects of such influences. Developments in literary technique, also apparent in the novels, have the dual role of being both cause and effect in relation to these patterns.

The novels of the first decade of this study, 1900–10, as well as the majority of the works in the second decade, differ from the later works in almost every respect. Occasional recurrences have been noted after 1920 of the elements that characterize the earlier novels, but these are steadily diminishing and, in a total accounting, minimal.

The first decade of the twentieth century—and some historians include the years up to the first world war—manifests some significant literary and cultural emphases and trends. The dominant ideas, quite naturally, derived from those of the preceding period but were in an unusual state of flux and conflict. An era seemed to be vanishing, with proponents of change ready to throw off the shackles of the old society—economic, social, religious, scientific, literary—while the defenders stanchly stood for the status quo. In literature this conflict was represented by the opposing forces of realism and romanticism. Romanticism had held sway for much of the preceding century, being represented in the later decades by such major authors as Walt Whitman, Herman Melville and, in the western field, James Fenimore Cooper. Although the output of romantic literature was still strong, it was on the wane, finding its adherents mainly in the popular, sentimental romances of Winston Churchill, Harold Bell Wright, and others. Its influence in major works of art was quite diminished. The surviving ideals of the romantic tradition were being forcefully defended at the close of the century by a small New York group led by Richard Henry Stoddard; the defense was, however, a final gasp of a dying tradition. Taking over the field were the works of Mark Twain, William Dean Howells, and those of the local color—regional artists like Bret Harte and Sarah Orne Jewett; these introduced the realist tradition and had already gained prominence and acceptance in literary circles. William Dean Howells, who had been preaching his mildly realistic gospel for two decades and had been accepted as the leading literary figure for almost as many years, was being edged aside at the turn of the century by realists with more extreme views about the techniques and philosophy of their art—more extreme in contrast to principles of romantic literature. The naturalistic ideology of Hamlin Garland and Theodore Drieser, literary successor to realism, was looming on the horizon. Some of the social and intellectual tensions were finding their way to the pages of novels, particularly in the literature of the reform movement. The quarrel between the classes, socialistic commentary on business and living standards, farm protests, municipal corruption, the conflict between individualism and collectivism: these were some of the ideas being represented in the literature of the period.

Realism and reform do not, however, figure as forces in the pioneer literature of the period after the turn of the century. Not one novel in the first decade can be so classified; the novels of the second decade follow suit, with the possible exception of the Cather works, which, while eschewing the stylistic traditions of the romantic school, nevertheless convey its idealistic values. The bulk of the works of this period adopt neither the techniques nor the ideals and purposes of realism. This generalization includes both the subdued reality of Howells and the starker reality of his successors. It might be expected that Hamlin Garland would have made some impression on frontier fiction since his early works—harsh and bitter and direct—dealt with the pioneer. However, his grim, plain portrayal of the pioneers and their lives, his protest and cry for reform, the theory of natural human rights which motivated his works—none of these carried over into the frontier novels of the first two decades.

The popular literature of the day, as recorded in lists of best sellers, evidenced the preference for sentimental fiction. A surge of interest in the historical novel highlighted the tendency toward fiction which had nothing to say about contemporary problems. This interest is related to the rising thrust for power and prestige in America. Certain standard patterns in the novels reflect this: association with and acceptance by royalty, the invincibility of the American male, the treachery and lack of development of the European.[2] The first is seen in the aristocratic emphasis of these works, the second forms the focus of the frontier novels, while the third idea also crops up occasionally. The novels were also shaped, at least indirectly, by the concepts which defended the existing order and traditions, thus determining the pioneer image. By concentrating on sentimental historical fiction, by avoiding the discussion of contemporary problems, by eluding accuracy of event and experience in favor of portraying the social-moral trappings of a superimposed tradition, the novels point to romanticism. This is a romanticism, however, that has been directed to the popular imagination through sentimentalized, watered-down principles.

The popular romantic tradition is reflected in the structure and style of the novels. The plots lack directness and simplicity; they are complicated inventions and depend upon circumstantial machinations for their development. Examples of this abound: the fanciful reasons that bring the hero and heroine to the frontier; the rapid and inconsistent learning of woodsman's skills; the unbelievable situations and obvious manipulation of action—

[2] Grant C. Knight, *The Strenuous Age in American Literature*, 21.

captures, impossible escapes, frivolity and drawing-room behavior in the face of danger; the sudden shift in allegiance and direction to return the main characters to the East; a happy, ideal ending which completes the tale. The reactions and conflicts are superficial despite the complexities of the plot. Attitudes, values and characterizations are conveyed in black and white. Depth of characterization is lacking. Characters adhere to the accepted patterns: the good guys never fail to live up to the highest creed; the bad guys are thoroughly so, except that an occasional one feels sudden, inexplicable remorse and redeems himself with a final act. This seems another facet of the happy, ideal ending.

There is little attempt to display life; issues and problems of life on the frontier are avoided except for cursory allusions to the Indian menace. Emotions are masked by sentiment; ideas, limited as they are, are conveyed by sermons and tributes. In short, the novels are unreal adventures generally detached from the drama of frontier life and featuring make-believe, ideally patterned people.

These novels do depict a local setting somewhat reminiscent of the early realists. Essentially, however, the frontier scene is only a backdrop. Its life is shown only sparingly: the local manners, the colloquial speech, the day-by-day working existence do not apply to the major characters. Instances when these do are exceptions, as in the novels of Winston Churchill and Owen Wister, which give some insight into frontier people. However, their orientation is basically romantic; they do not approach the sensational nature of Bret Harte's stories or the quiet directness of Sarah Orne Jewett. In most of the works, the life and manners of the frontier seem gross and exaggerated in comparison to the life and manners of the major characters and in this key respect do not fit the requirements peculiar to the local color school of realistic fiction.

These patterns of literary presentation themselves convey the quality and tone of the popular romantic tradition, but they are also the results of certain concepts of life of that period, concepts which act as the philosophical foundation to the overt structures and incidents. Some of these can be seen as part of a traditional American point of view and self-concept prevalent in that period, carrying over from the older society. Others were promulgated in defense of the existing order and thought against the trends calling for reform. Those ideas which preserve the status quo, which relate traditional social and personal relationships, are presented. The novels of the frontier, having taken on romantic structure and style, and having adopted the conservative and traditional defenses that go along with them, present a consistent portrait.

A broad acceptance of romanticism in popular literature in this period is motivated by two general reactions: traditional individualism and optimism, which were being strengthened by the events and the mood of the day; an impulse for self-improvement which, in turn, developed out of the traditions and events. The great mass of people, imbued with the optimism of inevitable progress and the creed of individual improvement—enhanced if not created by the frontier and its opportunities—was not materially influenced by the groundswell of protest calling for reform.[3] Progress and opportunity had been ever present; they could not be easily denied. This prevalent expectation, acting both as an opiate and a driving force, had buoyed up the people during the depression and hard times of the previous decade. The current prosperity, proof of their expectations even if it did not fully reach all of them, quelled the push for reform. In this quelling there was also a denial of realism in literature, the two being closely associated at the time.

The impulse for self-improvement which permeated this period was not solely economic in nature but encompassed cultural aspects as well. In relation to the development of literature, two reported facts are significant. The literary historian Robert E. Spiller, in discussing an author's failure to achieve success, notes that he did not appeal to the feminine audience. Women

[3] Merle Curti, *The Growth of American Thought*, 634.

formed the greatest part of the novel-reading public at the turn of the century.[4] Merle Curti discusses the broad advances in literacy accompanied by an upsurge in publishing. He cites the trend among middle-class women for cultural self-improvement through the courses and books offered by the Chautauqua Assembly and through literary clubs; these means were less available to country women, but they turned to mail order catalogues for lists of books. The novels listed in these were "guaranteed to be pure, inspiring and wholesome."[5] A majority of the novel-reading public may be assumed to include the middle-class women who were anxious to modify and enrich their lives and those women of upper-class status whose lives were altogether based on the "nicest" cultural traditions.

For the middle-class women cultural enhancement could mean only one thing. Certainly, in view of the dominant optimism and sense of progress, they would not accept the squalor, the disillusionment and despair expressed in the reform literature. Such a review of their own bare lives would not satisfy their aspirations for better things. For them, too, an improved life would not be founded on the impropriety of manners and morals suggested in the realistic fiction as compared with those demanded by the prevailing moral codes and standards of behavior. It was natural to try to adapt the standards of the admired group to those of the readers. The novels, relatively close to home, provided a bright focus as well as an escape from the dreariness of their lives. The ladies brought up in these ideals were also not interested in realistic or reform literature but for somewhat different reasons. For them the demands of the standards and codes were very real. They lived this life and expected the books they read to mirror it and not to provoke any impropriety. In addition, the novels offered the excitation of drama and adventure on the exotic, far-removed frontier. Together these women created an audience not to be ignored—a demand

[4] Robert E. Spiller, *Literary History of the United States*, 884.
[5] Curti, *op. cit.*, 602–604.

for these qualities in the popular literature. One can imagine them experiencing the frontier novels with pleasure, for they expressed the sentiment and romance, the standards and ideals, that they wanted and admired.

The characterizations and values displayed in the novels represent these standards and values, and convey a sense of romance. The genteel tradition of American literature and the principles of ideality are manifest. Life is seen in heroic, ideal terms. It is depicted devoid of work or activity—except heroic action—as a parlor game of words and manners. Only the charming aspects of the environment are shown; crude conditions do not exist. Love is a hallowed, sentimentalized experience; marriage is presented in like terms, while sex does not exist. Existence is dream-like. The major characters are of noble stature, both in character and heritage. They are well bred; their manners are gracious and cultured; they manifest romantic sensibilities, but their moral codes stress a complete purity which does not permit the slightest transgression. They exude personal dignity, decorum, and gentility. Thus the pioneer hero and heroine represent the ideal: all the virtues and fine sensibilities of a cultured, civilized world as well as the heroism and strength of the frontier. The crudeness of the backwoods is relegated to the contrasting minor characters.

The progress of the novels also shows the sense of propriety and romance. The hero is not permitted to act against these codes; he is not permitted to kill openly; a rare, relatively minor moral offense, e.g., a stolen kiss, causes great suffering. Evil is conquered by good and all ends happily. The hero marries the heroine and settles down to a comfortable, married, secure life, none the worse for his brief adventure away from civilization. It is a proper union; the moral and class conventions have not been broken. It is an ideal ending; the sentimental and romantic requirements of the reading public have been met. The total conception is another aspect of the fulfillment of contemporary requirements in the portrayal of the major characters in the popular fiction of this period. The hero represents—with his sensitivity, his culture, his superiority—the romantic ideal. In addition, he displays the strengths, abilities and courage required on the frontier. However, since the former receives the emphasis, the presentation is a rather distorted portrayal of the frontier and the pioneer.

The impact of "the strenuous age" was also felt. Americans were conscious of the nation's health and strength. The economic recovery from the depression of the previous decade seemed complete; the outlook of prosperity was enhanced by the drive of the newly rich mercantile class. The rapid successes of the United States on the imperialistic frontiers seemed to prove the nation's power and place in the world. And Americans were proudly aware of their national courage, perseverance and energy in the rapid conquering of the western frontier. Indeed, they were made very much aware of these virtues by the nationalistic back-patters of the period, not the least of whom was Theodore Roosevelt. His doctrine of the "strenuous life" which captured the people's imagination emphasized the manly and adventurous qualities and urged an aggressive, individualistic strength. He decried physical and moral degeneration brought on by a soft, easy life. Social evolutionists of the period gave intellectual credence to the stress on the strong, self-reliant man with the development of the theories that showed the process of natural selection of the fittest. Individual men as well as nations survived and succeeded only if they were strongest and most able. Frederick Jackson Turner's discussion emphasized this evolutionary process in the development of the nation and the national characteristics.

Inherent in the concept of the strenuous life and the social evolutionary theories was the belief in the progress of the individual, the ability of a man to make his own fortune. Success in the face of obstacles by dint of hard work and effort was a reality observable in both the frontier experience and the business world. The aggressive individual could rise above his environment, gaining power and strength in the process of assuring himself a place in the world. This principle relates to the social evolutionist theories of progress and growth as well as to the traditional optimism and individualism of the people. The success of individuals and the nation gave assurances that the future would be bright for all who put their backs to the wheel and their mettle to the test. Although the people may not have thought in quite these terms, their belief in the progress of the individual and the possibility of fortune through courage, persistence and hard work parallels these concepts.

A contradiction in direction exists in the emphases of the strenuous age and the genteel tradition. The aggressive, go-out-and-do-it strength is opposed to the unruffled decorum; the successful self-made man is a break in the status quo which the traditionalists seek to preserve. This seems to be a difference in levels of society as represented by this quotation:

> . . . [Roosevelt's] philosophy of the strenuous life ran with, rather than against, the main current of American life. We were an active rather than a contemplative people. Roosevelt gave verbal expression to a firmly held folk ideal.[6]

If the main stream of life was active and progressive, yet the established group was content with what it had and was at least condescending to both the activities of aspirants to positions of power and prestige and to the common people on the frontier. It ignored the folk ideal in the contemplation of the complete society it had created and wanted unchanged. However, on an intellectual level—and this has its effect on the literature—the differences are lessened by elements of the conservative. Their divergence is limited by their mutual success—except that the upper class in-group frowned on pursuing anything except gentility. The stress on virtuous hard work also tends to be a limitation of the strenuous life in a conservative way for it depresses the aggressive qualities of that life.

Associated with these concepts and a further conservative lim-

6 Spiller, *op. cit.*, 945.

itation upon them was the cult of the elite.[7] This was based on the belief that some individuals are superior to those about them, this superiority stemming from differences in innate ability. These individuals succeed inevitably and naturally. They have what it takes to endure and discipline themselves; they can and do undertake responsibility. While this concept of natural superiority was seen to uphold the belief in individual progress, it also acknowledged the inequality of men and further explained and justified existing social and economic inequalities. It gave these superior people the right to take what they could get, for they were better equipped to do so and it was natural for them to do so; by reverse reasoning, it gave those people already in control the right to maintain their positions and control of wealth. Thus this belief in a cult of the elite upheld the status quo of social and economic classes while seeming to represent greater opportunity. It was opportunity, but only for the superior few.

An expression of these several interrelated ideas is apparent in the novels. An animation exists on the frontier which is not found in the drawing rooms. Thus, the frontier represents the strenuous life and the pioneer its exponent. As the frontier demands strength, vigor, and perseverance, it offers great challenge to a man who has those qualities. Many of these heroes came to the frontier to escape the practices and judgments of a soft, ingrown and unjust society. The novels compare the Easterner with the frontiersman hero; this is done by showing the development of several of the heroes as well as by contrasting the hero and groups of pioneers with individuals and groups from the East. The Easterners are soft, weak, and often represent the immoral, unscrupulous villain. These portrayals enhance the value of the active life and demonstrate the superiority of the rugged, natural man while the characters of both the hero and the villain are symbolic of the results of the two kinds of life.

The hero's success and individual development also illustrate at the same time the belief in the self-made man and the doctrine

[7] Curti, *op. cit.*, 641.

of the elite. The heroes represent that special distinction, a superiority that sets them apart from the masses. They evince natural nobility as well as an aristocratic family background. Together these factors make their status insurmountable and their success inevitable. Their advance in life is predetermined. Individuals find their proper level and the experience on the frontier serves to sift the levels of society. In this respect, these novels illustrate an individualism of natural inequality. The force of life naturally separates these men.

A relationship can be seen with the doctrine of the strenuous life which argued for the factors of action and aggressive force in terms of success and progress. The demands of this life are such that only the very best of men can succeed and rise above the natural and human barriers that are placed before them. In that the hero manages to be successful in the face of obstacles—the crude frontier, loss of class status and role—after seeming to start from scratch, the novels further illustrate the ability of man to make his own way, particularly the superior man. Thus, the hero embodies the popular ideal of the self-made man and represents the tradition of individual advancement and inevitable progress.

In final analyses of these works, the frontiersman's progress is seen defined in romantic conservative terms rather than liberal, democratic ones. The genteel traditions are respected. The special nature of the pioneer hero is geared to the demands of this tradition. His progress and success while seeming to represent the self-made man tradition only emphasize the status and position of those who count: the social elite. The class inequalities are suggested not only by his own nobility of character and heritage but further by the distinctions and barriers between him and the mass of the pioneers. The strenuous life is merely superficially depicted in most instances, thus not jarring the genteel sensibilities of the readers. The activities of the heroes are heroic in nature and highly moral and principled, in keeping with the regimen of the romantic tradition. And, significantly, the strenuous life is given up for a return to the cloistered, settled, and cultured life. Thus the heroes are saved from ignominy and crude fate and returned unstained to their rightful places. The presentations, while unifying two seemingly opposite creeds in making the hero an exponent of both—the best of two worlds, are bound by these conservative ideologies which defined and strove to preserve the status quo of social values and class structure. Nevertheless, it can be seen that these ramifications also represent aspects of traditional individualism, optimism and expectation of progress fostered by the American mood of this period. They have merely been turned away from the popular folk imagination.

The floodgates of rebellion against the established order had been opened decades before in both literature and national life, but it was not until the nineteen twenties that the barriers of tradition crumbled before the onslaught. The spirit of reform which took the shape of both Progressivism and Socialism, the effect of Darwinism on science, religion and social theory, the development of realism and naturalism in literature—each had had its force but their impact was less than complete. Other, conflicting ideologies had also held sway, some of these representing conservative tenets, while still others searched out new, basically nonliberal directions. The line of resistance to change, though wavering and thin, seemed to hold; the forces of the past lingered on. American popular literature, steeped in sentimentality and romance, still had articulated the vanishing creeds and withheld the changing facts of life from its audience.

The war precipitated the final collapse of the old order and the undermining of the traditions. In contrast to the glorious ideals and bright hopes were the horrors, the bitter disillusionment of nonachievement, the sense of having been deceived and warped. The underlying cultural process for change had found its catalyst. The dominant note was protest: protest in the form of defiance, ridicule, disenchantment and disassociation, pleasure and self-expression; protest that shook the foundations of the old values and changed the tempo of the times. The reaction was to question and to act against the ideals and morality of the past. The optimism and complacent satisfaction that marked American life were denied. The overpowering commercialism and the industrialism which had been consolidated during the war, with their inherently mercenary values, were criticized; the companion cult of prosperity and interest in material goods were found despicable. This new economic order, the money-oriented society, was seen in hard contrast to the idealism of democracy with its standards of progress, opportunity, and equality. Beneath the surface were the realities of false values, coarseness, shallowness, and inequality. Closely related to this disillusionment was the collapse of international idealism, the peace lost to the forces of selfish reaction. Out of these flowed the other revolts against the symbols of the society being denied. Victorian propriety and virtue, the concept of middle class respectability, were ridiculed and defied. Sexual inhibitions were weakened as well, this being related to the looser moral patterns in the war situation as well as to the weakening of the traditional religious moral codes through secularization. Science was also a major factor: the popularization of Freudian and behavioristic psychology contributed to the decline of moral idealism.

The loss of ideals and values precipitated for many a disenchantment that led to a general alienation from society. The interest in political, economic, and social reform, which in the prewar period had taken the shape of crusades against dishonesty in government, sweatshops, child labor and delinquency among girls, was replaced by the reaction to the economic and political ramifications of the postwar scene. The disillusionment and disavowal engendered by the reaction to war and the national scene —dedication to prosperity, commercialism and a narrow national unity—rejected the reformist social criticism.[8] The sense of purpose and optimism was gone. Life was found in the pleasure of

[8] Vernon Louis Parrington, *Main Currents in American Thought*, 373.

the present and its denial, both of which expressed the disillusionment and protest of the day.

A negative note prevails in the major literature of the postwar period.

> For all their rage and frustration, the writers of the twenties, with few exceptions, showed little concern for reform. They were not conspicuous in the fight for the League of Nations or the cleansing of politics or the improvement of the lot of the workingman or the farmer. . . . It was somehow appropriate that the 1890's should be ushered in with *How the Other Half Lives,* and the 1920's with *Main Street* and *This Side of Paradise.*[9]

Many authors disassociated themselves from dealing directly with problems by depicting a fast and furious life of no values and no causes or by reporting all the hard, ugly facts of American life. Each method in its own way showed the author's disenchantment with the structure and values of American life, each encompassed a new social criticism of the veneer and values of that life, of its emptiness and falseness. The former group introduced codes completely alienated from the traditional values, emphasizing society's lost cause and lost purpose. The second, by simply exposing the cruel and vulgar aspects of life, by remaining unsympathetic and unmoved, showed their derision and low opinion. The novels do not, however, go beyond this negative passivity.

The literature of the times gave evidence of the loss of the symbols of the old society. The genteel tradition was disavowed: the veneer of manners and morality were gone; sex was no longer taboo. Their treatment was part of the general social criticism. The focus of literature moved farther from the upper class and the drawing room. The helpless heroine was fading along with these traditions, influenced as much by the woman's changing role in society as by the changes in literary tradition. Appropri-

[9] Spiller, *op. cit.,* 1118.

ately, any emphasis on a hardworking, strenuous life vanished along with the loss of enthusiasm for life.

The decline of literary sexual standards had begun early in the century, the novels of Crane and Dreiser taking the first major steps. Dreiser's *Sister Carrie* was, however, denied publication for twelve years until 1912. The attempted suppression of Cabell's *Jurgen* in 1919 was not only short lived but earned its author a wide reputation. By 1920 the best sellers had begun to show evidence of less rigid standards, giving sympathetic treatment to sinners and defiers of conventional standards. Historical romances, on the other hand, tended to retain standards of morality. By 1926 the historical novels also began to show these influences although the heroine usually remained pure while the hero, passionate and with a past, resisted his impulses.[10] Repressive forces continued in action but the wall of taboos had crumbled. The diversification of the American reading public accounted in part for this, there being a breaking down of the solid cultural and social group; publishers were ready to feed this new audience as well as recognize the new standards abroad in the land.[11]

The new literary climate spelled a rebirth of realism. Freed of the restraints of the ideals, ideas and manners of the old establishment, unconcerned with the ideals of the romanticists or with the heaviness of fate and consequence emphasized by the naturalists, disinterested in causes and passions, the serious authors reported what they saw about them. They were not necessarily dispassionate but their lack of passion, their disassociation, lent objectivity to their work. Gone also were the tensions and trials of the early realists and naturalists who had to fight the entrenched romantics. The new realism

> . . . had emerged out of the struggle for freedom of conduct and was concerned not with the conflict of great social forces that had dominated the first naturalistic generation, but with transcriptions

[10] Harrison Smith, *Twenty-five Years of Best Sellers*, 404–405.
[11] Spiller, *op. cit.*, 953–4.

of the average experience, with reproducing, sometimes parody-
ing, but always participating in, experience which made up the
native culture. . . .

Realism had become familiar and absorbed in the world of
familiarity . . . it had become the normal circuit.[12]

This sense of the familiar came also from the common experiences with which they dealt; they wrote of the common life in
the manner of reporting precisely what they saw.

In addition to creating new realms of literature, this emphasis
on the everyday experiences created new audiences. The popular
imagination responded to the self-portrait, as it were. As a consequence, popular taste veered away from sentimental to realistic
fiction toward the end of the third decade.[13]

The impact of these forces on the pioneer novels of the twenties and early thirties is as incomplete as might be expected.
Pioneer fiction, as was illustrated by the works of the first two
decades, tends to be out of the main stream of literary change
and social conflict. As has also been noted, historical fiction as a
rule was slower to react to these changes. These forces, however,
were by this time so strong and sweeping that the surge of the
floodtides began to swirl around the feet of the pioneer.

The most significant effect is the concentration on plain people
and their problems; men and women of humbler origins take the
center of the novels. As has been indicated in the chapter which
discusses class on the frontier, the dismissal of aristocratic aspects
in the characterizations is not immediate or complete. In several
of the early novels of the twenties there are compromises in the
identification. However, the tone and purposes of the novels have
shifted so that the activities of ordinary people are depicted. This
is not to say that the pioneer does not represent an ideal figure.
He is this, but not the romantic ideal of the genteel tradition. He
is a man of stronger parts, with an image that stems from more
earthy qualities.

[12] Alfred Kazin, *On Native Grounds*, 162–4.
[13] Philip V. D. Stern, *Books and Best Sellers*, 48.

Hand in hand with this shift is a necessary retreat from the genteel tradition representing the manners and culture of the upper class, ideal characters. As with the basic characterization, there are residual qualities carried over, but these diminish as the years pass. Necessarily, the plain people are involved in their work and in ordinary events for the most part. Included in this shift of values, following the outlined trend but more moderately, is the lowered level of morality. It is 1927 before a novel of pronouncedly sexual cast appears. In the preceding years the novels show the loss of inhibitions through references to secondary characters or past events, sometimes openly and at other times somewhat furtively, reminiscent of the rigid morality of the preceding decades. After 1927, there are two more novels in this decade with sexual emphasis; in the thirties the proportion increases—in both direct and indirect allusion—but the family nature of many of the novels tends to be a controlling factor.

Residual romantic overtones exist also in terms of the structure of some of these novels, particularly several of the early ones. However, the unbelievable situations, the unrefined characteristics, the extreme skills, and the idealistic nature of the hero—all tend to be lessened through the introduction of characters who exemplify qualities associated with more ordinary people. As the dramatic incidents become less dependent upon manipulated circumstances and more involved with common trials, the quality of adventure, which persists, loses the essence of melodrama and takes on the intensity of real-life situations. The exceptions to this are those novels, introduced in the latter segment of the twenties (also referred to in the preceding paragraph), which portray the lusty individualist. These novels, predictive of a more numerous quantity published in the forties, are believable in structure, technique, and development but are relatively exaggerated. The changing style of the novels also contributes to the increasing realism. Direct, plain language and stylistic effects complement the more direct depiction of the frontier life.

Another variant from the main stream of literature of the

twenties is the absence of disillusionment in the frontier novels. These works are marked by their sense of purpose and optimism, the enduring human strength and perseverance, the rabid and spirited individualism, and a general consciousness of destiny. Ideals are not denied. Several novels exhibit a sense of reform, in such a way as to indicate real concern for directions and purposes and not merely criticism and denial. In this respect these works seem like a reaffirmation—as if in contradiction, a minority report—of the traditional, homely verities of life. These novels which convey this without the remaining romantic trappings present a strong portrait indeed.

The economic crisis which ushered in the thirties left its mark on the entire social scene and affected the literary scene as well. Basic questions were asked about life in America in terms of both the economic system and the social structure. Values ignored in the previous decade, were taken up again and re-examined with purpose: the doctrine of inevitable progress, a central idea in American thought, was faced with new doubt; the material values—accumulation of goods, worldly success—came under attack; the principles and values of democracy were subjected to intense evaluation. A need was seen for national regeneration and reconstruction, although not all could agree on the path that should be taken. Social changes, and a new approach to problems of people and society were called for. Some adherents saw the answer in Socialism and Communism. Others called for a return to the old values that had originally created and strengthened the nation. Harm was seen in the pampering of the weak and jobless as an impairment of the moral and spiritual fiber; the American character, grown soft and flabby, needed discipline and hard work. The social-economic ferment, started in the thirties with the shock of crisis, carried over until the forties when the national energies were redirected towards winning the second world war and, later, trying to understand and win the peace.

The national crisis was evident in the social consciousness of the literature of the period. Diverse attitudes were displayed. There was expressed a new sensitiveness to social issues, to suffering and insecurity brought on by the realities of the depression. A sense of public responsibility and a reaffirmation of purpose was apparent in the works. More extreme novelists in this school depicted the class struggle in hard, raw terms and predicted or demanded social upheaval to correct the injustices inherent in the structure of society. The underlying spirit of reform that motivated these works was reminiscent in its general premises— if not its tone—of the earlier period of reform. The theory of human rights to opportunity and a meaningful existence, the faith in man's dignity, and the need to alter the social conditions that promote inequalities: these were inherent in both reform movements.

Although such socially conscious literature dominated the thirties, there were authors who remained aloof from the rush toward social change. One group of these continued to stress the traditional values, harkening back to the past and its glories. This complemented, perhaps, the return to the farm during the depression. Another group of authors chose to ignore the more acute issues of the day to concentrate on literary values, while still others expatriated themselves, continuing essentially the concepts of the previous decade.

The social protest of the times does not directly affect the novels of the frontier. Rather, these works tend to become instruments of the conservative defense, displaying the individualism, fortitude and power of the pioneer and, occasionally, using these as an argument against the pressures to put the government into private life. This display of the past is understandable and, perhaps, inevitable considering the trouble of the times. It served as reassurances to a bewildered people who had gotten used to their personal and national success. It also reasserted and reaffirmed the values of the past—perhaps nostalgically, perhaps deliberately—which seemed threatened now more than ever. This particular emphasis is brought home in those novels which emphasize the value of work and individual effort in assuring personal advancement. These make two corollary points significant to this discussion: one decries the over-consumption and frivolous, fancy living which takes the people away from the land; the second reacts against the government's work and relief program. The first is directly critical of the national frenzy of the twenties by pointing to the weakening and destruction of individuals; it calls for a return to the land and the verities of life—simplicity, hard work, and individualism. The second warns that the taking of the self-control and self-direction away from the people is demoralizing and weakens the national and personal fiber; it, too, calls for a return to the land, self-help, and individualism. There are also sporadic comments about government control by big business and, in turn, the hounding of the little man. This is seen as a cause of ruin while the frontier with its independence of action and social equality is seen as the salvation. Both of these points are related to a common conservative interest which partly emanates from the necessary historical frame of reference of the frontier and partly grows out of the social-political upheaval of the 1930's.

However, the signs of the times did not leave the pioneer novels untouched. Although there is a general reaction against the social change—or at least a neutrality—there is a greater consciousness of life of the frontier in terms of its problems and basic culture. An awareness of human beings, their dreams and struggles, is apparent. The people begin to emerge as real characters apart from the events and the frontier. Some evaluation is given to the development of the culture of the frontier, and in keeping with the lowered opinion of the upper class, there is some show of the impetus on the frontier to curb the development of class structure. A social consciousness is also apparent in the humanitarian attitudes represented in the novels. There is introduced an awareness of justice and fair dealings in human relations. Through the avoidance of the brutal and the cruel, a sense of civilized behavior is developed. The heroes who represent this approach, found particularly, but not solely, in the settlement-oriented novels, carry the burden of social responsibility of the times.

The most significant aspect of this consciousness in people and culture and sense of justice is the variation in the depiction of and reaction to the Indian. He is seen not merely in terms of threat or as a rare, incomprehensible animal, but in terms of his own culture and traditions. In the novels, the Indian is given sympathetic treatment: his culture is detailed in positive terms; his cause is stated and frequently promoted; he, himself, takes on character. This development parallels a change in government policy which recognized the Indian as a deserving, under-protected American and attempted to help him and to promote his culture through encouraging his tribal arts and life. This policy can be seen as part of the growing acceptance of the role of society through its government to assist the less privileged and the unfortunate.

The frontier novels of the forties are essentially a duplication of those of the preceding decade in basic direction. There is, however, less emphasis on the social problems even when contrasted to the minor stress in the novels of the thirties. The revolt novels generally disappeared with the coming of the war, social themes having lost their hold on the popular imagination. Cowley points out that every major war of our time has been followed by a movement away from socially-oriented writing.[14] The diverting effect of the war on the public's attention causes a tendency toward escapist literature. The two world wars directed American frontier fiction toward "straight" historical fiction—adventure and romance.

Taken as a unit, the novels of the final two decades of this study evince similar structural patterns. These generally develop out of those which were in evidence in the previous decade. Realistic writing is the accepted method. The craftmanship has

[14] Malcolm Cowley, *The Literary Situation*, 6.

advanced so that there is a greater control and unity of the dramatic situations. Gone are the contrived motivations, theatrical effects and elaborate descriptions, the overplotting, the clumsy diction. There is a better grasp of the frontier scene and the characterization. Clear, straight prose is used. Some novels attempt an impressionistic, introspective style. With the limitations removed and with the continued emphasis on the common life of the frontier, the realistic essence is conveyed.

The taboos of morality and manners, once broken, remain so. Sex takes its place among the incidents of human relations as much as in the novels of contemporary material with the exception that some works, perhaps as the result of the author's consciousness that he was dealing with a past in which the moral pattern was stricter, present a modified view. This modification is more often present in the family-oriented novels than those dealing with individuals, who could easily fit into modern garb in this respect.

The most marked advance in this group of novels is the finer characterization that is apparent. Apart from the superficial skills and traits, there is a greater effort to create a character of depth and unity, to deal with an individual. Although many of these novels go barely beneath skin-deep level, others attempt a deeper analysis. A psychological orientation, unknown to the early works, is apparent. The influence of psychology is evident in the occasional depiction of a character's inner life or in the attempt to explain his behavior through analysis of his past—even his childhood—and through discussion of his motivations and problems. Characters, as a rule, develop rather than remain static. They are not the same people at the novel's end that they were initially, having been influenced by the events and feelings that they have undergone. Characters also display purposes other than physical or material needs; they need emotional and spiritual satisfactions. These relate somewhat to the political-social qualities which also were represented in early works, but are considerably varied by a sense of quest, a search for fulfillment. Through such introspection and definition of the inner man, these works show the influence of modern literary patterns.

A parallel turn is also evident in the recent fiction, a turn which almost harkens back to the fiction of the romantic period. Realistic in structure and values, some of these works, nonetheless, portray a sense of romance and adventure; they might be termed realistic romances. These works do not emphasize issues and problems. Concentrating upon individual heroes, who are generally well constructed characters, these novels build upon adventure and romance, and the values found rampant in much contemporary popular fiction to create a lusty hero—perhaps a modern ideal—to suit a modern audience. This segment of popular fiction places stress on violence, fast action, shock effect and sex. This trend may relate to the escapist nature of the fiction of the war and postwar years. It does definitely help to develop a characterization of the independent, heroic pioneer like those of earlier days, except that today's hero has to be stronger in tone to meet today's standards of independence, heroism, nonconformity and moral nonrigidity. Although these elements are also found in the novels depicting the less extroverted hero, the farmer, these works modify the effect of this trend with their milder approach to characterization and action.

Throughout the half century that has been studied, each generation, each period of social-literary change has built its own standards into the pioneer hero. The conservative influences of each period are strongest in shaping the image, but, as the frame of reference shifts, so does the image. Moral values and the attitudes associated with social and personal relationships are most prone to change, and these are the very values and attitudes that are strenuously defended. The guardians of the traditional ways and views, responding perhaps to the nature and subject of the frontier novel, use it to portray and maintain these beliefs. Since the novels represent the national heritage, they are doubly subject to this response, particularly when the glory and spirit of the American achievement are being displayed. However, the force of changing standards cannot be denied—though delayed—and they are represented in the novels in the portrait of the pioneer. In these respects, the 1950 image is quite changed from that of 1900.

The core of characteristics and values around which these forces react forms a solid foundation, despite the variances of values and tone that suggest a different hero image. These include such concepts as independence and individualism, opportunity and challenge in a new country, strength, endurance and courage, determination, resourcefulness, and loyalty. These qualities develop and are developed from the popular folk traditions of the self-made man, the presence and right and power of individual opportunity, and the belief in ultimate progress for the persevering, the loyal, and the progressive. Evidence of them is found in the novels of the first decade, even though they are clouded, and, to the modern reviewer, dominated by opposing ideas. The concepts are certainly present in the thirties; indeed they are fortified by special attitudes and used as focal points to chart the road back from disaster. The neoromantic adventure stories of the recent decades portray these codes as the basis for the sharply individualistic behavior of the heroes; the chronicles of family and presettlement life of this period also manifest these values. The effect of this continuity in the novels of the frontier is to assert the place of these characteristics and values as part of the permanent image of the pioneer hero.

The total impact on the public consciousness of the pioneer in the novel is one of reaffirmation of the views which are cited as traditionally American by establishing them as the core of the image. They come through despite the battering of time. Thus, the novels enforce the concept of the traditional structure of the American character as well as the frontier's role in shaping it. The novels also convey a relationship with contemporary standards by associating the behavior and attitudes of the pioneer with today. This relates the past to the present, and solidifies the relationship of the traits and values of the pioneer with those of the reader.

Bibliography

PRIMARY SOURCES

Aldrich, Bess Streeter. *A Lantern in Her Hand.* New York, D. Appleton and Company, 1928.

———. *Song of Years.* New York, D. Appleton-Century Company, 1939.

———. *Spring Came on Forever.* New York, D. Appleton-Century Company, 1935.

Allen, Hervey. *Bedford Village.* New York, Farrar and Rinehart, Inc., 1944.

———. *The Forest and the Fort.* New York, Farrar and Rinehart, Inc., 1943.

Altsheler, J. A. *The Wilderness Road.* New York, D. Appleton and Company, 1901.

Atkinson, Eleanor S. *Johnny Appleseed.* New York, Harper and Brothers, 1915.

Bacheller, Irving. *D'ri and I.* Boston, Lothrop Publishing Company, 1901.

Binns, Archie. *The Land Is Bright.* New York, Charles Scribner's Sons, 1939.

———. *Mighty Mountain.* Portland, Oregon, Binford and Mort, Publishers, 1940.

Blake, Forrester. *Johnny Christmas.* New York, William Morrow and Company, 1948.

Bojer, Johan. *The Emigrants.* New York, The Century Company, 1925.

Boyd, James. *Bitter Creek*. New York, Charles Scribner's Sons, 1939.

———. *Long Hunt*. New York, Charles Scribner's Sons, 1930.

Boyd, Thomas A. *Shadow of the Long Knives*. New York, Charles Scribner's Sons, 1928.

Canfield, Chauncey L. *The City of Six*. Chicago, A. C. McClurg and Company, 1910.

Cannon, LeGrand, Jr. *Look to the Mountain*. New York, Henry Holt and Company, Inc., 1942.

Carmer, Carl. *Genesee Fever*. New York, Farrar and Rinehart, Inc., 1941.

Cather, Willa. *My Antonia*. Boston, Houghton Mifflin Company, 1918.

———. *O Pioneers*. Boston, Houghton Mifflin Company, 1913.

Churchill, Winston. *The Crossing*. New York, The Macmillan Company, 1904.

Colby, Merle E. *All Ye People*. New York, The Viking Press, 1931.

Colony, Horatio. *Free Forester*. Boston, Little, Brown and Company, 1935.

Cooper, Courtney R. *The Last Frontier*. Boston, Little, Brown and Company, 1923.

———. *Oklahoma*. Boston, Little, Brown and Company, 1926.

Cronyn, George W. *'Forty-Nine*. Philadelphia, Dorrance and Company, 1925.

Davis, Clyde B. *Nebraska Coast*. New York, Farrar and Rinehart, 1939.

Derleth, August. *Bright Journey*. New York, Charles Scribner's Sons, 1940.

———. *Restless Is the River*. New York, Charles Scribner's Sons, 1939.

———. *Wind Over Wisconsin*. New York, Charles Scribner's Sons, 1938.

Duffus, Robert L. *Jornada*. New York, Covici-Friede, 1935.

Edmonds, Walter D. *Drums Along the Mohawk*. Boston, Little, Brown and Company, 1936.

———. *In the Hands of the Senecas*. Boston, Little, Brown and Company, 1937.

———. *Wilderness Clearing*. New York, Dodd, Mead and Company, 1944.

Erdman, Loula G. *Edge of Time*. New York, Dodd, Mead and Company, 1950.

Ertz, Susan. *The Proselyte*. New York, D. Appleton-Century Company, 1933.

Ferber, Edna. *Cimarron*. New York, Doubleday, Doran and Company, 1930.

Fergusson, Harvey. *Wolf Song*. New York, Alfred A. Knopf, 1927.

Fisher, Vardis. *Children of God*. New York, Harper and Brothers, Publishers, 1939.

Fox, John, Jr. *Erskine Dale, Pioneer*. New York, Charles Scribner's Sons, 1920.

Frey, Ruby F. R. *Red Morning*. New York, G. P. Putnam's Sons, 1946.

Furnas, Marthedith. *The Far Country*. New York, Harper and Brothers, Publishers, 1947.

Gordon, Caroline. *Green Centuries*. New York, Charles Scribner's Sons, 1941.

Grey, Zane. *Betty Zane*. New York, Grosset and Dunlap, Publishers, 1903.

———. *The Last Trail*. New York, A. L. Burt Company, Publishers, 1909.

———. *The Spirit of the Border*. New York, Grosset and Dunlap, Publishers, 1906.

———. *The Thundering Herd*. New York, Grosset and Dunlap, Publishers, 1925.

Guthrie, A. B., Jr. *The Big Sky*. Boston, Houghton Mifflin Company, 1947.

———. *The Way West*. New York, William Sloane Associates, Publishers, 1949.

Hallet, Richard M. *Michael Beam*. Boston, Houghton Mifflin Company, 1939.

Hargreaves, Sheba. *The Cabin at the Trail's End*. New York, Harper and Brothers, Publishers, 1928.

———. *Heroine of the Prairies*. New York, Harper and Brothers, Publishers, 1930.

Hergesheimer, J. *Limestone Tree*. New York, Alfred A. Knopf, 1931.

Hough, Emerson. *The Covered Wagon*. New York, Grosset and Dunlap, Publishers, 1922.

———. *The Magnificent Adventure*. New York, D. Appleton and Company, 1916.

———. *North of 36*. New York, D. Appleton and Company, 1923.

Hueston, Ethel. *The Man of the Storm*. Indianapolis, The Bobbs-Merrill Company, 1936.

Laird, Charlton. *Thunder on the River*. Boston, Little, Brown and Company, 1949.

Lane, Rose Wilder. *Let the Hurricane Roar*. New York, Longmans-Green and Company, 1933.

Lewis, Alfred H. *The Throwback*. New York, Outing Publishing Company, 1906.

Lewis, Janet. *The Invasion*. New York, Harcourt, Brace and Company, 1932.

Linderman, Frank B. *Beyond Law*. New York, The John Day Company, 1933.

———. *Morning Light*. New York, The John Day Company, 1922.

Lovelace, Maud H. *Early Candlelight*. Minneapolis, University of Minnesota Press, 1929.

Lyle, Eugene P., Jr. *The Lone Star*. New York, Doubleday, Page and Company, 1907.

Mabie, Mary L. *The Long Knives Walked*. Indianapolis, The Bobbs-Merrill Company, 1932.

McKee, Ruth E. *Christopher Strange*. Garden City, New York, Doubleday, Doran and Company, Inc., 1941.

McNeilly, M. M. *Each Bright River*. New York, William Morrow and Company, 1950.

Miller, Caroline. *Lamb in His Bosom*. New York, Harper and Brothers, Publishers, 1933.

Minnigerode, Meade. *Black Forest*. New York, Farrar and Rinehart, Inc., 1937.

Moody, Minnie H. *Long Meadows*. New York, The Macmillan Company, 1941.

O'Connor, Jack. *Conquest*. New York, Harper and Brothers, Publishers, 1930.

Parrish, Randall. *A Sword of the Old Frontier*. Chicago, A. C. McClurg and Company, 1905.

———. *When Wilderness Was King*. Chicago, A. C. McClurg and Company, 1904.

Pendexter, Hugh. *The Red Road*. Indianapolis, The Bobbs-Merrill Company, 1927.

Putnam, George P. *Hickory Shirt*. New York, Duell, Sloan and Pearce, 1949.

Quick, Herbert. *Vandemark's Folly*. Indianapolis, The Bobbs-Merrill Company, 1922.

Raynolds, R. *Brothers in the West*. New York, Harper and Brothers, Publishers, 1931.

Richter, Conrad. *The Fields*. New York, Alfred A. Knopf, 1946.

———. *The Town*. New York, Alfred A. Knopf, 1950.

———. *The Trees*. New York, Alfred A. Knopf, 1940.

Roberts, Elizabeth M. *The Great Meadow*. New York, The Viking Press, 1930.

Roberts, Richard E. *The Gilded Rooster*. New York, G. P. Putnam's Sons, 1947.

Roe, Vingie E. *The Splendid Road*. New York, Duffield and Company, 1925.

Rolvaag, Ole E. *Giants in the Earth*. New York, Harper and Brothers, Publishers, 1927.

Schumann, Mary. *Strife Before Dawn*. New York, The Dial Press, 1939.

Seifert, Shirley. *Land of Tomorrow*. New York, M. S. Mill Company, Inc., 1937.

Singmaster, Elsie. *A High Wind Rising*. Boston, Houghton Mifflin Company, 1942.

Skinner, Constance L. *Debby Barnes, Trader*. New York, The Macmillan Company, 1932.

Small, Sidney H. *Fourscore*. Indianapolis, The Bobbs-Merrill Company, 1924.

Steele, Wilbur D. *Diamond Wedding*. Garden City, New York, Doubleday and Company, Inc., 1950.

Sterne, Emma G. *Some Plant Olive Trees*. New York, Dodd, Mead and Company, 1937.

Stevenson, Burton E. *The Heritage*. Boston, Houghton Mifflin and Company, 1902.

Stong, Phil. *Buckskin Breeches*. New York, Farrar and Rinehart, Inc., 1937.

Street, James H. *Oh, Promised Land*. New York, The Dial Press, 1940.

Sublette, Clifford M., and Harry H. Kroll. *Perilous Journey*. Indianapolis, The Bobbs-Merrill Company, 1943.

Swanson, Neil H. *Unconquered*. Garden City, New York, Doubleday and Company, Inc., 1948.

Terrell, John Upton. *Plume Rouge*. New York, The Viking Press, 1942.

Thompson, Maurice. *Alice of Old Vincennes*. Indianapolis, The Bobbs-Merrill Company, 1900.

Todd, Helen. *So Free We Seem*. New York, Reynal and Hitchcock, 1936.

Turnbull, Agnes S. *The Day Must Dawn*. New York, The Macmillan Company, 1942.

Van Every, Dale. *Bridal Journey*. New York, Julian Messner, Inc., 1950.

———. *Westward the River*. New York, G. P. Putnam's Sons, 1945.

Warren, Lella. *Foundation Stone*. New York, Alfred A. Knopf, 1940.

Weld, John. *Don't You Cry for Me*. New York, Charles Scribner's Sons, 1940.

White, Stewart Edward. *Gold*. Garden City, New York, Doubleday, Page and Company, 1913.

————. *The Long Rifle*. Garden City, New York, Doubleday, Doran and Company, 1930.

Wilson, Margaret. *The Able McLaughlins*. New York, Harper and Brothers, Publishers, 1923.

Wister, Owen. *The Virginian*. New York, The Macmillan Company, 1902.

Zara, Louis. *This Land Is Ours*. Boston, Houghton Mifflin Company, 1940.

SECONDARY SOURCES

Allen, Frederick Lewis. "Best Sellers 1900–1935: The Trend of Popular Reading Taste Since the Turn of the Century," *Saturday Review of Literature*, Vol. XVIII (December 7, 1935), 2–3, 24–26.

————. *Only Yesterday*. New York, Harper and Brothers, 1931.

Baker, E. A. *Guide to Historical Fiction*. New York, The Macmillan Company, 1914.

Baker, E. A., and J. Packman. *A Guide to the Best Fiction, English and American*. Third Edition. New York, The Macmillan Company, 1932.

Barck, Oscar T. Jr., and Nelson M. Blake. *Since 1900*. Revised Edition. New York, The Macmillan Company, 1952.

Beach, Joseph W., *American Fiction 1920–1940*. New York, The Macmillan Company, 1941.

Beard, Charles A., and Mary R. Beard. *The Rise of American Civilization*. New York, The Macmillan Company, 1939.

"Best Sellers," *The Bookman*, Vols. IX–XLVII (1899–1918).

"Best Sellers of the Month," *Publishers' Weekly*, Vols. XCV–CLIX, (January 1919–January 1951).

"Best Sellers of the Week," *The New York Times Book Review*, Vols. XCI–XCIX (August 1942–December 1950).

Blaine, Harold A. "The Frontiersman in American Prose Fiction 1800–1860." Unpublished Ph.D. dissertation from Western Reserve University, 1935.

Boynton, Percy H. *The Rediscovery of the Frontier*. Chicago, University of Chicago Press, 1931.

Cargill, Oscar. *Intellectual America*. New York, The Macmillan Company, 1941.

Chase, Richard. *Quest for Myth*. Baton Rouge, University of Louisiana Press, 1949.

Clifford, John. "Social and Political Attitudes in Fiction of Ranch and Range." Unpublished Ph.D. dissertation from the State University of Iowa, 1953.

Coan, Otis W., and R. G. Lillard. *America in Fiction*. Third and Fourth Editions. Stanford, Stanford University Press, 1949 and 1956.

Commager, Henry S. *The American Mind*. New York, Harper and Brothers, 1950.

———. "The Literature of the Pioneer West," *Minnesota History*, Vol. VIII (December 1927), 319–28.

Cook, Dorothy, *et al*. *Fiction Catalog* with Supplements. New York, H. W. Wilson Company, 1941.

Cotton, Gerald B., and Alan Glencross. *Fiction Index*. London, Association of Assistant Librarians, 1953.

Cowley, Malcolm. *The Literary Situation*. New York, The Viking Press, 1954.

Curti, Merle, Richard A. Shryock, Thomas C. Cochran, and Fred H Harrington. *An American History*, Vol. II. New York, Harper and Brothers, 1950.

———. *The Growth of American Thought*. New York, Harper and Brothers, 1943.

Daiches, David. *The Novel and the Modern World*. Chicago, University of Chicago Press, 1939.

Davidson, Levette J., and Prudence Bostwick. *The Literature of the Rocky Mountain West 1803–1903*. Caldwell, Idaho, Caxton Printers, Ltd., 1939.

DeVoto, Bernard. *Across the Wide Missouri.* Boston, Houghton Mifflin Company, 1952.

———. *The Year of Decision.* Boston, Houghton Mifflin Company, 1942.

Dewey, John. *Art as Experience.* New York, Minton, Balch and Company, 1934.

Dumond, D. C. *America in Our Time 1896–1946.* New York, Henry Holt and Company, 1947.

Dutcher, G. M., *et al. Guide to Historical Literature.* New York, The Macmillan Company, 1949.

Foerstcr, Norman (ed.). *The Reinterpretation of American Literature.* New York, Harcourt, Brace and Company, 1928.

Gabriel, Ralph Henry. *The Course of American Democratic Thought.* New York, The Ronald Press, 1940.

Goldman, Eric F. *Rendezvous with Destiny.* New York, Alfred A. Knopf, 1952.

Hackett, Alice Payne. *Sixty Years of Best Sellers 1895–1955.* New York, R. R. Bowker Company, 1956.

Handlin, Oscar, and A. M. Schlesinger, *et al. Harvard Guide to American History.* Cambridge, Belknap Press of Harvard University Press, 1954.

Harsh, Charles M., and H. G. Schrickel. *Personality-Development and Assessment.* New York, The Ronald Press, 1950.

Hart, Irving H. "Best Sellers in Fiction During the First Quarter of the Twentieth Century," *Publishers' Weekly,* Vol. CVII (February 14, 1925), 525–27.

———. "Fiction Fashions from 1895–1926," *Publishers' Weekly,* Vol. CXI (February 5, 1927), 473–77.

———. "The Most Popular Authors of Fiction Between 1900–1925," *Publishers' Weekly,* Vol. CVII (February 21, 1925), 619–22.

———. "The Most Popular Authors of Fiction in the Post-War Period, 1919–1926," *Publishers' Weekly,* Vol. CXI (March 21, 1927), 1045–53.

———. "The One Hundred Best Sellers of the last Quarter Century," *Publishers' Weekly*, Vol. XCIX (January 29, 1921), 269–72.

Hart, James D. *Oxford Companion to American Literature*. Second Edition. London, Oxford University Press, 1948.

———. *The Popular Book*. New York, Oxford University Press, 1950.

Hazard, Lucy L. *The Frontier in American Literature*. New York, T. Y. Crowell Company, Publishers, 1927.

Hofstadter, Richard. *The Age of Reform*. New York, Alfred A. Knopf, 1955.

Hornstein, Lillian H. "Analyses of Imagery: A Critique of Literary Method," *Publications of the Modern Language Association*, Vol. LVII (1942), 638–53.

Kazin, Alfred. *On Native Grounds*. New York, Harcourt, Brace and Company, 1942.

Kerr, Elizabeth M. *Bibliography of the Sequence Novel*. Minneapolis, University of Minnesota Press, 1950.

Knight, Grant C. *The Strenuous Age in American Literature*. Chapel Hill, University of North Carolina Press, 1954.

Langer, Susanne K. *Philosophy in a New Key*. New York, Mentor Books, 1951.

Leisy, Ernest E. *The American Historical Novel*. Norman, University of Oklahoma Press, 1950.

Lenrow, Elbert. *Readers' Guide to Prose Fiction*. New York, D. Appleton-Century and Company, 1940.

Lingenfelter, M. R. *Vocations in Fiction: An Annotated Bibliography*. Chicago, American Library Association, 1938.

Link, Arthur S. *American Epoch*. New York, Alfred A. Knopf, 1955.

———. *Woodrow Wilson and the Progressive Era*. New York, Harper and Brothers, 1954.

Logasa, Hannah. *Historical Fiction*. Philadelphia, McKinley Publishing Company, 1951.

———. *Regional United States*. Boston, Faxon Publishers, 1942.

Lynd, Robert S. *Knowledge for What?* Princeton, Princeton University Press, 1939.

Microfilm Abstracts. Ann Arbor, University Microfilms, vols. 1–15.

Modern Language Association. "Research in Progress," *Publications of the Modern Language Association,* Vol. LXXI (March–June, 1956).

Morris, Lloyd. *Postscript to Yesterday.* New York, Random House, 1947.

Mott, Frank L. *Golden Multitudes.* New York, The Macmillan Company, 1947.

Nield, Jonathan. *A Guide to the Best Historical Novels and Tales.* Fifth Edition, revised and enlarged. London, The Macmillan Company, 1929.

Northup, C. S. *Register of Bibliographies of English Language and Literature.* New Haven, Yale University Press, 1925.

Paine, Gregory. "The Frontier in American Literature," *Sewanee Review,* Vol. XXXVI (April 1928), 224–36.

Parks, George W. "Best Books and Novelists," *Publishers' Weekly,* Vol. CXI (March 12, 1927), 1068.

Parrington, Vernon L. *Main Currents of American Thought.* 3 vols. New York, Harcourt, Brace and Company, 1927–30.

Prescott, Frederick C. *Poetry and Myth.* New York, Harcourt, Brace and Company, 1927.

Quinn, Arthur H. *The Literature of the American People.* New York, Appleton-Century-Crofts, Inc., 1951.

Raglan, Lord. *The Hero: A Study in Tradition, Myth and Drama.* New York, Vantage Books, 1956.

Read, Herbert. *Art and Society.* London, Faber and Faber, 1937.

Richards, I. A. *Principles of Literary Criticism.* New York, Harcourt, Brace and Company, 1930.

Riegel, Robert E. *America Moves West.* Revised Edition. New York, Henry Holt and Company, 1947.

Roosevelt, Theodore. *The Winning of the West.* Vols. II and III. New York, The Current Literature Publishing Company, 1905.

309

Rosenblatt, Louise M. *Literature as Exploration*. New York, Appleton-Century-Crofts, Inc., 1938.

Schorer, Mark, *et al. Criticism*. New York, Harcourt, Brace and Company, 1948.

Schlesinger, Arthur M. *Political and Social Growth of the American People*. Third Edition. New York, The Macmillan Company, 1941.

Slosson, Preston W. *The Great Crusade and After*. New York, The Macmillan Company, 1930.

Smith, Harrison. "Twenty-Five Years of Best Sellers," *The English Journal*, Vol. XXXIII (October 1944), 401–408.

Smith, Henry Nash. *Virgin Land: The American West as Symbol and Myth*. Cambridge, Harvard University Press, 1950.

Spiller, Robert E., Willard Thorp, Thomas H. Johnson, and Henry Seidel Canby, (eds.). *Literary History of the United States*. 3 vols. New York, The Macmillan Company, 1949.

Stern, Philip Van Doren. "Books and Best Sellers," *Virginia Quarterly Review*, Vol. XVIII (January 1942), 45-55.

Sullivan, Mark. *Our Times, the United States, 1900–1925*. Vol. VI. New York, Charles Scribner's Sons, 1935.

Theissen, N. J. "An Annotated Bibliography of American Fiction," *Emporia State Teachers College Bulletin of Information*, Vol. XVIII (1938).

Trotier, A. H., and M. Harman (eds.). *Doctoral Dissertations Accepted by American Universities*. vols. 1–22. New York, The H. W. Wilson Company, 1933–55.

Turner, Frederick Jackson. *The Frontier in American History*. New York, Henry Holt and Company, 1920.

Van Doren, Carl, and Mark Van Doren. *American and British Literature Since 1890*. Revised Edition. New York, D. Appleton-Century Company, 1939.

Van Nostrand, Jeanne. *Subject Index to High School Fiction*. Chicago, American Library Association, 1938.

Van Patten, N. *Index to Bibliographies of American and British*

Authors—1923–1932. Stanford, Stanford University Press, 1934.

Wagenknecht, Edward. *Cavalcade of the American Novel.* New York, Henry Holt and Company, 1952.

Wellek, Rene, and Austin Warren. *Theory of Literature.* Second Edition. New York, Harcourt, Brace and Company, 1956.

Wigmore, E. "American Scene in Fiction," *American Journal of Nursing,* Vol. XXXVIII (August 1938), 933–34.

Winchell, Constance M. *Guide to Reference Books.* Seventh Edition. Chicago, American Library Association, 1951.

Wish, Harvey. *Contemporary America.* New York, Harper and Brothers, 1948.

Index